Historiography
of
Christianity
in India

JOHN C.B. WEBSTER

OXFORD
UNIVERSITY PRESS

OXFORD
UNIVERSITY PRESS

Oxford University Press is a department of the University of Oxford.
It furthers the University's objective of excellence in research, scholarship,
and education by publishing worldwide. Oxford is a registered trademark of
Oxford University Press in the UK and in certain other countries

Published in India by
Oxford University Press
YMCA Library Building, 1 Jai Singh Road, New Delhi 110 001, India

ISBN-13: 978-0-19-808920-9
ISBN-10: 0-19-808920-1

Typeset in Minion Pro 10.5/13
by Sai Graphic Design, New Delhi 110 055
Printed in India at Artxel, Noida 201301, U.P.

Contents

To
Leslie, Harry, and Emily Ann

Preface

This book brings together in one place seven essays I have written on the historiography of Christianity in India. Most appear as originally published with only slight modifications, to remove typographical errors, to present my ideas more clearly, or to reduce repetition. However, some duplication of material in chapters 1, 6, and 7 (such as, the historiographical background section of Chapter 6 which summarizes much of Chapter 1) has been unavoidable. I have also inserted some later research into Chapter 1, and Chapter 7 is more comprehensive than the version published elsewhere. The three longest essays portray the development of this field of study from its inception to the present. The other, shorter, essays deal with specific historiographical themes and issues: the contribution of the history of Christianity in India to other theological disciplines (Chapter 2); Christian identity (Chapter 3); historical deconstruction and reconstruction (Chapter 4); and the postmodern challenge (Chapter 5).

I wish to acknowledge and thank the organizers of the seminars at which these essays were first presented. I would also like to express my gratitude to the following for permission to publish previously published articles:

United Theological College in Bangalore for 'The History of Christianity in India: Aims and Methods' and 'The Contribution of the Historian to Theological Research in India' from the *Bangalore Theological Forum*; The Church History

Association of India for 'A Quest for the Historical Ditt' from the *Indian Church History Review*; Dharmaram Publications for 'The Identity of Indian Christians' from Francis Kanichikattil (ed.), *The Church in Context: Essays in Honour of Mathias Mundadan*, CMI; The Institute of Punjab Studies, Chandigarh, for 'The Women of Amritsar through Missionary Eyes' from Reeta Grewal and Sheena Pall (eds), *Precolonial and Colonial Punjab: Society, Economy, Politics and Culture: Essays for Indu Banga*; The Indian Council of Historical Research for 'Christian History as Indian Social History: A Review of the Literature' from Sabyasachi Bhattacharya (ed.), *Approaches to History: Essays in Indian Historiography*; another version of Chapter 7, 'Dalit Christian History: Themes and Trends', presented at the Centre for Historical Studies, Jawaharlal Nehru University will be published as 'Dalit Christian History as a Field of Study', in Tanika Sarkar, Pius Malekandathil, and Joy L.K. Pachuau (eds), *Christianity in Indian History: Issues of Culture, Power and Knowledge* (forthcoming).

The research for these essays was carried out in a large number of libraries, the staff of each of which deserves my thanks. None has been more helpful than that of United Theological College in Bengaluru, and Yale Divinity School here, in nearby New Haven, CT. Most of the chapters benefited from discussions in the seminars or the conferences at which they were initially presented. The concluding chapter was revised and improved, following comments by Indu Banga, Euan Cameron, Frederick Downs, O.V. Jathanna, and David Mosse. At the end, as has been our custom, my wife Penny reviewed the entire manuscript for clarity of expression. I am grateful to all these friends for their help, and I hold none of them responsible for the inadequacies that remain.

This book is dedicated to my two older brothers and my younger sister, all of whom, at key moments in my life, have been of great help and support to me.

Waterford, CT   JOHN C.B. WEBSTER
USA
August 2012

Introduction

This volume contains seven essays written between 1978 and 2011, presented in the order in which they were written. In rereading these essays together as a single body of work, three things stand out. The first is the importance of the academic location from which I have written. Location can not only determine which source materials are most readily available for research but can also shape the academic culture in which one is immersed; how significant Christian history is within that culture; which are the most important issues that its historians should address, and what career or other considerations can affect how and where one publishes.[1] Even though I wrote only Chapter 1 while actually resident in India, I have remained more a part of the Indian than of the Western academic scene. Each essay was published in India, primarily for Indian readers, with current academic and other developments in India providing the immediate context for

[1] A historian based in the West told me that, while historians of India located there may prefer to publish their work in India, the hard fact of life is that this preference does not bring the peer recognition and potential career advancement that publishing in the West does. Given that the India-based and the West-based publications are generally inaccessible to each other, there seem to be two separate conversations going on about the Indian history of Christianity, with much less cross-fertilization than is healthy for the development of the field.

writing. Within India, I have been located in both the distinctly Christian and the wider academic cultures, with one foot in each. My major historical works, like these essays, have been published by both kinds of publishers—Christian (ISPCK—Indian Society for Promoting Christian Knowledge) and academic (Macmillan, Manohar, Oxford).

The second aspect that stands out is a direct outgrowth of the first: the extent to which each essay was influenced by the particular audience or readership for which it was intended. All but two were presented initially as papers at conferences or seminars in India. My assumptions—about who would be present, how my work might affect them, what their responses might be—affected my assessment, not only of which assumptions and warrants I could take for granted as being acceptable, and which would need further justification, but also of which kind of language would be most appropriate for the occasion. Three of the most obvious differences which audience made were, first, whether I was writing 'Christian to fellow Christian' or to a wider 'academic to fellow academic' readership; secondly, whether I was writing just for other historians or primarily for people in other academic disciplines; and, thirdly, whether I was writing for people who would be likely to agree or to disagree either with what I had to say or with how I went about saying it. What was true of the audience at a seminar or a conference was equally true of the larger, but probably not dissimilar, readership for whom that paper would be revised and published.

The people most likely to read histories of Christianity in India are to be found, first of all, in Indian theological colleges or seminaries where it is a required course of study for the future clergy of the churches. Most of the non-Catholic theological colleges in India are affiliated to the Senate of Serampore College which largely determines the curriculum, sets most of the examination papers, and grants degrees to all of them. Some of these theological colleges and seminaries offer training at the Master of Theology (a preliminary research degree equivalent to the MPhil offered in universities) and the doctoral levels. While writing for them, I wrote as a 'Christian academic historian to Christian academics in several related disciplines who would be receptive to what I have to say'. A second category of readers is located in universities, primarily in India but also abroad, where the history of Christianity is viewed mostly as part of the history of India as a whole. For this readership, I wrote as an 'academic historian to fellow academic, mostly historians, who may not agree with what I have to say'. The third, and last major category of potential readers consists of those engaged in mission studies and particularly in the history of missions, most of whom are located in the West where rich mission archives are to be found. In this case, I would have to write as a 'Christian academic historian to Christian academics in related disciplines who are usually asking a different set of questions from mine'.

These readerships have not been equally important for me. I have been more influenced by fellow academics in the first two categories than by those in the third. For better or for worse, I have become an India specialist who tries to write for and pay special attention to what others in the first two categories have written that might impinge upon my own research. History, including Christian history, is not an individual but a collective endeavour of interdependent researchers. Each one of us moves in several circles at the same time, sharing in important conversations which can, potentially, influence the future direction and content of our own fields of study. So, the question is: when we write, which conversations do we wish to contribute to and help to shape? For example, as will become apparent in the next chapter, most of the early mission histories were written for a Western readership and published abroad; some even focused on debates which were taking place in Britain or the United States rather than in India. Those were the circles that mattered most to those historians and whose thinking they were most eager to influence. Even today, mission historians who focus on the history of missionaries, their visions, their work and their encounters, constitute a very productive and influential circle with which a historian of Christianity in India might well want to be in conversation. Because I have chosen to focus upon the history of the Christian people of India, my most significant conversation partners have been either in the first or in the second category of readers. While some of the chapters that follow were clearly written for the former and others clearly for the latter, all should be intelligible to both.

These readers know that, in India, Christianity has long had its internal conflicts as well as its advocates, its sympathizers, and its critics, some of whom have been quite hostile. Its history has, therefore, been so contested that it may be useful to cite some illustrative examples. Writing *Asia and Western Dominance* a decade after Independence, K.M. Panikkar severely criticized Christian missions for their intolerance [2] and attributed their failure in Asia to the missionary's 'attitude of moral superiority and a belief in his own exclusive righteousness'; to their close association with aggressive political and cultural imperialism; and to their own internal divisions.[3] Sita Ram Goel's *History of Hindu–Christian Encounters*, written thirty years later, sought to provide a 'connected account of how Hindu thinkers, saints, and sages have viewed Christianity and its exclusive claims' during 'the different phases of Christian aggression against this ancient religion and culture'.[4] His chapters describe a series of encounters and dialogues from ancient times to the post-Independence period. All were depicted as between 'the good guys' and 'the bad guys', with a clear reversal of roles from the older, triumphalist missionary histories. Arun Shourie's *Missionaries in India: Continuities, Changes, Dilemmas* also focused on the close collaboration between Christian missionaries and British officialdom in the imperial enterprise—a habit which, he said, the post-Independence Church, with its connections outside India, has not broken. For Shourie, 'normative Christianity' was embodied in the Minutes of Charles Trevelyan in the 1830s, and any changes since then have been merely tactical or cosmetic. Near the end of the book he laid down several criteria

2 'Intolerance of things Indian became henceforth the characteristic feature of missionary zeal in India.' K.M. Panikkar, *Asia and Western Dominance: A Survey of the Vasco Da Gama Epoch of Asian History, 1498–1945* (New York: Collins Books, 1969), p. 281. This book was originally published in England in 1959.

3 Ibid., p. 297.

4 Sita Ram Goel, *History of Hindu–Christian Encounters* (New Delhi: Voice of India, 1989), p. i.

which Christian churches in India had to meet if their bona fides were to be accepted, among which were repentance for past sins and refraining from converting others to Christianity.[5]

These views both reflect and affect some popular perceptions of the Christian past in India. Some historians of Christianity in India have addressed such views head-on,[6] while the great majority has treated areas of particular controversy—for example, mass conversion to Christianity; Christianity and Indian culture; Christian missions and imperialism—in ways that test the accuracy of those (and other) perceptions, but without direct reference to the controversies involved. My essays assume that the readership is familiar with these controversies, past and present, and can therefore appreciate the ways in which the historians mentioned here have chosen to deal with them.

This description of intended readership leads directly to the third striking feature of these essays when read together as a single body of work, namely, the prominence they give to the 'New Perspective' developed by the editorial board of the Church History Association of India (CHAI), back in 1974. At its bi-annual meeting in 1973, CHAI appointed an editorial board of six members to prepare and oversee the publication of a multi-volume history of Christianity in India. The board met in early 1974 and produced a lengthy prospectus for the project, which began by describing in broad terms the 'New Perspective' from which this history was to be written. It emphatically rejected the mission history and the more institutional 'Church history' approach, and was in favour of a socio-cultural history of the Christian people in India. This was to have three other components as well: an ecumenical rather than

5 Arun Shourie, *Missionaries in India: Continuities, Changes, Dilemmas* (New Delhi: ASA, 1994), pp. 229–30.

6 Recent examples would be Robert Eric Frykenberg's macro-study, *Christianity in India: From Beginnings to the Present* (Oxford: Oxford University Press, 2008); Chad M. Bauman's micro-study, *Christian Identity and Dalit Religion in Hindu India 1868–1947* (Grand Rapids: William B. Eerdmans, 2008); and Chandra Mallampalli's regional study, *Christians and Public Life in Colonial South India: Contending with Marginality, 1863–1937* (London: Routledge Curzon, 2004), all of which focus, in differing ways, on the issue of Christianity's 'Indianness'.

a denominational approach; the region as the basic working unit of study; and the national, which emphasized comparisons and linkages between regions and developments that were more national than regional.

This 'New Perspective' proved to be quite a watershed. It generated considerable excitement among historians in the first category mentioned above and was reflected in a number of theses. It also required some training in the methodology of socio-cultural history, since this type of history went against the grain of most of the source materials upon which historians of Christianity in India had been relying. I was a member of that original editorial board and had prepared a draft of the 'New Perspective' on the basis of the board's discussions. Because I had adopted this perspective in my doctoral thesis on *The Christian Community and Change in Nineteenth Century North India*,[7] I led some workshops at CHAI meetings to initiate other historians into the techniques and procedures of this new approach. Since then, I have been a strong advocate of this 'New Perspective' which requires continuous conversation with the first two categories of fellow academics mentioned above. That is the perspective from which the essays in this volume have been written.

'The History of Christianity in India: Aims and Methods' (Chapter 1) was first presented at a faculty research seminar at the United Theological College in Bangalore in 1978. Thus, its first audience and readership consisted of faculty colleagues in allied (Christian) theological disciplines. I had joined the department of the History of Christianity there the previous June and was responsible for introducing a new course into the Master of Theology (MTh) curriculum on 'Historical Method and the Historiography of the Indian Church'. The research done for this essay, was also done for that course, which was aimed at introducing future historians of Christianity in India to the discipline and its history. It remains, even to this day, the only history of the development of this field of study that I know of and continues to be required reading for students of that course.

---

7 This was later published in New Delhi by Macmillan in 1976.

The essay was originally published in the *Bangalore Theological Forum*, an inter-disciplinary theological journal, in 1978 and was then reprinted for the benefit of other historians in the *Indian Church History Review* in 1979. It had been my intention to write a follow-up article for publication in the West on 'The History of Christianity in India: Changing Perspectives', but I never completed it. However, some of the additional research I undertook for that article has been incorporated into the original essay for publication here. All the newly inserted material—including a new section on the Syrian churches in Kerala—is supplemental. It does not change the generalizations made or conclusions arrived at in the original version. Thus, despite the additions, this remains an essay of that time, place and readership. I have not attempted to 'update' it by bringing a twenty-first century perspective to bear upon the same material.

'The Historian and Theological Research in India' (Chapter 2) was also presented at a faculty research seminar at the United Theological College in the summer of 1983, when I returned to teach for a term as a visiting professor. The essay dealt with the basic working assumptions underlying historical research in general, and research on the history of Christianity in India in particular. It was my first attempt at an internal dialogue between my Christian theology and my practice as a historian of Christianity in India. It was then published in the *Bangalore Theological Forum*. I return to this theme in part again in the concluding chapter of this book.

The next three essays deal with specific issues of historiographical import in studying the history of Christianity in India. 'The Identity of Indian Christians' (Chapter 3) was not written for a conference or a seminar but for a collection of essays to honour Fr A. Mathias Mundadan CMI (Carmelites of Mary Immaculate) on the occasion of his sixtieth birthday. Fr Mundadan is a long-time friend, has been a member of the CHAI editorial board since its inception, and its chief editor since 1984. He was also the author of a book on the identity of Indian Christians which influenced my decision to write on that subject. Like the other essays written to honour him, mine was intended for a Christian readership. In it, I examined the manner in which four historians—including both

Fr Mundadan and I—have treated the subject of Indian Christian identity. The essay illustrates how complex and important the identity issue is for Indian Christians. It also reveals the extent to which identity is a relational term, so that the implicit, if not explicit, question about it is always: Identity defined in relation to what or to whom? My essay offers an 'answer' that is, in all honesty, more faith-based than empirically-based, precisely because the empirical is so problematical and yet so impossible to ignore.

In 'A Quest for the Historical Ditt' (Chapter 4), presented initially to a CHAI conference in 2002 and subsequently published in *Indian Church History Review*, I drew a sharp distinction between history and tradition. Ditt, the person credited with starting the rural Dalit mass conversion movement in the Punjab in 1873–4, has been used to make or illustrate important points about the conduct of the Christian mission in India, as was most obvious in J. Waskom Pickett's influential *Christian Mass Movements in India*.[8] I started my quest for the historical Ditt with Pickett and moved back in time to see what I could learn about him from the earliest references available, using earlier sources to critique later ones. I then turned around and traced the development of the traditions about Ditt from their earliest appearance up to the time of writing. I found it to be a very illuminating exercise in historical deconstruction and reconstruction, which might well be applied to other important persons or events in and beyond the Indian history of Christianity.

'The Women of Amritsar through Missionary Eyes' (Chapter 5) was presented in 2004 at an Institute of Punjab Studies seminar held at Panjab University, Chandigarh, in honour of Indu Banga and was later published in the proceedings of that seminar. Banga, a former colleague and long-time friend, has done considerable work in the history of Indian women and it seemed appropriate to contribute an essay on that subject. I happened to be working on a major history of Christianity in North-west India at that time and had at my disposal a good body of source materials produced by the missionaries of the Church of England Zenana Missionary Society. I felt that these Christian sources, if used properly, could

---

8 New York: The Abingdon Press, 1933.

shed some useful light on the situation of women in the city of Amritsar and, therefore, on the general social history of the Punjab, during the late nineteenth and early twentieth century. The essay is included in this collection because it also served as a response to some of the important issues of method being raised by post-modern and post-colonial scholarship.

In 2009, under the chairmanship of Sabyasachi Bhattacharya, the Indian Council of Historical Research undertook a historiography project in order to assess the 'state of the field'. I was invited to contribute an essay on Christianity. When we met, he and I agreed that its title should be 'Christian History as Indian Social History: A Review of the Literature' (Chapter 6). In 2011, the essay was published along with nine others on very different themes in *Approaches to History: Essays in Indian Historiography*, which he edited. That essay included some background historiographical material which has been deleted here to avoid repeating what has already been provided in Chapter 1.

In many respects, this essay serves to bring the historiography of Christianity in India in Chapter 1 up to date. It was, however, written for a much broader academic readership than was the earlier essay. In addition—and partly as a consequence—it is much narrower and sharper in focus, being confined to academic histories of Christians or of Christianity that have contributed to an understanding of Indian social history. Mission and Church histories have thus been largely excluded. The number of books consulted proved to be surprisingly large and, so, articles on the subject were left out. I sought to make this essay more than merely an annotated bibliography, and found that a topical arrangement of my material was best suited to achieve that purpose. At the end, I have offered a few suggestions for the study of Indian social history in the light of what this particular body of historical literature had revealed.

'Dalit Christian History: Themes and Trends' (Chapter 7) was prepared for an international conference on 'Christianity in History: Encounters, Engagements and Experiences' at the Centre for Historical Studies at Jawaharlal Nehru University in February 2011. Since I had already reviewed the literature on Christian history as Indian social history for the ICHR and since the prospectus for this conference encouraged similar 'state of the field' analyses, I thought that this conference would be an excellent occasion for presenting a similar study of historical writing on Dalit Christians, a subject of special interest to me. That essay was then reduced from 12,000 to 8,000 words for publication. That shorter version, under the title, 'Dalit Christian History as a Field of Study', appears elsewhere along with other papers from the conference. What is included here is a slight modification of the original essay.

That essay attempted to trace the development of Dalit Christian history as a field of study in relation to both the changing situation of Dalit Christians and the developments in the study of modern Indian history generally at the time of writing. The framework I used was basically chronological, decade by decade, from the 1970s to the present; within that framework, it was initially thematic and then regional. Unlike the essay for the ICHR, it included not only books but individual chapters and articles as well. During the course of the essay, I attempted to make comparisons and generalizations about the approaches adopted, the findings arrived at, and the conclusions drawn from them.

In the light of all that has preceded it, the concluding chapter offers some reflections on a few of the basic assumptions underlying research and writing on the history of Christianity in India. It seeks to respond to four questions and the varying concerns which have surrounded them in recent years: Why should we study the history of Christianity in India? Is it possible to have an accurate reading of that history (epistemological assumptions)? Which trends in the writing of Indian history are of special value to the historian of Indian Christianity (theoretical assumptions)? Which Christian theological assumptions have, and should, undergird its study as well? The aim of the chapter is less to propose an agenda for the future writing of such histories than to gain greater clarity concerning the foundations upon which such research and writing takes place.

These are not the only essays written on the historiography of Christianity in India, but there are not many others. Even introductory chapters to research monographs deal more with context and possible theoretical issues than with the background historiography of the subject under study. The most thorough free-standing essay on the subject is A. Mathias Mundadan's 'The Changing Task of Christian History: A View at the Outset of the Third Millennium', which was presented initially at an international conference. In what is at heart a visionary work, Mundadan offered, first of all, his own view of the history of Christianity as:

> the history of the encounter of the gospel message of Jesus with different peoples and their ever-newer religious-cultural and sociopolitical contexts. It is the history of the impregnation of these contexts by the gospel, the assimilation of the cultures of the peoples by the gospel and that of the gospel by their cultures, and the history of the consequent changes in the Christian movement and of the cultures of the people.[9]

This view led him not only to ask such questions as, 'Has the gospel had a real encounter with the Indian people, with their culture, with their world view, with their religious outlook? Has the Christian gospel really touched the soul of India, and has an Indian Christian culture emerged?',[10] but also to set forth, at the conclusion of his work, his own agenda for writing particular Christian histories as well as global Christian history. Mundadan also provided a review of historiographical trends in the West as well as in India, in which he both critiqued my 1978 essay (Chapter 1) for admittedly limiting itself to works in English, and supplemented what I had done by commenting on some earlier works, especially in Portuguese.

Some of the chapters presuppose an introductory knowledge of the history of Christianity in India and particularly of some of its internal disputes and controversies. A very brief overview providing a broader context for some of the events referred to in those chapters may, therefore, be useful to those unfamiliar with that history. There is a belief which has been neither proven nor disproven, that Thomas, one of Jesus's original disciples, came to south India, preached, baptized some converts, and died a martyr there. That belief forms the basis for the claim that the oldest church

9 A. Mathias Mundadan, 'The Changing Task of Christian History: A View at the Outset of the Third Millennium', in W.R. Shenk (ed.), *Enlarging the Story: Perspectives on Writing World Christian History* (Maryknoll: Orbis Books, 2002), p. 23.

10 Ibid., p. 24.

in India—like the oldest churches in the West—was of apostolic origin. By the fourth century, there were Christian migrants from Edessa in south India whose churches became connected ecclesiastically with the East Syrian Church. When the Portuguese arrived in 1498, there were Christian communities on the Kerala coast using Syrian rites for worship (hence Syrian Christians).

In 1510, the Portuguese established their rule along the western coast of India with their capital in Goa. In 1514, the Pope gave the kings of Portugal the right of patronage (Padroado). This included not only presenting candidates for bishop and other church offices, but also the financial responsibility for sponsoring and maintaining churches and missions in African and Asian lands 'conquered and to be conquered'. Under the Padroado, a number of Roman Catholic religious orders came to evangelize India, of which the most prominent were the Jesuits. In the 1540s, Francis Xavier evangelized and baptized thousands of fisherfolk on the southern tip of India. Soon after arriving in Madurai in 1606, Roberto de Nobili adopted an ascetic Brahmin lifestyle, learned Sanskrit, and entered into religious dialogue with learned pundits as a means of evangelizing the upper castes. Under Archbishop Menzes, the Padroado sought not only to bring the Syrian rite churches in Kerala under its control and into obedience to Rome, but also to change some of their most basic beliefs and practices. He achieved temporary success at the Synod of Diamper in 1599 but, in 1653, a large number of Syrian Christians broke away and resumed their ties to the East Syrian Church. The Catholic Church itself became divided into two jurisdictions—one for those using the Syrian rite and the other for those using the Latin rite common to the rest of India. As Portuguese power declined and its kings were unable to carry out the financial responsibilities of the Padroado, a lengthy power struggle took place between the Padroado and Rome. This was resolved in Rome's favour in 1886 when the Catholic hierarchy was established in India. This gave the Catholic Church in India a new lease of life.

The British, unlike the Portuguese, were ambivalent about having anything to do with the spread of Christianity in India. The first Protestant missions in India were established in Danish colonies. The first was in Tranquebar, south of Madras (1706). From there, it was spread by German and Indian missionaries into other parts of what is now Tamil Nadu. The next was the Serampore Mission (1800) near Calcutta established by William Carey. Only when the East India Company's charter was renewed in 1813 and 1833 were mission societies allowed to operate in British territories. Many came in during the course of the following century, moving inland from the coast and dividing up 'mission fields' between them so as to avoid competition. During the second half of the nineteenth century, Dalits, in particular, began converting in large numbers (the 'mass movements') and, in the early twentieth century, the tribal peoples of the hill areas of North-east India also began to convert in increasing numbers. Like the Catholic religious orders, the Protestant missions were dominated by foreign missionaries. However, beginning in the late nineteenth century, Indian Christian leaders began to challenge the 'Missionary Raj' and, during the twentieth century, a gradual transfer of power took place which, in many respects, paralleled that occurring in the nation at large. Soon after the British transferred power to independent India in 1947, the churches in India also became independent of foreign control. What happened to the Christian people of India and to their relationships with their fellow Indians in these processes of change will be described in some of the essays that follow.

CHAPTER 1

The History of Christianity in India
*Aims and Methods**

The Church History Association of India, at its October 1973 meeting, appointed an editorial board to prepare a multi-volume history of Christianity in India written from a single perspective. The editorial board consisted of six historians—three Protestant, two Roman Catholic and one Mar Thoma, all of whom had already published in the field of Indian church history. Their opening statement at their first meeting in February 1974 was that the perspective from which the history of Christianity in India had been written up to then was 'in serious need of revision'.[1] But how, precisely, had the history of Christianity in India been written and with what end in view? The purpose of this essay is to answer that question. This is not intended to be an exhaustive bibliographic essay since

---

* This chapter was previously published in *Bangalore Theological Forum*, vol. X, July–December 1978, pp. 110–48; reprinted in *Indian Church History Review*, vol. XIII, December 1979, pp. 87–122. This is a revised version.

1 See, 'A Scheme for a Comprehensive History of Christianity in India', *Indian Church History Review*, vol. VIII (December 1974), pp. 89–90. One phrase from the mimeographed version was accidentally omitted in this printing.

the literature on the subject is far too vast for it.[2] Instead, it will concentrate upon general histories and refer to more specialized works only where such works represent significant new departures or illustrate important general trends. It is also confined to histories written in English.

EARLY HISTORIES

The first general history of Christianity in India was a short work by Mathurin Veysierre de la Croze published in 1724. De la Croze was a French Protestant in the employ of the King of Prussia as a librarian and antiquary. His very anti-Catholic history focused on the Christians of Malabar—whom de la Croze found to be very similar to Protestants—and the Roman Catholic attempts to bring them under Papal authority. He simply ignored the rest of Catholic history in India and ended his work with a brief account of the first Protestant mission to India which was begun only in 1706.[3]

The first major history of Christianity in India was James Hough's multi-volume work which was published in 1839, 1845, and, posthumously, in 1860. Hough was one of the early 'Evangelical Chaplains' of the East India Company who sought not merely to minister to the needs of resident Europeans but also to evangelize the Indian people and build up the Indian Church. When he arrived in Palamcottah (Palayankottai) in 1816, he found the old SPCK (Society for Promoting Christian Knowledge) mission there in a state of neglect. He visited the neighbouring villages; revived a number of mission schools which had failed for lack of support; started seminaries to train school teachers; established a local branch of the Bible Society; and began both a Tamil translation of the Bible and a Tamil dictionary. Before he left in 1821 he

2 In 1976, Fr E.R. Hambye prepared a bibliography at the request of the editorial board for the use of the authors of the multi-volume history. This bibliography is 183 single-spaced foolscap pages in length. E.R. Hambye, *A Bibliography on Christianity in India* (Bangalore:Church History Association of India, 1976).

3 M.V. de la Croze, *Histoire du Christianisme des Indes* (La Haye: les frères Vaillant et N. Prévost, 1724).

handed over the work of 'reorganization, revival and extension of the Missions in Tinnevelly',[4] which he had carried out mostly at his own expense, to the Church Missionary Society, and specifically to C.T.E. Rhenius who had arrived there in 1820. After staying in England from 1822 to 1824 Hough returned but found that, owing to poor health, he had to leave India for good in 1826. Before leaving he had occasion to visit the Syrian Christians and the CMS Mission of Help in Travancore in 1825 and 1826.

In England, Hough put his Indian experience to good use as a controversialist for the Protestant missionary cause. While in Madras in 1824, he had written a reply to Abbé J.A. Dubois's *Letters on the State of Christianity in India*[5] which had been published the previous year and which was considered damaging to the cause of missions. During the 1830s, after he had settled permanently in England, Hough wrote a number of letters to the editors of various periodicals defending and vindicating Protestant missions against their 'Romanist' attackers. One of these was the Rev. (later Cardinal) Nicholas Wiseman who, in his 1836 *Lectures on the Principal Doctrines and Practices of the Catholic Church*, had argued at some length that the success of Roman Catholic and the failure of Protestant missions, especially in India, was clear evidence of divine favour and hence proved the truth of the Catholic and the falsity of the Protestant rule of faith.[6] Given all this contro-

---

4 Eugene Stock, *The History of the Church Missionary Society: Its Environment, Its Men and Its Work*, vol. 1 (London: Church Missionary Society, 1899), p. 202.

5 James Hough, *A Reply to the Letters of the Abbé Dubois, on the State of Christianity in India* (London: L.B. Seeley and Son, 1824). Hereafter, *Reply*.

6 Nicholas Wiseman, *Lectures on the Principal Doctrines and Practices of the Catholic Church* (London: Joseph Booker, 1836) pp. 163–260. Jackman's comments on Wiseman as a historian, while not based upon these particular lectures, do apply to them. 'In his lectures, he used history in a didactic sense. He produced evidence to underline a lesson, to illustrate a specific point of view. The philosophical conclusions existed from the beginning; the evidence merely illustrated the truth.' S.W. Jackman, *Nicholas Cardinal Wiseman: A Victorian Prelate and His Writings* (Dublin: Five Lamps Press, 1977), p. 116.

versy with the Catholics, a 'History of Christianity in India seemed [to Hough] to present the only hope of fortifying the public mind against their assaults' and so he began work on his history.[7] Since Hough's opponents had made extensive use of Dubois' *Letters*, Dubois' arguments helped to shape Hough's history.

Abbé Dubois, a priest of the Paris Missionary Society,[8] writing at the ebb tide of Roman Catholic missions in India, used the authority of his long experience in India to show that it was not possible, humanly speaking, to make 'real converts to Christianity among the natives in India'.[9] His arguments were essentially three in number. The first was that native prejudice against Christianity was so strong that conversion was virtually impossible. Brahmin control over the Hindu mind and the rigidity of the caste system were largely responsible for this.[10] Second, Dubois argued that if Roman Catholicism, which, because of its close conformity to native usages and prejudices, was more congenial to the Hindu mind, but which had failed to make progress, 'no other sect can flatter itself with the remotest hopes of establishing its system'.[11] Third, Dubois believed that those Hindus who had become Christians were not *real* converts. They clung to the old superstitions and usages; they did not practise equality or charity; they had not remained faithful in adversity; many had become Christians for material advantage.[12] Moreover, Dubois contended that the major innovation of Protestant evangelists—the translation and distribution of the scriptures—instead of winning people to Christianity, would increase their prejudice against it. There is much in the Bible that Hindus would find offensive (for example, Jesus was the son of a carpenter and his disciples were fishermen), and a lot

---

7 James Hough, *The History of Christianity in India from the Commencement of the Christian Era*, vol. I (London: R.B. Seeley and W. Burnside, 1839), p. iii. Hereafter, *History*.

8 Hough wrongly referred to him as a Jesuit. *Reply*, p. 1.

9 Abbé J.A. Dubois, *Letters on the State of Christianity in India* (London: Longman, Hurst, Orme, Brown and Green, 1823), pp. 1–2.

10 Ibid., pp. 97–102.

11 Ibid., p. 24.

12 Ibid., pp. 63–75.

more which they would find incomprehensible.[13] He also faulted Protestant Bible translations as inaccurate and lacking in literary elegance; they were therefore treated with laughter or scorn rather than with respect.[14]

The stated purpose of Hough's history was to

> ... furnish the Christian Public with a body of facts, an answer to the Romanists' vaunting of the successes of their own Missions, and their assertions of the failure of Protestant Missions; and hence to prove the fallacy of their conclusions, that theirs must be the cause of truth, and the Protestants' the cause of error.[15]

To achieve this aim, Hough made a neat distinction in his *History*. The first two volumes, published together in 1839, dealt with the Syrians and the Roman Catholics, up to 1750 in the former case, and up to the end of the eighteenth century in the latter. In these two volumes, the central event was the Synod of Diamper, which was 'the leading event of the Romish Missions in Malabar, and it develops the character of their entire history',[16] and to which Hough devoted almost half of this portion of his *History*. Hough saw the Syrians as an apostolic[17] church, completely independent of Rome. He treated their history in this period as, first, a prelude to subjugation, and then, as a struggle for freedom from subjugation to Rome. His main interest, however, was clearly the Roman Catholics, and he presented their history as one of deception, betrayal of the Gospel, and ultimate failure in Rome's pursuit of domination in India.[18] These volumes end with quotations from

13 Ibid., p. 32.

14 Ibid., pp. 37–41.

15 *History*, vol. III, p. i.

16 Ibid., vol. I, p. xiii.

17 It was apostolic not in the sense of being founded by an apostle, as Hough did not believe that St. Thomas had come to Malabar, but in the sense that it conformed to the teachings of the Bible in its polity and in its basic tenets. Ibid., vol. I, pp. 110–17, 151; vol. II, p. 12.

18 'In the two former volumes I have shown, from their own authorities, that their entire course in India has been one of deception; a system of accommodation to the most absurd notions and the foulest abominations of the Heathen; that they have systematically concealed

and a refutation of Dubois's *Letters*. By way of contrast, the history of Protestant missions in India, which is the exclusive concern of the remaining volumes,[19] is a story of success. Where occasional failures occurred, they were explained by referring to the peculiar circumstances responsible.[20] This portion of the *History* was organized on a mission-by-mission basis with special chapters on each of the first four Anglican bishops in India. Volumes three and four, published together in 1845, provide decade-by-decade accounts from 1706 to 1816; the fifth volume, which Hough's son edited from his papers after his death in 1847 and published only in 1860, carried the account up to 1826.

Hough's use of sources is also noteworthy. His usual practice was first to establish the authoritativeness of the sources he relied upon and then to treat them as authorities, often reproducing their contents. He sought to meet the charge of bias, particularly in regard to Roman Catholic history, by using Roman Catholic sources.[21] He also showed a marked tendency to rely upon one or two, often secondary, sources for major sections in his *History*. Thus, he made

---

from the Hindoo the essential peculiarities of revealed Truth; and that their Indian Missions, with reference to the propagation of Christianity, have proved, according to the confession of Jesuit Missionary [Dubois] of thirty years' standing, *a total failure*.' Ibid., vol. III, pp. i–ii.

19 Hough referred to the subsequent histories of the Syrian Church and its connection with the CMS Mission of Help, and of the Roman Catholic Church only when describing the opposition which various Protestant missions had to face.

20 Usually, this was lack of support from home, for example, *History*, vol. IV, p. 215.

21 An exception would appear to be his extensive use of de la Croze and Geddes, both of whom were Protestant, in his account of the Synod of Diamper. However, both of them drew upon Gouvea's *Jornado*. Gouvea belonged to the same order as did Menezes and is considered to have written a panegyric rather than a history of Menezes's trip and the Synod. Later, Protestant historians used Gouvea's efforts to show how zealous and masterly Menezes was in order to indicate how bigoted and ruthless Menezes really was! See Eugene Tisserant, *Eastern Christianity in India*, adapted from the French by E.R. Hambye (Bombay: Orient Longman, 1957), p. 56; and Jonas Thaliath, *The Synod of Diamper* (Rome: Institutum Orientalium Studiorum, 1958), pp. x, xi, 2 and 173 on de Gouvea.

extensive use of William Robertson's *An Historical Disquisition Concerning the Knowledge which the Ancients had of India* (4th ed., London, 1804) for contacts between India and the West; Michael Geddes, *The History of the Church of Malabar* (London, 1694); and de la Croze's *Histoire du Christianisme des Indes* (La Haye, 1724) for the history of Christianity in Malabar; *Jornada do Arcebispo de Goa Dom Frey Alexio de Menezes* by António de Gouvea (Coimbra, 1606) for Dom Alexis de Menezes, the then-Portuguese Archbishop of Goa; some Jesuit letters translated by John Lockman in 1743, and Paulinus of St. Bartholomew's *India Orientalis Christiana* (Rome, 1794) for the Madura Mission of Roberto de Nobili; R.P. Norbert, *Mémoires Historiques* for the Pondicherry missions; J.L. Niecamp's *Historia Missionis Evangelicae in India Orientali;* and then the annual reports of the SPCK for the Tranquebar Mission; and, for the remaining Protestant missions, he relied almost completely upon their annual reports. He also drew upon his own personal experience when describing the Syrian Christians or the history with which he was involved when in India. Hough's choice and use of sources led more to a work of comprehensiveness than of originality; as a result, the last three volumes consisted of a series of mission chronicles.

The major preoccupation of Hough's work was missionary methods. He had no disagreement with Dubois on the question of native prejudice against Christianity. Their views on Hindu 'superstition', the role of the Brahmins in maintaining such superstitions, and on caste as the chief obstacles to conversion were basically similar.[22] Although, in his *Reply* to Dubois's *Letters*, Hough had made the point that the Brahmins were losing their hold over the people's minds as Indians were being exposed to European arts and sciences,[23] and had begun patronizing them, one does not find this point elaborated in his *History*.

Hough took serious issue with Dubois's contention that, if the Roman Catholics could not succeed in converting India, no one else could, by faulting the methods which the Catholics in general and the Jesuits in particular had used for converting people.

22 *History*, vol. III, pp. 1–52.
23 *Reply*, pp. 38–43.

While he found in St. Francis Xavier's missionary character much that was admirable, Hough believed that many of his missionary methods (for example, the content and manner of instruction of converts) were the unavoidable outcome of the false system of belief 'which enthralled his mind'.[24] Menezes, according to Hough, used force, threats, bribery, lies, treachery and arrogance to achieve his aims in Malabar which were 'to assert the Pope's supremacy, and not to extend the dominion of Jesus Christ'.[25] Hough often found de Nobili and the Madura Mission guilty of deceit (for example, in claiming to be Brahmins and in 'forging' a fifth Veda),[26] while their policy of accommodation concealed rather than highlighted 'the peculiarities of the Gospel'.[27] Hough condemned the Roman Catholics and their methods for deviating

24 *History*, vol. I, pp. 207–9.

25 In writing later about the visit of Thomas Middleton, the first Anglican bishop in India, to Malabar, Hough drew the following comparison: 'We cannot pass without bidding the reader mark the differences between the conduct of Menezes, Archbishop of Goa, in 1598 and 1599, and that of Bishop Middleton, towards the ancient church. The former came to it with the wiles of the deceiver and the rod of the oppressor; the latter came with the words of truth in his mouth, and the olive branch of peace in his hand. Archbishop Menezes destroyed all the copies of the Syriac Scriptures that he could find, together with her [the Syrian Church's] formularies, history and every ancient record he could find, for the purpose of obliterating every vestige of her identity with the Church of Antioch and forcing her into communion with Rome. Bishop Middleton, on the contrary, deprecated any alteration in the Syrian Church brought about by foreign interference, or any conformity of it even with the Church of England, to the loss or injury of its own distinctive peculiarity. He admired its wonderful preservation, though he deplored its grievous errors and sad degradation. He wished it to be *the Church of Travancore*; and that it might be more worthy to occupy that position, and become the centre of light to the heathen around, it was the purpose of his heart to furnish it with an ample supply of the Syriac Scriptures, and other means for the reformation of itself. Whether any of these two prelates acted more in accordance with the character of a Christian bishop, let the reader judge.' Ibid., vol. V, p. 74.

26 Ibid., vol. II, pp. 221, 231, 237–8.

27 Ibid., vol. II, p. 251.

from Scripture; their ultimate condemnation, however, was their failure to which Dubois had borne testimony in his *Letters*. This failure was the result of their having 'obscured the light of Divine Truth' and put 'stumbling blocks . . . in the way of its reception, by the superstitions and ceremonies with which they have thought to recommend it'.[28] Thus, 'the failure of their labours ought to be attributed rather to their own unfaithfulness to the Lord, than to the people's insurmountable prejudices'.[29]

The methods of the Protestants were completely different and so, too, were the results of their work, measured not in the quantity but in the quality of their converts.[30] The Protestants' methods were scriptural. They sought to win converts not by force or guile but by the simple preaching of the Gospel; not by conforming but by contrasting the Gospel to the prejudices of the people; by translating the Scriptures as best they could, not into the flowery 'high' language full of literary conceits as the Jesuits had done, but into the simple language which ordinary people used and understood; [31] by using simple forms of worship rather than substituting one form of idolatry for another. The result had been a good number of *real* converts who had braved persecution, led Christian lives and died Christian deaths,[32] many of whom Hough described in his final three volumes. The conclusion was obvious: Roman Catholicism and all its ways stood condemned,[33] while Evangelical Protestantism was vindicated. In addition, Protestant missions required the full support of the British Christian public. British rule in India had provided both an opportunity and a responsibility for British Christians which was literally

28 Ibid., vol. II, p. 502.

29 Ibid., vol. II, p. 504.

30 See, for example, ibid., vol. III, pp. 51–2, 279–84.

31 Ibid., vol. II, pp. 232–3, 241–4; vol. V, pp. 218–21.

32 Hough, like many early-nineteenth-century Evangelicals, seemed to be fascinated with the death scenes of pious Christians. For example, ibid., vol. V, pp. 174–5 and 188–9.

33 Hough was not beyond pointing to explicit morals of the Indian story for his English readers as, for example, in using Menezes's take-over of the Syrian Church at Diamper to show what reunion with Rome would actually involve. Ibid., vol. II, pp. 133–42.

God-given.[34] While Hough was opposed to using the power of the State either to convert or to provide inducements to convert,[35] he did expect those in authority in India to be practising Christians, to lend their prestige and personal support to the Christian cause, to allow Indians to learn about Christ in schools, and to withdraw official support of idolatry.

Hough wrote his *Reply* to Dubois at a time when the Protestant missionary cause was fighting to win acceptance both in England and in India. However, by the time his *History* came out, Protestant missions were not only an accepted fact of life but were also gaining in strength and influence. As a result, Hough could and did write a history of the foundation-laying period of Protestant missions in India with a sense of confidence in their future success. His *History* became a standard reference work for future historians who drew upon the large amount of detailed information in its over three thousand pages and who often shared its author's views on the relative merits of Catholic and Protestant missions. His view of the history of Christianity in India as an account (with commentary) of missionary agencies and missionary methods, measured in terms of both (Anglican) Evangelical Truth and the results achieved, was in keeping with the needs of a generation of Evangelicals who were striving both to evangelize India as effectively as they could and to meet with the challenge of the Oxford Movement and Roman Catholicism at home.

LATER NINETEENTH CENTURY PROTESTANT HISTORIES

Three other general histories were written during the nineteenth century which, when taken together with Hough's and some denominational histories, provide a basis for characterizing the century's approach to the history of Christianity in India. The first of these, Sir John William Kaye's *Christianity in India: An Historical Narrative*, was written in 1859 in the midst of contro-

---

34 Ibid., vol. II, pp. 411–12.
35 Hough criticized the Dutch in Ceylon for their policy of giving jobs only to Christians. Ibid., vol. III, p. 92.

versies between Evangelicals and their opponents not only over
the role of Christian missions—and especially of the government
connection with Protestant missions—in causing the 1857 revolt,
but also concerning the social and religious policies which the
Government of India should, therefore, pursue in the future.[36]
Kaye, Secretary at the India Office in London, was of the view that
the public needed the means for making a more correct judgement
on the past and future of India.[37] He wrote as a Christian urging
moderation upon other Christians and as a defender (and possible
architect) of the particular policy of religious neutrality which was
being adopted by the Government of India. History was an ideal
vehicle for clarifying what he considered as being both the issues
and the relevant components in a desirable policy, because of the
importance he gave both to changes and to precedents.

The subject matter of Kaye's history was the progress of
Christianity in India, 'more especially as it has been affected by the
efforts of the Protestant Church and the measures of the British
Government'.[38] He devoted one chapter to pre-eighteenth-century
history, one to the Tranquebar Mission, and the remainder to
British religious life, religious policies, missions in India, and
especially to the relationship of the British Government of India
to the missionary cause. His subject matter was intentionally biographical, as he saw this as a period of mostly pioneers[39]—whether
British politicians, governors, chaplains or missionaries—and concentrated in Bengal, especially in Calcutta, to the virtual exclusion
of the rest of the country, because Calcutta was the centre of British
power in India.

For his early, non-British chapters, Kaye drew heavily upon
Hough, whose views he shared but which he stated with much
greater wit.[40] His chapter on Serampore was based on John

36 For an analysis of these controversies, see Thomas R. Metcalf, *The
Aftermath of Revolt: India, 1857–1870* (Princeton: Princeton University
Press, 1964), pp. 72–5, 82–110.

37 Sir John William Kaye, *Christianity in India: An Historical
Narrative* (London: Smith, Elder and Co., 1859), pp. xii–xiii.

38 Ibid., p. 1.

39 Ibid., p. xiv.

40 The following comments on de Nobili and the Madura Mission

Marshman's manuscript which was published in the same year as Kaye's own work.[41] For the rest, he used official and private papers, as well as occasional mission reports. He treated his sources with more critical detachment and with a broader awareness of historical context than did Hough. The result was an analytical history, rather than a chronicle, written in a very readable literary style. Like Hough, Kaye was not reluctant to pass moral judgements upon people or events.

Kaye showed that there was little enthusiasm in India or England for missions until the very end of the eighteenth century. Meanwhile, in the process of empire-building, the Government of India took over from the governments it had superseded responsibility for religious endowments, collecting a pilgrim tax and maintaining Hindu and Muslim religious institutions. Gradually, the Evangelical chaplains in India and the Clapham Sect in England changed the British attitude towards missions and then towards the government connection with Indian religions. According to Kaye, from 1813 to 1833, the British began to assert their own Christian faith, while from 1833 to 1853, they sought to emancipate themselves from their earlier connections with Hindu and Muslim religious institutions.[42] Kaye differed from the advocates of a 'Christian policy' for India in arguing that the diffusion of Christianity had depended upon British success which, in turn, had been due in part to their early prudence in making Indians feel that their religions were safe under British rule. Thus,

> What I am contending for is, if the people of India had not felt that *their* religions were secure against the assaults of the British Government,

---

illustrate this: 'They did their best to render conversion as easy as possible, by heathenizing Christianity to the utmost possible extent. Indeed it may be questioned whether the Jesuit missionaries were not themselves the only real converts. It is almost enough to say of the scandalous nature of their proceedings, that they brought a blush to the hard cheek of Menezes.' Ibid., pp. 32–3.

41 Ibid., p. xv. It appeared in 1859 under the title, *The Life and Times of Carey, Marshman and Ward: Embracing the History of the Serampore Mission.*

42 Sir John William Kaye, *Christianity in India*, pp. 482–3.

the British Government could not have asserted, as it has done, *its* own religion, without obstruction from the conflicting faiths by which it was surrounded.[43]

Consequently, Kaye argued that the government could not stop religious endowments without committing a breach of faith, nor should it promote Christianity by teaching it in government schools, lest people feel threatened. Instead, government neutrality posed the best hope for Christian missions.[44] Kaye closed with a plea for patience, moderation and for the kind of gentleness towards and respect for Indians that befits a Christian, instead of the cruelty and contempt characteristic of a dominant race.[45]

Kaye's was not only a very timely piece of historical writing for the post-1857 situation but also a very competent one. As the preceding summary of his argument indicates, for Kaye, the history of Christianity in India was primarily a matter of Church–State relationship. For later historians, his book became a standard reference work on that subject.[46]

The next general history, *The History of Protestant Missions in India, from their Commencement in 1706 to 1871*, was written in 1875 by the Rev. M.A. Sherring, for many years a missionary in Banaras of the London Missionary Society. The aim of this work, written to 'stimulate the zeal of the Churches at home on behalf of the great enterprise of Missions in India',[47] was 'to show historically what Protestant Missions have accomplished in India since their commencement'.[48] In this respect, Sherring's book was typical of most nineteenth-century histories. However, while others concentrated on the activities and achievements of their

43 Ibid., p. 480.

44 Ibid., pp. 489–91.

45 Ibid., p. 503.

46 For example, Arthur Mayhew used Kaye as one of his main sources for the pre-1858 period section in his *Christianity and the Government of India 1600–1920* (London: Faber & Gwyer, 1929).

47 M.A. Sherring, *The History of Protestant Missions in India, from their Commencement in 1706 to 1871* (London: Trubner and Co., 1875), p. viii.

48 Ibid., p. vii.

own particular missions, Sherring attempted to do this for all the missions together.

The major theme of Sherring's book was the spread of Protestant Christianity from one corner of India to the rest of it. After an opening chapter on the Tranquebar Mission, Sherring provided a region-by-region survey starting with Calcutta and greater Bengal (including Assam, Orissa and Bihar), proceeding north through the United Provinces to the Punjab, then down the west coast to South Travancore, and finally up the east coast to Andhra Pradesh. Each chapter of the survey begins with a description of some peculiarity, either of the people or of the missions in the region under survey, before moving on to a brief historical account of the various mission societies at work there and ending with a composite statistical table for 1871. The final chapter describes the direct and indirect results of Protestant missionary work and concludes with an assessment of the various missionary methods employed.

Sherring's sources were extremely limited. He relied heavily upon Hough and on the reports of the missionary conferences held at Ootacamund in 1858 and Allahabad in 1872–3. These he accepted without criticism, often quoting them at length. Of special significance is the unashamed triumphalism which pervades his work.

> The aggressive spirit of Christianity has never been more strongly exhibited than in its conflict with various forms of Hindooism in India during the present century ... It has combated superstition in its wildest forms. It has attacked Brahmanism in its famous seats of learning. It has contended with bloody rites, with foolish customs, with caste prejudices. It has followed idolatry to its most sacred spots ... Under the persistent assaults of Christianity, continued with sustained vigour from year to year, Hindooism has become fairly wearied ... At one time strenuous resistance was shown, and controversy raged throughout the land. But that day is past. Idolatry is not an active foe ... Christianity is looked upon as a young giant with whom it is dangerous to contend, and whom it is best to leave alone.[49]

The concluding chapter attributes the recent awakening of India in all its many aspects to the activities of Protestant missions. For

49 Ibid., pp. 133–4.

Sherring, the history of Christianity in India was the triumphant story of missions, missionaries, and missionary methods.

Sherring's work exemplifies the Euro-centric perspective on the history of Christianity in India which was to continue throughout the remainder of the nineteenth and well into the twentieth centu ry. Denominational histories of Western missions and missionary biographies—the two most common forms of historical writing during this period—followed Hough and Sherring in using history to promote Protestant missions. In these histories, India was reduced to a mere setting, and the sad state of her people explained by reference to the evil effects of the Hindu and the Muslim religions. The instruments of her salvation—measured in terms both of converts and socio-cultural change—were the aggressive band of Protestant missionaries labouring faithfully and efficiently in her midst, whose story formed the main body of each history.

Sherring's history also reflects the changed spirit with which historians were writing. The reminiscences, memoirs and historical narratives of the initial foundation-laying period of a mission society's work in India written in the first half of the century concentrated upon struggles in the face of tremendous challenges posed by the Indian environment—the terrain, the climate, local religious and cultural traditions, and the problematic nature of the resident European population. They were being replaced by histories which faced the future with increasing confidence. Christian missions in India were now taken for granted, at least in Western circles; they were getting permanently established in many parts of India and were expanding their operations; they were winning larger numbers of converts and were stimulating an increasingly apparent social and religious ferment among the still-unconverted. Writers of mission histories and biographies were, therefore, optimistic about the inevitable and none-too-distant triumph of Christianity in India. Whatever controversy there was focused upon such questions of mission strategy as the evangelistic potential of Christian educational institutions, or the wisdom of mass conversion of 'untouchables', rather than upon the very existence of Christian missions themselves.[50]

50 An excellent example of this perspective, as well as of continuing

The last general history written during the nineteenth century was Julius Richter's *A History of Missions in India*, which appeared first in German in 1906 and then in English translation in 1908. Richter, then editor of 'Die Evangelischen Missiones' and later Professor of Missiology at Berlin University, also wrote similar histories of Missions in the Near East (1910), Africa (1922) and China (1928). While he had less direct connection with India than any of the authors considered thus far, having paid only one visit prior to writing his history, he did treat his subject with a spirit of detachment lacking in other works.

Richter divided his work into two parts. After devoting an introductory chapter to the land, people, religion, and caste structure of India, he used three chapters to describe the development of missions in India. In this section, like Hough before him, he lumped together the Syrians and the Roman Catholics and traced their history only up to the end of the eighteenth century. Unlike Hough—who was much closer to the eighteenth century—Richter made a clear distinction between the Tranquebar Mission and 'modern missionary work' which was inaugurated by William Carey.[51] Like Kaye, he devoted an unusually large portion of the modern section of his history to Bengal, even naming two of the four sub-divisions of the chapter, 'The Age of William Carey' and 'The Age of Alexander Duff'. The second part of the history was arranged topically. This dealt with the religious challenges which missions faced in India as well as with missionary organization and methods (that is, vernacular preaching, literary work, mission

---

Protestant anti-Catholicism, was George Smith, the period's most prolific writer on missions in India. See his many missionary biographies as well as his general history, *The Conversion of India: from Pantaenus to the Present Time A.D. 191–1893* (London: John Murray, 1893). For an excellent list of nineteenth-century histories and biographies, the titles of which are often quite revealing, see the footnotes of Kenneth Scott Latourette, *A History of the Expansion of Christianity*, vol. VI: *The Great Century in Northern Africa and Asia, A.D. 1800–A.D. 1914* (New York: Harper & Brothers, 1944), pp. 99–186.

51 Julius Richter, *A History of Missions in India* (trans.) Sydney H. Moore (Edinburgh and London: Oliphant, Anderson and Ferrier, 1908), p. 131.

schools, women's work for women, medical missions, and missions to lepers). The final chapters describe some of the results of missions in India.

In Richter's history, one notes several methodological advances upon earlier histories. First of all, although Richter was extremely sparing in the use of footnotes, it is evident that he used a wider range of source materials than did his predecessors. Richter could, and did, draw upon a body of literature on India and on missions in India which had been developing over the second half of the nineteenth century, as well as upon the official census conducted every decade since 1881. A second advance was a certain critical distance between the author and his subject. Both the triumphalism of Sherring's work and the value judgements with which Hough's and Kaye's works abound were more controlled, although not absent, in Richter's. Moreover, where controversies existed—as in running schools for non-Christian children—Richter presented both sides as fairly as he could so that the issues involved were clear.[52] The third advance was his recognition that India did play a role in the history of missions. Hough had provided a (less scholarly) chapter on India while Sherring had mentioned the various influences of Protestant missions upon Indian society. Richter went a step further by describing the challenge posed by the religious beliefs and institutions of India. For Richter, 'The great problem of missionary work is: How can Christianity overcome and supplant native forms of religion?'[53] Therefore, he had to address himself to the question: 'What has been up to the present the attitude of Indian religions towards Christianity, and what prospects are there for their ultimate overthrow?'[54] He sought to answer his questions by analysing categories of Indians who held different types of beliefs. Clearly, the role India played was largely that of a 'problem to be overcome'; even Richter's concluding section on 'The Building up of the Christian Church in India' is a story of those shifts in mission policy and administration which were granting the Indian

52 Ibid., pp. 313–20.
53 Ibid., p. 241.
54 Ibid., p. 243.

churches more independence, rather than about what Indian Christians sought to have their churches become.

Thus, Richter was very much the proponent of Protestant missions and his history was very present-oriented. He used his history not so much to inspire support as to define the problems and issues which he felt missions were facing. For Richter, therefore, the history of Christianity in India was a history of (mostly Protestant) missions, missionaries and missionary methods.

The preceding analysis of nineteenth-century histories of Christianity in India indicates that, despite certain shifts of emphasis or advances in method, these histories shared several characteristics. The first and the most obvious is that they were written by Western authors and published in the West for a Western readership. Hence, at least in this proprietary way, these histories 'belonged' to the West rather than to India. Second, the history of Christianity in India was viewed as the history of missions and missionaries from the West, of their work, their methods, their successes and failures in India. They were not histories of the Indian Church but of Western attempts to create one. Only in the struggles of the Syrian Christians against the Portuguese hierarchy does one get a glimpse of an Indian *Church*, while individual Indian Christians, even when accorded considerable space, were generally assigned subordinate, 'assisting', or 'mission results' roles. This is also characteristic of the many Protestant denominational histories from this period which bear such titles as *Our India Missions*;[55] *The Story of the Delhi Mission*;[56] *Forty Years of the Punjab Mission of the Church of Scotland, 1855–1895*;[57] and *The Story of Fifty Years' Mission Work in Chhota Nagpur*,[58] to mention only a few. These histories were written for those (Westerners) who controlled and supported Protestant missions in India so that they might appreci-

55 By Andrew Gordon in 1886. *A Thirty Year's History of the India Mission of the United Presbyterian Church of North America, Together with Personal Reminiscences* (Philadelphia: Andrew Gordon, 1886).

56 Published by the Society for the Propagation of the Gospel (Westminister, 1908).

57 By John F.W. Youngson (Edinburgh: R. & R. Clark, 1896).

58 By Eyre Chatterton (London and New York: Society for Promoting Christian Knowledge, 1901).

ate *present* work and *current* issues by viewing them in a historical perspective. Since missions and missionaries dominated the
churches in India in the nineteenth century and were expected to
continue to do so for the foreseeable future, their histories were,
quite naturally, equated with the history of Christianity in India.

Given this equation of Protestant missions in India with
Christianity in India, it is not by accident that the third feature of
these histories is that, in them, neither the Syrian Christians nor
the Roman Catholics have a nineteenth-century history.[59] Not only
were those churches non-Protestant but they were also so torn by
internal divisions in the nineteenth century as to pose no serious
threat, or have anything positive to teach to those Protestants preoccupied with missions and mission work. Fourthly, India played
virtually no role in these nineteenth-century histories. India was
a setting on which the great missionary drama was acted out or a
kind of laboratory in which a variety of missionary methods were
tested. The peoples of India had no history of their own in these
accounts; they were not actors but were simply acted upon. In fact,
one is given the impression that 'by waking them up from their
long slumber', Christian missions gave them a history where previously they had none. Finally, these histories were based almost
exclusively upon mission sources which were generally treated
uncritically.

These histories bear a striking resemblance to contemporary
British histories of India in general which were also written to
instruct, inspire or convince a Western readership. While histories
of India concentrated upon the political, military and administrative history of rulers, and particularly upon British rulers, histories
of Christianity in India dealt with (particularly recent Protestant)
missionary policies, campaigns, and administrative measures.
Percival Spear's comment on British historical writing in the late
nineteenth and early twentieth centuries applies equally, as we
have seen, to histories of Christianity in India.

---

59 This is not true of the second edition of Richter's history, published
in 1924 and only in German, which included a chapter on Roman
Catholicism in the nineteenth century. (I owe this information to Hugald
Grafe.)

British historians in general were concerned with British activities and regarded the vicissitudes of Indian society as being outside their ken. Indian society being unprogressive and perhaps decadent the important thing was what the British did and how what they did affected the Indians.[60]

There is also the same kind of dependence upon 'official' sources produced by foreign administrators themselves found in the histories of Christianity. In fact, the parallels are so exact as to suggest that a common imperial viewpoint concerning India shaped nineteenth-century histories of both the religious and the mundane realms.

EARLY TWENTIETH CENTURY ROMAN CATHOLIC HISTORIES

While the Protestant historians described above were experiencing their 'Great Century' as they wrote, the same cannot be said of the Roman Catholic historians. Their 'Great Century' in India had run from the mid-sixteenth to about the mid-seventeenth century, while the nineteenth century was a period of recovery from intervening disasters as well as of prolonged jurisdictional disputes between the Portuguese Padroado (Patronage) and the Sacred Congregation for the Propagation of the Faith in Rome. These circumstances and their concept of the Church gave Catholic historians perspectives on the history of Christianity in India which were somewhat different from those of Protestant historians. They did not produce general histories of Christianity in India comparable to those of Hough, Kaye or Richter. M. D'Sa's short two-volume *History of the Catholic Church in India*[61] may be considered the first written in English, covering the history of the entire Catholic Church in India, while Joseph C. Houpert's *Church History of India*

60 T.G.P. Spear, 'British Historical Writing in the Era of the Nationalist Movements', in C.H. Philips (ed.), *Historians of India, Pakistan and Ceylon* (London: Oxford University Press, 1961), p. 409. See also, the other articles in this volume, especially, 'The Administrators and Historical Writing on India', by E.T. Stokes, pp. 385–403.

61 Bombay: The Lalka Printing and Litho Works, 1910, 1924.

and Ceylon A.D. 52–1942 provides only a brief Catholic vision of Indian Church history as a whole.[62]

The Rev. M. D'Sa, in all probability an Indian secular priest in the diocese of Damaun, wrote within a frame of reference which was not only Roman Catholic but also Portuguese and Padroadoist. Although the two volumes were divided into a large number of often very small chapters, they were, in fact, quite different. The first, devoted to the period from 52 to 1652, was an account of the establishment and spread of Christianity in India, and it largely avoided scholarly and ecclesiastical controversy. The second, which carried the history from 1652 up to 1924, and was, in the author's eyes, the more controversial of the two,[63] consisted largely of Papal and Portuguese documents pertaining to the jurisdiction of the Padroado in India. Thus, what began as a history of the Catholic Church ended up as a historical defence or justification of the Padroadoist stand on the jurisdictional disputes which plagued the Roman Catholic Church in India during the nineteenth century.

Most of D'Sa's first volume was organized around the lives and activities of the bishops and archbishops of Goa. He devoted three short chapters to the pre-Portuguese period at the outset, and the concluding chapters to the works of the various religious orders then in India. St. Francis Xavier, the Mughal Mission, and 'The Syriac Church' received separate chapters, but one is still left with the impression that all important developments were initiated from Goa. For example, de Nobili was virtually ignored in this volume and, in the second one, was referred to only in the context of the later disputes over the 'Malabar Rites'.[64] The chapter on 'The Popes and the Church in India' was made up mostly of quotations showing that the Popes were pleased with what the Portuguese were doing to spread the faith in India and that they themselves

62 (Trichinopoly: The Catholic Truth Society of India, 1942). This is a revision of an even briefer work terminating in 1930 and published in 1933.

63 M. D'Sa, 'Preface', *History of the Catholic Church in India, Volume II: A.D. 1652–1924* (Bombay: The Lalka Printing and Litho Works,1924).

64 Ibid., vol. I, p. 170; vol. II, pp. 31–41.

were bound by the Padroado arrangement. The next chapter on 'The Kings of Portugal and the Church in India' showed that the Popes' confidence in the Portuguese was well justified. D'Sa not only accepted as quite natural the union of Church and State that was implicit in the Padroado arrangement, but also considered it largely responsible for the success of Christianity in India. He opened his history by saying that, 'In justice it must be said that the conquests of Portugal were so many conquests of religion',[65] and elaborated further when discussing the Kings of Portugal and the Church in India by saying, 'It was his [the King's] army of brave Portuguese soldiers that enabled Fr Antonin do Porto, Michael Vaz, St. Francis Xavier and other zealous missionaries to break down idols and destroy pagodas without molestation'.[66] D'Sa devoted his second volume almost exclusively to the jurisdictional controversy between the Padroado and the Propaganda.[67] He concluded it—as he had the first volume—with brief organizational histories of the various religious orders in India. He provided ample footnotes in both volumes, citing both primary and secondary sources, but gave no bibliography.

D'Sa largely avoided the controversial issues raised by the historians discussed thus far, and, as a result, his explanations often appear complacent and simplistic. For example, he attributed de Nobili's methods mainly to an excess of zeal[68] and explained conflicts between the Roman Catholic and the 'Syriac' Churches

65 Ibid., vol. I, p. 1.

66 Ibid., vol. I, p. 204.

67 Under the Padroado agreement of 1514, the Portuguese were responsible for maintaining missions and churches in India; in return they had the right of ecclesiastical patronage which included the nomination of bishops. When the Portuguese were no longer able to fulfill the financial obligations of this agreement, the Vatican, through the Sacred Congregation for the Propagation of the Faith (the Propaganda), sent out their own missionaries whose churches were organized under Vicars Apostolic. Thus there were two competing, and in some places overlapping, jurisdictions in India. Negotiations went on from 1833 to 1886 when a concord was reached which enabled the Propaganda to establish dioceses and appoint bishops outside the Padroado jurisdiction.

68 Ibid., vol. I, p. 170.

solely in terms of either personal disagreements or of the clash between Catholic truth and Nestorian heresy.[69] The destruction of Hindu idols and 'pagodas' as well as other denials of religious liberty did not call forth any explanation at all. Perhaps controversy made D'Sa feel uncomfortable, as his preface to the second volume suggests;[70] perhaps his loyalty to the Padroado made him accept things which others would question; perhaps he did not want to disturb the Catholic faithful for whom his history was written. However, since D'Sa cited Hough's *History*,[71] he could not have been totally unaware that there were strong differences on these and other questions.

Joseph C. Houpert SJ used both his general history and a more detailed history of his own Madura Mission[72] as vindication for Roman Catholic Christianity. His view of the Church as, on the one hand, 'the visible society of believers united in a constitutional monarchy under one head the Pope as Vicar of Christ' and, on the other, as 'the assembly of God's people imperfect still but growing in perfection ... [as the Church] takes men as they are and by degrees raises them to higher levels'[73] undergirded the two major themes of his histories: institutional continuity and missionary expansion. With regard to the former, Houpert considered the Church in India to have been Catholic from the very outset, for a time Nestorian in name only, and then divided by the 'Jacobite schism' in the seventeenth century and the coming of Protestant 'counter-missions' in the eighteenth century.[74] With regard to the latter theme, he saw the aim of mission as establishing the Catholic Church on a permanent basis, with the religious orders as the chief agents of mission. He defended the missionary methods they had used, especially those of de Nobili and his successors in the Madura Mission, and concluded his general history with a descrip-

69 Ibid., vol. I, pp. 172–85.
70 Ibid., vol. II, Preface.
71 Ibid., vol. I, p. 180.
72 *A South Indian Mission: The Madura Catholic Mission from 1535 to 1935*, new ed. (Trichinopoly: St. Joseph's Industrial School Press, 1937).
73 Joseph C. Houpert, *Church History of India and Ceylon*, pp. 1, 97.
74 Ibid., pp. 9–10, 40–2, 66.

tion of the present Church as sociologically complex, economically poor and dependent on foreign help, as well as on the defensive in relation to other Indians.

D'Sa's and Houpert's primary preoccupations—missionary expansion and methods; the institutional development of a hierarchical church; questions of jurisdiction between religious orders as well as between Padroado and Propaganda—are also reflected in the many other histories of dioceses and religious orders in the late nineteenth and early twentieth centuries.[75] While, as in the Protestant case, foreigners were the chief actors and India served basically as a stage in Catholic histories, the histories themselves do not share quite the same imperial ethos. Most of the authors—both as non-Anglo-Saxons and as Catholics—could not participate fully in the triumphalism of the British Raj. Moreover, the 'Golden Age' of Roman Catholicism in India had come and gone, and was identified more with Portugal than with Great Britain.

EARLY SYRIAN ORTHODOX HISTORIES

The history of the Syrian churches in Kerala was the first to attract Indian Christian writers. It also generated the earliest and largest body of modern historical literature on Christianity in an Indian language (Malayalam). However, the first history of the Syrian Church in India to be written in English was in 1694 by an Englishman who had never been to India. Michael Geddes, Chancellor of the Cathedral Church at Sarum, was a prolific writer of tracts and books, most of which were critiques of the Roman Catholic Church.[76] This history is no exception, as its full title indi-

75 Many of these histories, like their Protestant counterparts, were inspirational or promotional in character, whereas Adrien Launay's five-volume *Histoire des Missions de L'Inde: Pondichéry, Maïssour, Coïmbatour* (Paris: Ancienne Maison Charles Douniol, 1898) parallels Richter's history in its focus upon missiological issues.

76 These include works on the Council of Trent, the Protestant Martyrs in Spain, a Church History of Ethiopia and one titled *A View of the Methods by Which the Roman Church Keeps Her People from Coming to the Knowledge of the Great and Manifold Errors and Corruptions Which are in her Faith, Worship and Spirit* (London: A. and J. Churchill, 1706).

cates: *The History of the Church of Malabar from the Time of its being first discovered by the Portuguezes in the Year 1501. Giving an Account of the Persecutions and Violent Methods of the Roman Prelates, to Reduce them to the Subjection of the Church of Rome. Together with the Synod of Diamper, Celebrated in the Year of our Lord 1599. With some Remarks upon the Faith and Doctrine of the Christians of St. Thomas in the Indies, agreeing with the Church of England, in opposition to That of Rome.*[77] The main body of the work consists of the decrees of the Synod of Diamper taken from Gouvea's *Jornada* because, as Geddes pointed out, in condemning them, the decrees revealed much about the doctrines and practices of the Malabar Church that otherwise would not have come to light[78] and showed that 'there has always been a considerable visible Church upon Earth, that never believed the Doctrines of the Pope's Supremacy, Purgatory, Transubstantiation, Adoration of Images, Auricular Confession &c.'[79] The decrees were preceded by a history of the Malabar Church's relation with the Portuguese from 1501, most of which was devoted to Menezes's trip to Malabar climaxed by the Synod of Diamper and to a list of fifteen 'doctrines in which the Church of Malabar agrees with the Church of England and disagrees with Rome'.[80]

The Syrian Christians of Malabar,[81] the first history in English by a Syrian Christian writer located thus far, was published in England in 1869. Its author, Edavalikel Philipos, was a cathanar of the Jacobite Syrian Church and a staunch supporter of Mar Joseph Dionysius against Mar Matthew Athanasius in the dispute over who was the legitimate Metropolitan of the Jacobite Syrian Church in Travancore and Cochin. Philipos's was a short work written in a question-and-answer form. It began by setting forth the doctrines of his Church and its relationship to the early councils of

77 London: Sam. Smith and Benj. Walford, 1694.

78 Ibid., p. 109.

79 Ibid., Dedication Page.

80 Ibid., p. G3.

81 Edavalikel Philipos, *The Syrian Christians of Malabar: Otherwise Called the Christians of S. Thomas* (ed.) G.B. Howard (Oxford and London: James Parker & Co., 1869).

the Church. The Indian portion of the history, that covers only a third of the thirty-two pages, describes the coming of St. Thomas in AD 52 and Thomas of Cana in AD 345, the Synod of Diamper and its aftermath, ending with the then-current controversy, in which he condemned Matthew Athanasius as a deceiver, and the Travancore government for its policy of non-interference in ecclesiastical matters.[82]

Only in 1892 did a full-length history, *The Syrian Church in India*, appear. Its author, George Milne Rae, a former professor at Madras Christian College, had it published in England as his aim was simply to inform Western readers about this church by writing its history. His focus was first upon its origin and then upon its relationships with churches in the West. With regard to the former, he argued, largely on the basis of the *Acts of Thomas*, that St. Thomas did not come personally to south India. However, since Thomas was the founder and patron saint of the Church of Edessa, when members of that Church migrated to south India, Thomas became by extension the founder of the church there, too. This, Rae called 'the migration of tradition'.[83] The rest of the history he divided into three periods: the Nestorian, the Roman, and the Jacobite. During the Nestorian period, the Syrian Christians established themselves in India as a caste of good standing.[84] The Roman period was characterized by subjugation. The Jacobite period involved a switch of allegiance from Nestorian Edessa and Babylon to Jacobite Antioch and thus from the tradition of St. Thomas to a heretical tradition of St. Peter. However, Rae devoted most of this period to the 'Mission of Help' of the Church Missionary Society (CMS) (1813–37) aimed at reforming the Jacobite Church from within; to the divisions in the Church that followed; and to the dubious role that the Patriarchs of Antioch played in those disputes. His history ends with the 1889 court case that the traditionalists won over those reformers who were influenced by the CMS missionaries, and to a critique of the ways in which the two Hindu judges used historical

82 Ibid., p. 25.
83 George Milne Rae, *The Syrian Church in India* (Edinburgh and London: William Blackwood and Sons, 1892), p. 128.
84 Ibid., p. 183.

data to reach their majority decision. Rae's own conclusion was that the Syrian Church in India would be much better off if they cut ties with the Patriarchs, to whom they sent money and from whom they received nothing in return, and if they took 'their Church affairs' into their own hands lest their members be absorbed by the stronger Catholic and Protestant churches nearby.[85]

C.M. Agur's lengthy *Church History of Travancore*, which appeared a decade later, had a less conspicuous agenda to push than its predecessors had. Agur, a Tamil Protestant native of Travancore working in government service, sought to create an interest among his fellow countrymen in the history of their churches 'in view to their further development'[86] and published his history in India in 1903. In his view, the central fact about the Travancore churches was their marvellous growth. This, he attributed primarily to the zeal of many missionaries, both Indian and foreign.[87] He treated the history of the Syrian Church, the Roman Catholic Church and the Protestant Church separately, devoting more space to the last than to the former two combined, despite the shorter history of Protestantism in Travancore. His section on the Syrian Church was not about growth. Instead, he followed Rae not only in his analysis of the St. Thomas tradition and in labelling the three periods of Syrian Church history as Nestorian, Roman and Jacobite, but also in paying a lot of attention to the Church's external ecclesiastical relationships. Where he differed from Rae was in supplying more information about the nineteenth-century Syrian congregations; about what the competing metropolitans actually did for their congregations; and about the current condition of the Jacobite Syrian and the Reformed Syrian churches following their separation. Like Rae, he saw the connection with Antioch as a weakness because it created divisions in Travancore but offered no compensating benefits. Unlike Rae, he saw some signs of reconciliation and reform in both parts of the now-divided

---

85 Ibid., pp. 355–6.

86 C.M. Agur, *Church History of Travancore* (New Delhi: Asian Educational Services, 1990), p. vi. This book was originally published in Madras in 1903.

87 Ibid., p. 69.

church, and so, concluded that 'Surely then we may say that the Syrian Church in Travancore has yet a glorious future.'[88]

The last of these early general histories of the Syrian Church to be included in this overview is E.M. Philip's *The Indian Church of St. Thomas*. Philip, a nephew of Edavalikel Philipos, felt it was important to write such a history from the Syrian Christian point of view,[89] arguing that it was a genuinely orthodox church of long standing and so deserved both sympathy and high regard.[90] Like its predecessors, this history concentrated upon the Church's external ecclesiastical relationships as well as upon the disputes over the legitimacy of its various metropolitans in India. Philip finished the book in 1907 and tried, but failed, to get it published in Britain. Instead, it was published in India after his death in 1914, first in Malayalam (1929) and then, much later, in English (1950).

Philip took direct issue with Rae (whom he frequently referred to as 'our critic') on three key points. He upheld the tradition that St. Thomas himself came to India in AD 52, citing indirect evidence in its favour and arguing that, while it could not be proven, Rae had failed to disprove it with his conjectures.[91] He also rejected Rae's neat division of the Church history into Nestorian, Roman and Jacobite periods, largely because he was not convinced that the Syrian Church to which the Kerala Christians were ecclesiastically linked had been consistently Nestorian prior to 1500; he saw it as a mix of Jacobite and Nestorian, with the Jacobite being the stronger part of the mix.[92] He was also firmly committed to the ecclesiastical tie with the Jacobite Patriarch of Antioch as historic; invaluable (as when the Patriarch visited Kerala in 1875–6 and reorganized the Church there);[93] and integral to the identity of the Jacobite Syrian Orthodox Church.

---

88 Ibid., p. 196.

89 E.M. Philip, *The Indian Church of St. Thomas* (Nagercoil: The London Missionary Society Press, 1950), p. i.

90 Ibid., pp. 5–6.

91 Ibid., p. 47. He also placed the arrival of a group of migrants under Thomas of Cana in AD 345, four hundred years earlier than did Rae. Ibid., pp. 70–5.

92 Ibid., pp. 130–58.

93 Ibid., pp. 259–61.

Philip devoted more than half of his history to the nineteenth century, and particularly to the CMS 'Mission of Help' and its consequences for the Jacobite Syrian Orthodox Church. While the mission had perhaps begun with the best of intentions as an act of friendship and solidarity at a time when the Syrian Church was especially vulnerable, it had proved to be anything but that in practice. Philip saw the C.M.S. missionaries working in col- lusion with the British Residents in Travancore—who had great influence with the Travancore government—to grant recognition to or to dismiss Metropolitans sent by the Patriarch of Antioch, and so divide and weaken his Church. He produced evidence to show that they insulted, violated, and robbed the Jacobite Church of both members and treasure. He considered their 'Mission of Help' to be similar in aim though gentler in methods to Menezes's earlier attempt to take over the Syrian Church.[94] He decided that the Syrian Christians were treated far better by the tolerant Hindu rulers of Travancore than by fellow Christians from Portugal and England.[95] In his concluding retrospect, Philip wrote that the Church's 'staunch attachment to her ancient oriental customs, and forms of worship and government is not more striking than the marked dislike she has consistently displayed to all Western inno- vations, whether Romish or Anglican.'[96] Philip clearly shared that dislike and this portion of his history has been criticized as being unfairly one-sided as a result.[97] His was a 'committed history' full of moral judgements which could not simply be dismissed because

94 Ibid., pp. 326–30.
95 Ibid., p. 418.
96 Ibid., p. 416.
97 While by no means exonerating the CMS missionaries, the following two histories of the 'Mission of Help' do take issue with Philip on the role which the mission played in the history of the Syrian Church. P. Cheriyan, *The Malabar Syrians and the Church Missionary Society, 1816–1840*. (Kothayam: The Church Missionary Society's Press & Book Depot, 1935); Eugene Lester Ten Brink, 'The C.M.S. Mission of Help to the Syrian Church in Malabar, 1816–1840: A Study in Protestant–Eastern Orthodox Encounter', unpublished PhD dissertation (Hartford: Hartford Seminary Foundation, 1960).

of both the line of argument and the substantial documentation it provided.

Although the Syrian Church had a very different history from that of the Catholic or the Protestant Churches, it is striking how similar nineteenth-century historical writing about them was. In all three cases, the roles of foreign actors and of those at the top of the ecclesiastical hierarchies really constituted the histories, while the community was largely ignored. Both the Syrian and the Catholic Churches were plagued by jurisdictional disputes and these became major focal points for their historians. What distinguished this body of historical writing from the others was, on the one hand, its preoccupation with questions of origins and legitimacy, and, on the other, two important innovations: C.M. Agur's reaching out to a new readership by publishing in India for his fellow countrymen, and the spirit of what might be called 'ecclesiastical nationalism' in which E.M. Philip wrote his history.

TWENTIETH CENTURY DEVELOPMENTS

The period between the outbreak of World War I and the achievement of Indian Independence was a period of great change for the Church and for India generally. Under Gandhi's leadership, the Indian National Congress ushered in a new era by broadening its base of support enormously, completely changing its structure and tactics, and posing so serious a challenge to British rule that the British decided to leave in 1947. As a result of the impact of the nationalist movement upon Indian life, ecclesiastical statesmen came to see that the future of Christianity in India would be very different from its past, and that their major task now was to prepare the Church in India for an uncertain future. It is, therefore, not surprising that during this period not only were no general histories of Christianity in India written and that the number of denominational histories declined, but also that the Syrian churches—which were for all intents and purposes free from foreign domination—became of increasing interest to historians.[98] It would seem from

98 H. Mingana, *The Early Spread of Christianity in India* (Manchester: The University Press, 1926); P. Cheriyan, *The Malabar Syrians*; F.E. Keay,

two articles on the study of church history written in the 1930s that, as the Indian Church came to replace the foreign missions as the centre of Christian concern during this period, Indian Churchmen felt that they had more of value to learn from the past experience of the Church in the West than from their own past.[99] Nevertheless, in response to the recommendations made by the Church History deputation sent to Asia by the International Missionary Council in 1931–2, the Church History Association of India was founded in 1935. It devoted its energies primarily to the location, collection and preservation of source materials. It did plan a three volume history, which was to maintain the now traditional denominational division, as well as some short sketches of pioneers and leaders of the Church, most of whom were foreigners, but neither of these projects came to fruition.[100] In 1941, 'The History of Christianity in India' became a separate optional course in Church History for theological students in colleges affiliated to the Senate of Serampore College.[101] Thus, while this pre-Independence period did not see much attention paid to the history of Christianity in

---

A History of the Syrian Church in India (Madras: SPCK 1938); Rev. Fr Placid, The Syrian Church of Malabar (ed.) K.E. Job (Changamacherry: St. Joseph's Orphanage Press, 1938).

99 In 1933, A.J. Appasamy listed four issues on which the Indian Church needed guidance from the past, and he drew upon the Western experience to illustrate his point: church union; 'relating Christianity to the accepted doctrines and philosophical systems of India'; the sanyasi or monastic ideal; and great epochs of creative growth. To the first two of these, C.E. Abraham, writing in 1936, added the numerical expansion of the church under the impact of the mass movements, and the rise of communism and socialism in India. A.J. Appasamy, 'The Study of Church History in India', National Christian Council Review, vol. LIII (March 1933), pp. 123–8 (April 1933), pp. 185–93. C.E. Abraham, 'The Study of Church History in India', The International Review of Missions, vol. XXV (1936), pp. 461–9.

100 'Reports: Church History Association of India, Burma and Ceylon Report for the Year 1935', National Christian Council Review, vol. LVI (March 1936), pp. 160–6.

101 It remained an optional course until 1969 when it became a required course. United Theological College, Year Book July 1940, p. 17; Year Book July 1941, p. 21; Year Book 1969–70, p. 42.

India, some steps were taken in India towards the development of this field of study.[102]

Soon after Independence, two short general histories of Christianity in India appeared which indicate some of the significant continuities with and changes from the earlier histories already examined. Both were written by Indians and both were published in England. The first, written in 1952, was *The Cross over India* by Rajaiah D. Paul, the General Secretary of the recently formed Church of South India. Paul stated in his preface that he was not writing a history of Christianity in India. He saw his work as 'a meager, almost cursory, attempt to assess the process and worth of the Christian enterprise in my country in the past and its position at present, with an even slighter attempt to indicate what conditions may be in the near future'.[103] He began with a chapter on 'The Beginnings of Christianity in India' to show that 'the Indian Church, or at least one portion of it, is historically one of the most ancient Churches in the world; though, for all practical purposes, it must be considered to be one of the "younger churches"—to use the phraseology now familiar since Jerusalem 1928 and Tambaram 1938'.[104] After a brief survey of later history which included a (now familiar) chapter on 'Campaigning Methods' in the nineteenth and early twentieth centuries, Paul devoted the longest chapter to a series of biographical sketches of some early Protestant converts under the title, 'Some Heroes of the Indian Church'.[105] He then

102 C.W. Ranson's report on theological education in India, written in 1945, considered Church History to be 'the part of theology in which the Church in India is weakest', and noted that 'the dearth of books on the history of the Church in India is a heavy handicap to students. We still await a good comprehensive history of the Church in this country.' C.W. Ranson, *The Christian Minister in India, His Vocation and Training* (London: The United Society for Christian Literature, 1946), pp. 210–11.

103 Rajaiah D. Paul, *The Cross over India* (London: SCM Press Ltd., 1952), p. 10.

104 Ibid., p. 13.

105 He wrote five other books of biographies of Indian Christians: *Chosen Vessels: Lives of Ten Indian Christian Pastors of the Eighteenth and Nineteenth Centuries* (Madras: The Christian Literature Socciety, 1961); *Triumphs of His Grace: Lives of Eight Indian Christian Laymen of*

listed the achievements and failures of the Church in India and concluded with a chapter on the present situation entitled 'The Church in the New India'.

Paul mentioned only three sources in his footnotes and provided no bibliography. His work is significant not for its scholarship but for the perspective from which it was written. This was the first Indian nationalist history of Christianity in India. It was a history of the Indian Church (which he, like his predecessors, clearly equated with the Protestant churches) rather than of foreign missions; Indian, rather than foreign, heroes were singled out for special attention; the role of the Indian churches in the ecumenical movement was given a separate chapter. Both the Indianization of the Church and the Independence of India were presented in a very positive light. Yet Paul's nationalism was both very Christian and very definitely moderate. It was Christian in that he was a strong advocate of evangelism and of the distinctily *Christian* contribution which the Church had made and should continue to make to India. It was moderate in that, while Paul favoured the political and cultural Indianization of the Church, he was, on the whole, appreciative of the contribution which foreign missionaries had made in the past, and he believed that "The Church in India cannot afford to dissociate herself from the Church in the West, and in the interests of Christianity should not be allowed to do so'.[106]

The other history written soon after Independence was *Christians and Christianity in India and Pakistan* by P. Thomas, a Syrian Christian, who wrote it in order to meet a need for 'a book giving a connected account of Christianity in India from the time of the Apostle Thomas, who preached the Gospel in India, to the

---

the Early Days of Protestant Christianity in India, Every One of Whom Was a Triumph of His Grace (Madras: The Christian Literature Society, 1967); Changed Lives (Lucknow: Lucknow Publishing House, 1968); They Kept the Faith: Biographies of Gopeenath Nundi, Pyari Mohan Rudra, and Lal Behari Day (Lucknow; Lucknow Publishing House, 1968); and Lights in the World: Life Sketches of Maulvi Safdar Ali and the Rev. Janni Alli (Lucknow: Lucknow Publishing House,1969).

106 Rajaiah D. Paul, *The Cross over India*, p. 123.

present day'.[107] Thomas sought to overcome the denominational point of view of earlier Western writers by laying emphasis upon 'the Greater Church of Christ'. He also sought 'to put the history of Indian Christianity in its correct perspective' by describing the pre-Portuguese period in greater detail and by avoiding the earlier Western writers' 'marked antipathy towards Indian traditions, especially of Kerala'.[108] Thomas certainly succeeded in avoiding the strong Protestant emphasis of the earlier histories: he gave approximately equal space to Syrian, Latin Catholic and Protestant history, and also refrained from treating Protestant missions as the climax or the last word in missions. Furthermore, he devoted a chapter to 'The Early Malabar Church' to fill the gap he found in other works.

In his chapters on St. Thomas and the early Malabar Church, Thomas relied upon the usual Western sources and the above-mentioned Kerala traditions which he regarded as completely reliable.[109] For the rest of the book, the sources are rarely mentioned even when quoted, although a fifteen-book bibliography was provided at the end. Thomas obviously drew heavily, if not excessively, upon Edward Maclagan[110] for his chapter on 'Christianity in Mughal India'; upon Banerji[111] for his chapter on Begam Samru; and upon Kaye for much of his material on pre-1857 Protestant history. The post-1857 portion of his chapter on 'Progress of Christianity under the British' is so impressionistic that, aside from a few quotations to illustrate Christian responses to the nationalist movement, one wonders whether Thomas used any sources at all.

---

107 P. Thomas, 'Preface', in his *Christians and Christianity in India and Pakistan: A General Survey of the Progress of Christianity in India from Apostolic Times to the Present Day* (London: George Allen and Unwin Ltd., 1954).

108 Ibid.

109 This same uncritical attitude towards tradition is reflected in the estimates he gave of the number of converts won by St. Francis Xavier (700,000) and Roberto de Nobili (100,000). Ibid., pp. 62, 72.

110 *The Jesuits and the Great Mogul* (Tunbridge Wells: Burns Oates and Washbourne, 1932).

111 Brajendranath Banerji, *Begam Samru* (Calcutta: M.C. Sarkar & Sons, 1925).

For Thomas, the history of Christianity in India was the history of neither Christian missions—as it was for the nineteenth-century histories—nor of the Indian Church—as it was for Rajaiah Paul— but of the Christian community in India. This particular emphasis is reflected in the title;[112] in Thomas' non-denominational approach to his subject; in his discussions of the part which Christians played at certain times in Indian history; in his descriptions of Christian communities (especially in Malabar); and in the statement concerning the future with which the book ends.

> All this augurs well for the future, and as long as the present [Indian political] leadership lasts Christians as a community have little to fear. But whether the same liberal traditions [of government] will be followed after the passing away of the present generation, the future alone will show.[113]

Thomas's history, like Paul's before it, was significant not for the quality of the scholarship upon which it was based but for the Indian perspective from which it was written. In the years when Christians were still adjusting to life in an independent secular democracy, Thomas used history to affirm that Christians had a place in the new India, just as Rajaiah Paul had used history to define the important role which he believed the Church had to play in the present and the foreseeable future.

In 1961, the Christian Students' Library brought out the first general history of Christianity to be published in India primarily for an Indian readership. It was a textbook for Indian theological students in the Serampore system, titled, *An Introduction to Indian Church History* by Cyril Bruce Firth, a missionary in India of the London Missionary Society since 1930 and, at the time of writing, the Principal of the Union Kanarese Seminary in Tumkur. Firth sought to 'trace the outline of Indian Church History from the beginning down to the present time'.[114] In this outline, the first

112 Thomas mentioned Pakistan in his title but did not deal with it in the book.

113 P. Thomas, *Christians and Christianity in India and Pakistan*, p. 244.

114 Cyril Bruce Firth, *An Introduction to Indian Church History* (Madras: Christian Literature Society, 1961), p. iii.

eighteen centuries received as much attention as did the nineteenth and the twentieth. There was also a good balance between Syrian, Roman Catholic and Protestant history from their respective beginnings in India to the post-Independence period. The organization was chronological up to the nineteenth century and topical thereafter as far as the Protestants were concerned.[115] The two chapters on the nineteenth- and twentieth-century histories of the Syrian and the Catholic churches (an innovation) dealt primarily with institutional developments. Only the title of his concluding chapter, 'The Emerging Indian Church', which is almost exclusively Protestant in content, betrays a denominational preference. For the rest, the book is, indeed, very balanced.

Firth drew heavily upon both the nineteenth-century histories discussed earlier, except Kaye,[116] and the monographic literature which had grown up during the years since Richter's history was written. Of these more specialized histories, the ones he quoted most frequently were: A. Mingana, *The Early Spread of Christianity in India* (1926); E.M. Philip, *The Indian Church of St. Thomas* (1956); L.W. Brown, *The Indian Christians of St. Thomas* (1956); and E. Tisserant, *Eastern Christianity in India* (1957), on the Syrian Christians. J.C. Houpert, *A South Indian Mission: The Madura Catholic Mission from 1535 to 1935* (2nd ed., 1937); and D. Feroli, *The Jesuits in Malabar* (2 vols., 1939, 1951), on the Roman Catholics. J.W. Pickett, *Christian Mass Movements in India* (1933); E.G.K. Hewat, *Christ and Western India* (1950); B. Sundkler, *Church of South India* (1954); and E.A. Lehmann, *It Began at Tranquebar* (1956), on the Protestants. On the other hand, references to primary sources are very few in number.

Firth was both critical and fair in his treatment of his sources, especially of the first eighteen centuries. His discussion of the St. Thomas tradition is still one of the most lucid and perceptive available. His treatment of such controversial subjects as Menezes and Diamper or de Nobili and the Madura Mission focuses attention on the issues involved in quite a dispassionate way. The nineteenth

---

115 In this, he generally followed Richter.
116 The Church–State issue in the nineteenth century was of little interest to Firth.

century posed greater problems for him because, as he has indicated in his Preface, the subject became so vast. Firth saw a lack of comprehensiveness as his problem and sought to use a topical approach to deal with it.[117]

As the title indicates, Firth's is an institutional history of the Church. One reads about its expansion, important activities, leading personalities, major problems and inner life, ending with the story of its gradual cultural and administrative transformation from 'foreign mission' to 'Indian Church'. The shift in the unit of study from mission to Church corresponded to the institutional changes which the Church had undergone by 1961; so, too, did the shift from a readership of foreign 'donor' to Indian 'future leader'. While Firth's view of the Church was much broader than that of his nineteenth-century predecessors—embracing as it did the non-Protestant as well as the Protestant churches—his retention of the institutional framework meant that it could not be much more Indian than theirs.

The publication of Firth's *Introduction* coincided with two other events which affected the writing of the history of Christianity in India. The first of these was the revival in 1959 of the Church History Association of India (CHAI), which had been dormant since 1940, and the publication of the first issue of its *Bulletin* as a small research journal in August 1961.[118] The Association's membership rose from five to twenty-five that year and in just a few years exceeded one hundred.[119] In 1963, the Southern and the Northern Branch were formed, the former holding its first conference in June 1963, and the latter in October 1965. The first All-India conference was held in 1971. During this period Roman

117 Cyril Bruce Firth, *An Introduction to Indian Church History*, p. iii.

118 World War II, as well as the death or retirement of CHAI's early leadership, was held responsible for the Association's decline. Earlier, the *Bulletin* had been only a newsletter. 'Report: The Church History Association of India (A History of the Association from 1935 to 1960)', *The Indian Journal of Theology*, vol. IX (1960), pp. 166–8.

119 D.A. Christadoss, 'Church History Association of India: A Statement of Work: 1941 to 1961', *Bulletin of the Church History Association of India* (August 1961), p. 5 (hereafter *Bulletin*); and 'From the Secretary's Desk', *Bulletin* (February 1963), p. 19.

Catholics joined the Association,[120] as did a number of Hindus and Sikhs.

Also, at this juncture (1960), Kaj Baagø arrived from Denmark to teach Church History at United Theological College in Bangalore. Even though the revival of the Church History Association of India and the publication of its *Bulletin* were not his work, probably no single person deserves more credit for the professionalization of Church History in India than he does. Baagø's contribution to this process was fourfold: developing post-graduate studies in Church History at United Theological College; making additional source materials available to students and scholars in India, especially by microfilming materials available in archives abroad;[121] starting *The Indian Church History Review* in 1967 as a much more substantial successor to the *Bulletin of the Church History Association of India*; and, especially, posing a serious challenge to the perspectives from which the history of Christianity in India had been written.

In September 1962, Baagø wrote an article, 'On the Teaching of Church History in India', in which he noted how foreign the teaching of Church History was and how necessary it was to teach it from an Indian point of view.[122] Although the article was concerned with general Church History, this became Baagø's concern for Indian Church History as well, because he wanted Church historians to become part of the movement for the indigenization of the Indian Church. Baagø did not write a general history of Christianity in India, but indigenization was a major theme of his

120 'The Regional Conference in Bangalore June 1963', *Bulletin* (November 1963), p. 1. When it was first formed, the Archbishop of Calcutta had expressed an interest in it but that was about all. 'Reports: Church History Association of India, Burma and Ceylon Report for the Year 1935', *National Christian Council Review*, vol. LVI (March 1936), p. 166.

121 Kaj Baagø, 'The Microfilming of Indian Church History Archives', *Bulletin* (September 1965), pp. 2–6. Baagø also compiled *A Bibliography* for the Library of Indian Christian Theology (Madras: Christian Literature Society, 1969).

122 *Bulletin* (September 1962), p. 7.

A History of the National Christian Council of India 1914–64,[123] which is still one of the very few overviews of twentieth-century history based on primary sources available. It also forms the subject matter of most of his other works, which are concentrated on the late nineteenth and twentieth centuries and of which *Pioneers of Indigenous Christianity* is the largest and most important.[124] His understanding of indigenization was far more radical than that of any of his predecessors.

> Indigenization does not mean the mere adoption of certain Indian customs—sitting on the floor, building churches in Dravidian style, etc. The Indian Church may adopt such customs and still remain a foreign body. Neither is indigenization simply the introduction of certain Sanskrit terms in Bible translations or sermons, however important this might be. Real indigenization means the crossing of the borderline. It means leaving, if not bodily at least spiritually, Western Christianity and the Westernized Christian Church in India, and moving into another religion, another culture, taking only Christ with oneself. Indigenization is evangelization. It is the planting of the gospel inside another culture, another philosophy and another religion.[125]

In his historical writing, therefore, Baagø paid special attention to Indian efforts to emancipate the Church from foreign domination, whether in the realms of administration or theology, and to establish continuities between Indian churches and Hindu philosophy, culture and religion. In both these processes, the central figures were the well-educated Indian Christian 'leaders' or 'rebels' who were cast in the roles of heroes, while the main hindrance to prog-

123 Kaj Baagø, *A History of the National Christian Council of India 1914–64* (Nagpur: National Christian Council, 1965).

124 Kaj Baagø, *Pioneers of Indigenous Christianity* (Madras: Christian Literature Society, 1969). Others are: 'The First Independence Movement Among Indian Christians', *Indian Church History Review*, vol. I (June 1967), pp. 65–78; 'The Discovery of India's Past and Its Effect on the Christian Church in India', in John C.B. Webster (ed.), *History and Contemporary India* (Bombay: Asia Publishing House, 1971), pp. 26–45; *The Movement around Subba Rao: A study of the Hindu–Christian movement around K. Subba Rao in Andhra Pradesh* (Madras: Christian Literature Society, 1968).

125 Kaj Baagø, *Pioneers of Indigenous Christianity*, p. 85.

ress was either missionary opposition or missionary domination of Church structures. For example, the National Christian Council could not and did not come out in support of the Indian nationalist movement until the Council itself was dominated by Indians;[126] the main reasons why the Christo Samaj, which represented 'The First Independence Movement Among Indian Christians', failed, was missionary opposition and the dependence of too many Indians upon missionary support.[127] Moreover, the indigenization of Christianity was brought on by developments outside the Church such as the rediscovery by Hindus of their past in the area of theology,[128] and the Indian nationalist movement in its political and cultural aspects in the case of institutional changes.[129] In short, Baagø's nationalist perspective on the history of Christianity in India—in contrast to that of Rajaiah Paul—parallels that of the early extremists (for example, Tilak, Lajpat Rai, Brahmabanhav, etc.) who tended to equate the Indian with the Hindu; to lay stress more upon Hindu than upon Christian or Western forms and inspirations; to heighten the inherent conflicts between the Indian and the Western.

In Baagø's view,

> Church History is not merely the history of the Christian religion, it is the history of the movement connected directly or indirectly with the name of Christ. It comprises therefore in a way all religions and philosophies and cultures and is, rightly conceived, a universal history. It stretches back to the beginning of mankind's history and it points towards a kingdom of God upon earth.[130]

Nevertheless, Baagø remained basically a Church historian. He wrote primarily about developments within the Church and relied

126 Kaj Baagø, *A History of the National Christian Council of India*, pp. 18, 63–64.
127 Kaj Baagø, 'The First Independence Movement Among Indian Christians', p. 77.
128 Kaj Baagø, 'The Discovery of India's Past and its Effect on the Christian Church in India', pp. 32–42.
129 Kaj Baagø, *A History of the National Christian Council of India*, passim.
130 Kaj Baagø, 'Indigenization and Church History', p. 27.

almost completely upon Christian sources for doing so. However, as indicated by his study, published in 1968, of a Hindu-Christian movement outside the Church led by Subba Rao in Andhra Pradesh,[131] Baagø was clearly moving towards the limits of his field as he defined it when he left it to join the Danish Foreign Service.

The gradual professionalization of 'The History of Christianity in India'—through the creation of programmes of advanced learning; the development of libraries and archives; the establishment of a scholarly association with its own journal, conferences, and debates on questions of aims and methods in this field—has not been fully reflected in the general histories of Christianity written since Firth. Two Roman Catholic histories written for the Eucharistic Congress at Bombay in 1964 came too soon for these developments to have much influence. Aloysius Soares's *The Catholic Church in India: A Historical Sketch*, although written in an ecumenical spirit with a chapter on Protestantism and dependent upon P. Thomas for quite a bit of material,[132] is for the most part an institutional history in which questions of hierarchy and jurisdiction loom large.[133] (Soares was much less sympathetic to the Portuguese and the Padroado than was D'Sa.) George Moraes's *A History of Christianity in India from Early Times to St. Francis Xavier: A.D. 52–1542*[134] was quite a lengthy study of a period about which comparatively little was known. The result was a combination of useful summaries of material drawn from Portuguese sources (for example, on the St. Thomas Christians, various missions, and the Padroado itself) on the one hand, and either large quantities of extraneous material (for example, on the details of Portuguese military and diplomatic activity or the history of syphilis in India), or conjectures, often laboriously made (for example, connecting St. Thomas and St. Bartholomew) on the other, which

131 See footnote 123.

132 Aloysius Soares, *The Catholic Church in India: A Historical Sketch* (Nagpur: Government Press and Book Depot, 1964). This, he acknowledged in his Preface.

133 Soares stated that his was not a connected history but a series of highlights in Church History. Another major highlight for Soares, then President of the Catholic Union of India, was the present.

134 Bombay: Manaktalas, 1964.

represented a broadening of, rather than a change in, the earlier Western institutional perspectives.[135] Stephen Neill's *The Story of the Christian Church in India and Pakistan*[136] was written, it would seem, to elucidate some of the missiological problems that history raises. But, while using some articles of *The Indian Church History Review* and attempting to bring the history of the Church into a somewhat closer relation with Indian history than had Firth, it did not face up to the challenge Baagø had posed. His perspective, therefore, was, for all intents and purposes, the same as that of Firth.

Christianity in India: A History in Ecumenical Perspective (1972) was a landmark in the sense that it was written by Roman Catholic, Syrian, and Protestant historians. However, it was a composite rather than a single history written from a single perspective. Some of the chapters were based on primary and others on secondary sources; some authors used a large number of footnotes and others gave only a bibliography. There are chapters which are chronicles,[137] vindications,[138] fairly detached studies of limited subjects,[139] and broad interpretative surveys of major periods.[140] T.V. Philip's chapter on 'Protestant Christianity in India since 1858' and his 'Conclusion' showed most clearly the great changes which had taken place in the 1960s. Almost all his secondary

135 The broadening comes in Chapter VII which contains a lot of descriptive material on the St. Thomas Christians in the sixteenth century, not found in earlier general histories.

136 Stephen Neill, *The Story of the Christian Church in India and Pakistan* (Madras, Delhi: CLS-ISPCK, 1972).

137 N.J. Thomas, 'The Eastern Orthodox Church in India 1653–1972', in H.C. Perumalil and E.R. Hambye (eds), *Christianity in India: A History in Ecumenical Perspective* (Alleppey: Prakasam Publications, 1972), pp. 194–210.

138 George M. Moraes, 'The Catholic Church under the Portuguese Patronage', in ibid., pp. 129–70.

139 E.R. Hambye, 'Medieval Christianity in India: The Medieval Church', in ibid., pp. 30–7.

140 A. Meersman, 'The Catholic Church in India since the mid-19th Century', in ibid., pp. 248–66; T.V. Philip, 'Protestant Christianity in India since 1858', in ibid., pp. 267–99.

sources came from the 1960s and his perspective was very close to that of Baagø. For him, this period was one of emancipation: first, from the old system of belief and oppression (as in the case of the depressed classes and the tribal people) and, then, from foreign domination. Philip concluded with a statement which was a total rejection of the nineteenth-century approach both in its Indian-centredness and in its ecumenical outlook.

> Till recently, the Church in India has been understood in terms of Western missionary expansion. Church historians are only now beginning to recognize the fact that while foreign missions have played an important role in the life and growth of the Indian church, its history is best understood as an independent story. This history, from an early period of the Christian era up to the present, is the common possession of all Christians in India. The history of Christianity in any part of India is an integral part of the history of the church anywhere in the country. The history of the Church in India is much larger and richer than our denominational histories, whether Roman Catholic, Protestant or Orthodox. The Indian Church has a history and a tradition of its own. This understanding of the unity of history is essential for maintaining its integrity and wholeness.[141]

Recent Histories from an Indian History Perspective

Meanwhile, similar developments were taking place in the field of Indian history generally, although on a much vaster scale. The Indian History Congress was organized in 1935 and, with a few exceptions, has held annual meetings at which scholars have presented papers. It has never published a journal but, instead, has published the proceedings of its annual meetings. *The Journal of Indian History* has been in existence since 1923 and in recent years has been supplemented by *The Quarterly Review of Historical Studies* (1961); *The Indian Economic and Social History Review* (1963); *The Indian Historical Review* (1974)—the last two of which are of a very high standard—as well as by numerous smaller journals. Although the Comprehensive History of India project

141 Ibid., p. 300.

of the Congress, begun in 1943, has produced so far only two volumes—one on the Nandas and Mauryas and one on the Delhi Sultanate—the sheer quantity of books on Indian history by Indian historians has increased enormously, especially in the last fifteen years. In 1963, the University Grants Commission organized a seminar on Postgraduate Teaching and Research in History in order to stimulate improvement in the quality of historical studies at the university level.[142] Subsequently, training seminars have been held for college teachers as well.[143] In the former, a lot of attention was given to clarifying aims and developing courses of study; in the latter, emphasis was placed upon historiography and research methodology. The creation of the Indian Council of Historical Research in 1972 has given added impetus and financial resources to historical research. In short, the field of Indian history has developed enormously, both quantitatively and qualitatively, in recent years.

The changes in the aims and methods of Indian historians since the end of the nineteenth century have also been very great and so can only be briefly touched upon here. The first significant change was brought about by the inevitable nationalist reaction to British rule and to British historical writing on India. This took the form of a greater exploration and glorification of the Indian as opposed to the British imperial past on the one hand and an attempt to 'set the record straight' concerning the British record in India on the other.[144] The perspectives from which nationalist histories have

142 *Report of the Seminar on Postgraduate Teaching and Research in History* (New Delhi: University Grants Commission, 1964).

143 Published reports are available for two: John C.B. Webster (ed.), *The Study of History and College History Teaching* (Patiala: Punjabi University, 1965); John C.B. Webster (ed.), *History for College Students* (Chandigarh: Panjab University, 1966).

144 See R.C. Majumdar, 'Nationalist Historians', in C.H. Philips (ed.), *Historians of India, Pakistan and Ceylon* (London: Oxford University Press, 1961), pp. 416–28. Johannes H. Voight provides a fascinating case study of one aspect of this process in 'Nationalist Interpretations of Arthashastra in Indian Historical Writing', in S.N. Mukherjee (ed.), *St. Anthony's Papers Number 18: The Movement for National Freedom in India* (London: Oxford University Press, 1966), pp. 46–66.

been written have varied from the obscurantist and religious reviv-
alist to the secular liberal and Marxist. Secondly, Indian historians
have broadened the range of historical studies from the political,
military and administrative to the social, economic and cultural in
order to gain a deeper understanding of the history of the Indian
people rather than just of their rulers. With this, there has come
a corresponding broadening of the range of sources which historians have used. In no other area have more significant advances
been made than in this. Finally, with respect to the methods of
historical research, there is a growing number of historians who
consider history to be one of the social sciences and who, therefore,
make considerable use of social science theory when formulating
research questions, and of social science techniques, especially
statistics, in analysing their sources.[145]

Some historians of India—not all of them Christian—have
written valuable monographs, or portions of monographs, on
Christians and Christianity in India. In 1965, Muhammad Mohar
Ali, a Bangladeshi Muslim historian, published his doctoral dissertation, *The Bengali Reaction to Christian Missionary Activities
1833–1857*. As his conclusion indicates, Ali was more interested in
the history of Bengal than in the history of Christian missions or the
Christian Church. Since this was a neglected area of Bengal history,
he studied it.[146] His work dealt with the response, first, of the Hindus
in and around Calcutta, and then, of the zamindars in the mufussal
areas. Sisir Kumar Das's *The Shadow of the Cross: Christianity and
Hinduism in a Colonial Situation* (1974) did much the same thing.
Das, then Reader in Bengali at Delhi University, examined the
confrontation of these two religions and its impact upon Bengali
literature, from Ram Mohan Roy to Rabindranath Tagore. David
Kopf in *British Orientalism and the Bengal Renaissance* (1969)
examined the roles of William Carey and Alexander Duff, among
others, in the process of modernization from 1773 to 1835. Robert

145 See S. Gopal, 'The Fear of History', *Seminar*, no. 221 (January
1978), pp. 71–4.
146 This is implied in the Preface. Muhammad Mohar Ali, *The Bengali
Reaction to Christian Missionary Activities 1833–1857* (Chittagong: The
Mehrub Publications, 1965), p. vii.

L. Hardgrave, Jr, in his *The Nadars of Tamilnad* not only devoted a full chapter to the role Christianity played during the first half of the nineteenth century but also referred thereafter to the contributions of individual Nadar Christians to the history of the Nadars' rise to prominence during the past 150 years. In these, and other such, studies,[147] it was the missionaries who received by far the most attention; except in Hardgrave's study, the Indian converts were either totally ignored or relegated to secondary roles. My study of social change as well as of Christianity, *The Christian Community and Change in Nineteenth Century North India*, analysed the foreign missionary and the Indian members of the community, separately and in relation to each other and, together, to the rest of North Indian society. All these studies make use of non-mission and non-church sources, whether newspapers, novels, government reports, or anti-Christian tracts. In them, various techniques of literary (Das) or sociological (Kopf, Hardgrave, Webster) analysis, including statistics (Webster)—often used by Indian historians—are employed. In all of them, except perhaps my own which tries to have it both ways, one sees the history of Christianity in India from the Indian rather than from the Christian end of the looking glass, so to speak. The result has been an academic history of Christianity in India in the sense that the historians' intended readership was more academic than churchly, and their own aims and methods were shaped more by the academy or university than by the Church.

Towards a New Perspective

The foregoing analysis suggests that several important changes have taken place in the historiography of Christianity in India during the past 150 years. The first of these is the marked change in the

---

147   Robert L. Hardgrave, Jr, *The Nadars of Tamilnad* (Berkeley and Los Angeles: University of California Press, 1969). For other studies see, for example, Sushil Madhava Pathak, *American Missionaries and Hinduism: A Study of their Contacts from 1813 to 1910* (Delhi: Munshiram Manoharlal, 1967); Kanti Prasanna Sen Gupta, *The Christian Missionaries in Bengal 1793–1833* (Calcutta: Firma K.L. Mukhopadhyay, 1971).

kinds of people involved in this endeavour. During the nineteenth century, the historians, publishers and intended readers were all Western and, so far as the general histories were concerned, Protestant. During the course of the twentieth century, Indians— and Catholics and Syrians—joined the ranks of the historians, publishers and intended readers. Of even greater significance, however, is the fact that by the 1960s, both the historians and their readers were no longer exclusively Christian. Hindus and Muslims had started writing doctoral dissertations on various aspects of the history of Christianity in India for an academic, and largely non-Christian, readership. The increased diversity of historians and readers has meant that a much wider range of aims and perspectives, and even biases, is being brought to bear on the subject now than was the case seventy-five or even twenty-five years ago, so that the churchly preoccupations of the nineteenth century (Protestant versus Catholic; Church and State; missionary methods; Padroado versus Propaganda), as well as of the twentieth century (the indigenization, unity, and mission of the Indian Church) are not the sole concerns of historians and their readers as they once were. This broadening of the social and intellectual context in which the history of Christianity in India is now written increases the complexities and, therefore, the difficult choices, that historians must face in selecting aims, subject matter, and appropriate methods of research and presentation. Christian historians who desire to 'indigenize Church History' must now keep this broader, and broadening, social and intellectual context in mind.

Clearly related to this change is the trend towards the greater professionalization of the field. Hough and Kaye were amateur historians who worked mostly on their own. Today, there is a growing community of academic historians with well-organized means of sharing the fruits of their research with each other. Along with this professionalization has come a kind of 'revolution of rising expectations' with regard to the quality of the histories produced; historians are now under more pressure than before to meet with rising professional standards of excellence. The implication of this development is not that from now on all histories of Christianity in India must be scholarly histories, but rather, that all histories, whether scholarly or popular, must be based upon scholarly history or be dismissed as impressionistic and distorted, or as mere religious tracts.[148]

The third change which has taken place is that historians of Christianity in India are now using a far greater diversity of source materials than they were previously. The number of specialized secondary works in the form of books and articles has increased enormously since Hough's day, as have efforts to gather and make available primary sources. Even more significant is the fact that academic historians no longer rely exclusively upon Christian sources but use such non-Church sources as press reports, government documents, regional language literature, and Hindu and Muslim religious publications in order to understand those aspects of the history of Christianity which interest them. The result has been not only new perspectives upon the Christian past but also new critical problems in dealing with evidence. It is no longer possible for historians to share Hough's or Sherring's total confidence in the trustworthiness of mission reports when faced with the conflicting evidence found in Hindu or Muslim or government sources.

Finally, the pace of change itself has changed. From Hough to Firth, the biggest change in perspective was in their contrasting views of the Roman Catholic Church. For the rest, the continuities are far more impressive. Each historian relied heavily upon his predecessors for information, for methods, and for perspectives. They all used Christian sources almost exclusively and adopted a moderately or an extremely uncritical attitude towards them.[149] Hough's preoccupation with missionary methods was just as strong in Richter, and was by no means absent in Paul or Firth. Everyone, from Hough to Paul, used the same scheme of periodization, dividing 1900 years of history into the Syrian, the Roman Catholic and the Protestant eras. Kaye's Bengali bias reappeared in Richter; all the Roman Catholic histories surveyed shared a Bombay–Goa bias. Most important of all, the institutional framework continued from

---

148 This was brought home to me in a remark made in a review of my book to the effect that, 'All too often comments on religious movements themselves become tracts for the times'. 'The Missionary Impact', *The Sunday Statesman*, 6 June 1976.

149 Sherring and Thomas were the worst in this regard.

Hough to Firth. Of course, Paul and Firth laid greater stress on the Indian Church than on the foreign mission as the institution of significance, but even they saw the shift from the latter to the former as a rather smooth and orderly transition, thus stressing institutional continuity rather than a break from the past.

Then came the revolution of the 1960s: a rapid diversification of the community of historians and readers; marked advances in the professionalization of Indian Church History and Indian history generally; and the sharp change in the perspectives introduced by Kaj Baagø and other advocates of indigenization on the one hand and the academic historians on the other. So sudden has this change of pace been that many historians of Christianity in India, trained before the 1960s, have been unable to adjust to the new situation. The result is a kind of mixture of aims and methods found in the most recent general history of Christianity in India, *Christianity in India: A History in Ecumenical Perspective* (1972), and in the articles which have appeared in *The Indian Church History Review* over the past twelve years. Only a few articles have been written on pre-Portuguese history. Catholic historians have confined their attention almost (but not quite) exclusively to pre-nineteenth-century history, whereas Protestants, again with a few exceptions, have confined theirs to the nineteenth and twentieth centuries. While mission and institutional studies— Catholic and Protestant—continue to abound, there is also a good number of social and cultural histories of Christian communities and articles on Christian attitudes towards and involvement in social and political movements. The same kind of mixture exists in Indian history generally, as a smaller revolution took place there too in the 1960s but, whereas Indian historians appear now to be sharply divided on methodological and ideological grounds,[150] similar tensions have not yet appeared among historians of Christianity.

It is in the context of the recent rapid development of the field that one must see the pronouncement of the Church History Association of India's editorial board—mentioned at the outset of

150 See S. Gopal, 'The Fear of History'; Romila Thapar, 'The Academic Professional', *Seminar*, no. 222 (February 1978), pp. 18–23; Ashis Nandy, 'Self-Esteem, Autonomy and Authenticity', ibid., pp. 24–7.

this essay—that earlier perspectives on the History of Christianity in India stand 'in serious need of revision'. The editorial board criticized earlier historians for having treated the history of Christianity in India as 'an Eastward extension of Western ecclesiastical history. Stress has been laid upon either its internal history or upon its 'foreign mission' dimension so that the Church is viewed as a relatively self-contained unit which acted upon and was acted upon by the society outside.'[151] In its place they proposed 'to write the history of Christianity in the context of Indian history' by focusing attention upon the socio-cultural history of the Christian people of India, by using a framework which is both ecumenical and national, and by using the region as their basic working unit. This is indeed a 'New Perspective' requiring new research methods, but it is also one which is in keeping with the developments which have taken place in the field during and since the 1960s.[152]

151 'A Scheme for a Comprehensive History of Christianity in India', p. 89.

152 Ibid., pp. 89–90.

CHAPTER 2

The Historian and Theological Research in India*

In discussing the historian's contribution to theological research in India, I have chosen to examine the assumptions on which a historian works rather than the actual contribution of historians to theological research in India. There are two reasons for this rather unhistorical approach to the subject. First, in spite of the fact that the history of Christianity in India is a growing field with a very good journal of its own,[1] its actual contribution to theological research in other disciplines in India has probably been slight and, in any case, would be difficult to document. Whether such a state of affairs is due to the idiosyncratic nature and/or poor quality of the historians' work to date, or to intellectual isolationism among practitioners of other theological disciplines, is a question well worth pondering but difficult to answer convincingly. The second reason is that I am more interested in giving direction to future research than in worrying about what could or should have happened in past research. Perhaps non-historians can make a better assessment of the potential usefulness of the historian's

* This chapter was previously published as 'The Contribution of the Historian to Theological Research in India', *Bangalore Theological Forum*, vol. XVI, January–April 1984, pp. 38–57. This is a revised version.
  1 *Indian Church History Review*, published twice annually.

contribution to their work if they become aware of the assumptions upon which historical research is founded than if they simply review the record. I will therefore address myself to three questions: (1) what are the working assumptions upon which the historian actually does research? (2) Are the working assumptions of the historian of Christianity different in any way from those of other historians? (3) Are there any special assumptions which should guide the work of historians of Christianity in India? Since there are deep disagreements among historians on each of these three questions, this essay must, of necessity, be a personal statement.

ASSUMPTIONS ABOUT HISTORY

The first and most fundamental of the historian's working assumptions concerns subject matter. What the historian seeks to understand is the human past and, specifically, events and changes in the past. An interest in change and continuity over time and thus in chronology informs the basic questions which the historian asks about the past: what happened, when, where, how, why, and with what consequences? In seeking answers to those questions about specific events and changes in the past, the historian makes reference to other events and changes which occurred prior to, or simultaneously with, those under investigation. In other words, historical understanding is an understanding of events and changes *in their context*.

A second, and perhaps equally important, working assumption is that an understanding of the past is possible, but only within limits. While historians differ in their procedures, there is a general research process through which they all tend to go in order to arrive at an understanding of the past. First, one must decide what one wishes to find out about the past. This involves selecting an area for research and, sooner or later, developing a series of fairly general questions to guide one's inquiry in that area of research. Next, one must locate and, if necessary, select those primary sources which are relevant to one's inquiry. After ascertaining the authenticity of those sources, one examines them critically in order both to gather evidence and to assess the reliability of that evidence for the purpose of the investigation being undertaken.

The crucial importance of this stage of the research process cannot be overestimated: a deep familiarity with the relevant primary sources—as well as with their relative strengths and weaknesses—is the necessary foundation upon which historical research is based. That is when the historian not only gets facts but also begins to see possible relationships between the facts his/her investigation has yielded. These possible relationships—whether derived from the writings of previous scholars, or from one's own examination of the sources, or from a combination of the two—are then put in the form either of more detailed and precise questions, or of hypotheses to be checked out with reference to the evidence. The inferences or explanations at which one arrives through this questioning, testing and checking process should be those which are supported best by *all* the evidence. These are then related to all the other inferences and explanations which the inquiry has necessitated and produced by a similar process until an understanding of the events or changes under examination is arrived at. This understanding is the historian's interpretation of that particular segment of the human past which he/she has researched.

As this description of the research process indicates, there are several factors that limit the understanding which a historian can have of the past. The very questions which one asks introduce an element of subjectivity that limits the understanding arrived at; this is a situation which will not be redeemed by refusing to ask any questions at all, because facts are not self-determining and do not speak for themselves. Next, the historian's understanding is limited by the sources he/she consults. The counsel for perfection is to consult all the available sources, and historians do go to considerable pains to discover new sources, as well as to devise new techniques by which reliable evidence can be obtained from those sources that do remain. Unfortunately, none of these methods is foolproof, so, yet another element of subjectivity enters. Finally, the process of drawing inferences and arriving at explanations and interpretations is also full of difficult choices and decisions for which each historian must accept responsibility. It is for these reasons that the conclusions of earlier historians are being revised by present-day historians, whose conclusions will, in turn, be revised by future historians.

Yet, despite these limiting factors—which, incidentally, apply to an understanding as much of the present as of the past—the historian's quest for truth about the past is not totally in vain. Historians do not operate in the realm of pure subjectivity or ideological relativism where it must be assumed that one person's interpretation of the past is as valid as that of another. One can test the quality of the questions which guide a particular piece of historical research by comparing them with those posed by other historians who have done research in the same or similar fields, as well as by comparing the answers to which those questions led with the findings of other historians. While originality is certainly an important criterion of quality for making assessments of this kind, significance is an even more important criterion. Significance is an indicator of the revelatory power of a question—or a combination of questions—in illuminating context or trends; in testing theory; or in providing depth of perception into the basic problems of human existence. Moreover, the discipline involved in answering historical questions has some built-in checks against avoidable bias. Counsels to consult as wide a variety of sources as possible; to compare the evidence provided by different sources; to be careful and clear about the warrants used in arriving at conclusions; to be faithful to *all* the facts; and to stay within the limits warranted by the evidence—all serve as additional criteria for distinguishing between good and bad research.[2] In other words, the discipline of historical research can not only rule out certain explanations of the past—thus making us fairly certain concerning what did not happen—but can also lead us, in many instances, to conclusions about the past which are highly probable. Some histories, by virtue of the continuing significance of the questions asked as well as of the quality of research and communicative power used in answering them, do gain a much wider and much longer acceptance than others.

2 An excellent discussion of the components and canons of historical judgement is given in chapter 2 of Van A. Harvey, *The Historian and the Believer: The Morality of Historical Knowledge and Christian Belief* (Toronto: The Macmillan Company, 1966).

The third and most controversial working assumption of the historian concerns history as a social science, since this is at the heart of a very important debate concerning the purpose of historical research and the best methods to use in carrying out the historian's task. Is history a theory-building discipline or is its primary objective to understand concrete changes and events in all their richness, complexity, and distinctiveness? Do the methods of the social scientist—quantitative methods in particular—produce more solid evidence and, therefore, sounder explanations, than the empathetic intuition of the humanistically-oriented historian? Should the historian make use of the theories and concepts developed by social scientists in formulating research questions and then in providing explanations of the past, or would this lead to an inevitable and obvious distortion? I shall deal with each of these questions briefly and, in doing so, make reference primarily to sociology as that is the social science with which I am most familiar and of which historians seem to be making the greatest use.

The tradition of history as a science goes well back into the last century. However, the former notion that historians, by a careful criticism of sources, would increase knowledge and eliminate error broke down when the fruits of their research—instead of increasing our understanding of the past—confused it by revealing complexities, complications, even contradictions. The hope of linear progress in the accumulation of historical knowledge through the discovery of an ever-larger number of facts seems to have been replaced by the view that history can make its contribution to developing theories of society. What the social sciences lack, so goes the argument, is the depth which the time-dimension provides and it is the historian's job to make good that deficiency. Closely related to this view is the view which sees the historian's task as interpreting the past according to surviving evidence and conceptual frameworks based on tested social science theory. Just as such a theory can be used for interpreting portions of the human past, so, presumably, can historical study provide further testing and revision of such conceptual frameworks.

There are, however, two important criticisms of this view of history as a theory-building discipline. The first is that, given both the complexity of the human past and the paucity of source materials upon which a knowledge of it must be based, such theory-building is impossible, if not downright pretentious. In making such a criticism, one does not have to go to the opposite extreme of affirming that the historian deals only with the particular and the unique. Historians do make generalizations, but as a means of describing specific trends at particular times and places, not in order to formulate general theories or universal laws on the basis of which one could make predictions with respect to such trends. The second criticism concerns the compromising of what is, basically, the inductive nature of historical research. Often, sociologists make theory the starting point of their research, using it to define a research problem, with the resulting hypotheses to be tested in an abstract, generalized, even predictive language. In this approach, so much critical deductive work is done on inherited theory before empirical work begins that it would almost seem that the sociologist has everything figured out in advance. The historian tends to begin empirical research in a more open-ended frame of mind, sharpening and focusing questions or hypotheses in the process of—rather than prior to—examining the primary sources; making adjustments suggested by the evidence until there is a 'fit' between questions or hypotheses and the evidence provided by the sources. Moreover, the historian, in seeking to understand a particular segment of the human past, rather than testing the validity of one or two carefully developed general theories, will probably draw more heavily upon other studies of that segment's historical context than upon relevant theoretical literature.

Even though, as the preceding analysis indicates, I tend to see that the social scientist uses the concrete in the interests of the abstract while the historian tends to do just the opposite, there is no denying the enormous influence which the social sciences have had upon historical writing. I would agree with Barraclough's remark that

> If we seek . . . to specify ways in which the social sciences have affected the attitudes and presuppositions of historians, there is no doubt that the first and most general result was a major shift of focus, from the particular to the general, from events to uniformities, and from narrative to analysis.[3]

3 Geoffrey Barraclough, *Main Trends in History* (New York: Holmes and Meier, 1979), p. 51.

He then enumerated several ways in which sociology and anthropology have influenced historical writing during the past two decades. The first influence is by forcing the historian to pay much more attention than previously to the 'underlying structural framework within which events and personalities operate'.[4] Another is by introducing a greater precision of thought into historical writing; by urging quantification upon historians; and by offering a number of conceptual models with which to interpret historical evidence.

If one is interested in writing the history of large groups or aggregates of people instead of individuals and the small ruling élite, one must come to terms with the social sciences. The question is not whether, but how, to use them. Social structure is part of the context with reference to which historical events are explained, but it is not the whole context. Quantitative data can provide some precise information about the past, but a few well-chosen illustrative examples may provide greater depth of insight. Commenting upon the American scene, one social historian has written, 'In general historians have found quantification more useful in organizing data to raise vital questions for analysis than actually in providing such analysis.'[5] In like manner, conceptual models borrowed from the social sciences can provide greater precision in explaining the past, but a well-turned phrase or a quotation from the past may prove more illuminating. Generally, the models which have proven most helpful have been 'middle range' models limited to particular times and places rather than those of general theory. As these comments suggest, historians tend to disagree on such points and many of us tend to be eclectic and pragmatic: we use what works.

4 Ibid., p. 54.

5 Peter N. Stearns, 'Toward a Wider Vision: Trends in Social History', in Michael Kammen (ed.), *The Past Before Us: Contemporary Historical Writing in the United States* (Ithaca: Cornell University Press, 1980), p. 227.

ASSUMPTIONS ABOUT THE HISTORY OF CHRISTIANITY

Historians of the Church or of Christianity share the working assumptions about history as a discipline as described earlier. What distinguishes them from fellow historians is the particular aspect of history which constitutes their primary subject matter. Like their colleagues working in other areas of historical inquiry, they make some conscious or unconscious decisions of great consequence in the process of delineating or defining their particular subject of study. What is Christianity? What is the Church? At least two important sets of working assumptions are built into those questions. In both instances, these assumptions are theological and so provide important links between history and other theological disciplines.

The first set of assumptions concerns the nature of the Church or of Christianity as an empirical phenomenon. Hubert Jedin in his introduction to a ten-volume history of the Church took as his starting point 'the theological idea of the Church' defined in its dogma. This theological idea, he said, refers solely to

> The Church's divine origin through Jesus Christ, to the hierarchic and sacramental order founded by him, to the promised assistance of the Holy Spirit and to the eschatological consummation at the end of the world; the very elements, in fact, in which her essential identity consists, namely her continuity in spite of changing outward forms.[6]

The evidence of the promised assistance by the Holy Spirit is the preservation of the Church from error, the production and maintenance of holiness within her, and the performance of miracles.[7] This very explicit definition of the Church serves to delimit the Church historian's field of inquiry and to determine the basic components of that field. One may wish to take issue with this working definition of the Church on theological grounds, or because it has

6 Hubert Jedin, 'General Introduction to Church History', in Karl Baus (ed.), *Handbook of Church History, Volume I: From Apostolic Community to Constantine*, Hubert Jedin and John Dolan (gen. eds), (New York: Herder & Herder, 1965), p. 1.

7 Ibid., p. 2.

built into it some questionable conclusions of historical research, or for other reasons, but it does have the merit of being a highly operational definition. It indicates that the historian is studying an empirical institution with well-defined elements and clear-cut boundaries so that he/she knows who and what is included; who and what is excluded; who and what is important; who and what is not important. Vatican II loosened up but did not change this definition substantially; one can now write Church History as the history of the people of God, of their religious life, and not only about the hierarchy, institutions, and dogmas of the Church, but the latter still remain of the essence of the Church.[8]

In his essay, 'Church History is the History of the Exposition of Scripture', Gerhard Ebeling has provided the outlines of a Protestant understanding of Church History. He viewed the Church as an assembly of believers, established, nourished and bound together by the proclamation of the Word of God. Since the proclamation of the Word of God is constitutive of the Church, 'the constantly renewed interpretation of Holy Scripture' becomes the subject matter of Church History.[9] Ebeling did not restrict 'interpretation' to preaching or doctrine, but considered it applicable to a wide variety of actions ranging from prayer and ritual to wars of religion, martyrdom, and witch burning, as long as they stood in some spoken or unspoken, conscious or unconscious, positive or negative, relation to Holy Scripture. 'It is the task of the Church historian to uncover this relation of the event to Holy Scripture, and to assign its place and estimate its significance.'[10] While this view of the Church and of Church History is poten-

8 See 'Dogmatic Constitution on the Church', in Walter M. Abbott (ed.), *The Documents of Vatican II* (New York: Guild Press, 1966), pp. 14–101. The Twenty-first Ecumenical Council, convened by Pope John XXIII on 11 October 1962 at the Vatican, produced sixteen documents on such subjects as the Church, Revelation, Ecumenism, Mission, and Non-Christians for the guidance of the Church during four extended sessions that ended on 8 December 1965.

9 Gerhard Ebeling, *The Word of God and Tradition: Historical Studies Interpreting the Divisions of Christianity* (trans.) S.M. Hooke (London: Collins, 1968), p. 26.

10 Ibid., p. 28.

tially all-encompassing (even though unspoken, and especially unconscious, relationships between events and Scripture would be extremely difficult to establish convincingly), it does give a central place in Church History to the conscious, articulate interpretations of Holy Scripture and hence to the more intellectual dimensions of the life of the Church.[11]

The constitution of the Church of South India offers yet another view of the Church with somewhat different practical implications for the Church historian. It defines the Church as:

> the Body of Christ and its members are members of His Body; and that those are members according to the will and purpose of God who have been baptized into the name of the Father and of the Son and of the Holy Spirit, and, receiving the calling and grace of God with faith, continue steadfast therein, maintaining by the same faith through the various means of grace which He has provided in His Church, their vital union with the Head of the Body, and through Him their fellowship one with another.[12]

According to this definition, the Church is people whose life together is structured in no necessary way; who are distinguished from others by baptism and by continuing together, steadfast in the calling and grace they have received from God. While Jedin's and Ebeling's views of the Church, respectively, tend towards the primacy of institutional and of intellectual history, the Church of South India definition points in the direction of social history. It also has the virtue of being flexible and operational, once the historian gets over the hurdle of deciding who has been steadfast and who has not.

As these three views of the Church indicate, theological assumptions about the nature of the Church as an empirical phenomenon guide the historian's understanding of what precisely the subject matter of his/her study is. One cannot escape the dilemma of being

---

11 Ebeling virtually admitted this in pointing out that 'the Church historian must pay greater attention to the history of the interpretations of Holy Scripture in a stricter sense than has hitherto been the case'. Ibid., p. 29.

12 *The Constitution of the Church of South India* (Madras: Christian Literature Society [CLS], 1972), pp. 4–5.

sectarian in one's (working) definitions by deciding to study the history of Christianity, instead of Church History, because theological understandings of the nature of Christianity are many, varied and, ultimately, sectarian. In the ecumenical age in which we live, the problem of these conflicting theological understandings becomes most acute for the historian at the point where decisions are made about who is to be included and who is to be excluded from the history of the Church or of Christianity. In Jedin's definition, those not in the institution are excluded, while the potentially more inclusive definitions of Ebeling and of the Church of South India, respectively, beg the question of what a *faithful* interpretation of Scripture is and of who has been steadfast. Perhaps under these circumstances, the best the historian can do is concentrate upon those people who have been baptized and either consider themselves, or are considered by others, to be Christians, and treat organization, theology, etc., as a superstructure.

The other set of theological assumptions concerns the nature of the Church or of Christianity as a divine event. All three definitions of the Church discussed above include a divine as well as a human dimension of the Church when referring both to its origin and to its continuing life. This begs the question, first, of whether God acts in history and, if so, then of how this affirmation can become part of a framework of inquiry for studying the history of the Church or of Christianity. Given the assumptions—presented in the first section of this essay—about history as a discipline, the historian who wishes to operationalize the view that God has been acting in the history of the Church or of Christianity would have to: (1) include a question about the activity of God in the specific time and place under study when defining the scope of his/her inquiry; (2) develop a set of indicators or 'signs' of God's activity so that the question of its presence in given situations can be answered empirically; (3) give the reality to which the presence of those indicators point central significance in the wider context of events under study when developing historical explanations.

The historian can take the first step in this process only if he/she believes that such a question is, in principle, answerable in empirical terms. Since it is through faith that one believes God acts in history, the issue of whether and how such a faith can be applied to the concrete events and changes which the historian is studying becomes a theological issue. At least two aspects of this come out in the dialogue between M.M. Thomas and H.H. Wolf on 'Christ at Work in History'. The first is whether God is hidden or revealed in historical events. M.M. Thomas argued that 'faith can discern the work of Christ in contemporary secular history and that this discernment of faith is the basis of Christian spiritual discrimination and Christian ethical responsibility in secular life'.[13] H.H. Wolf, fearing that Christ, through such a discerning of his work, could become confused with and finally get swallowed up by an ideology, argued that, 'Speaking in general, Christ is at work in history; but we can never take certain phenomena or situations as norms or manifestations of his work'.[14] The other aspect of the issue concerns the sphere of Christ's discernible activity. While rejecting Thomas's view that Christ's work could be discerned in secular history, Wolf did indicate that the promises of Christ could be 'constantly rediscovered by listening to his Word, and from the life of the Church',[15] and that 'forgiving sins, liberating men from death, bringing reconciliation, and beginning a new mankind in Him' were the present activities of the living Christ.[16]

The second step in operationalizing the view that God acts in history leads to further difficulty and controversy. Which are the most reliable indicators of the activity of God in specific events and changes in the past? Answers to that question will vary according to theological perspective. One may draw a sharp distinction between 'sacred' and 'secular' history by limiting one's list of signs of God's activity to the internal life of the Church and still come up with different sets of indicators, as Jedin and Wolf did. Kenneth

13 M.M. Thomas, *Some Theological Dialogues* (Madras: CLS, 1977), p. 68.

14 Ibid., pp. 53–4, 63. This issue is also discussed, although less helpfully, in the final section of the World Council of Churches document, 'God in Nature and History', in C.T. McIntire (ed.), *God, History and Historians: Modern Christian Views of History* (New York: Oxford University Press, 1977), pp. 326–8.

15 M.M. Thomas, *Some Theological Dialogues*, p. 56.

16 Ibid., p. 62.

Scott Latourette, in his presidential address before the American Historical Association in 1948, offered liberal evangelical indicators of Jesus's influence upon subsequent history, such as, changes in individual character as well as the joint efforts undertaken by Christians for Christian reasons to spread literacy, combat slavery, emancipate women, and provide improved health care.[17] These offer quite a contrast to M.M. Thomas's indicators, described most fully in his *The Christian Response to the Asian Revolution*. Christ is at work in the Asian revolution, said Thomas, using (1) the modernization process to create the basic conditions (personal freedom, social justice, higher standards of living, a sense of national identity) of 'greater human dignity, enhanced human creativity and mature human living';[18] (2) the accompanying cultural changes which were leading Asian people to 'a new awareness . . . of the personal dimensions of individual and collective existence' to prepare them to choose between Jesus Christ and alternative saviours offering different schemes of salvation;[19] and (3) all these changes occurring primarily outside the Church in order to judge and recall the Church to repentance and renewal.[20] Yet, both Latourette and Thomas acknowledged that each of their indicators was not the product of divine activity alone; that each could be an indicator of something else more mundane at the same time; and that what might be considered a valid indicator today could prove with the passage of time to have been a very poor indicator indeed.

Once the historian has made a judgement, which is at least as much theological as historical, concerning which reliable indicators of God's activity to look for and has found those indicators present in the sources, he/she is then ready to take the third and final step in determining what divine dimension there was in a particular complex of events and changes in the Church's past.

17 Kenneth Scott Latourette, 'The Christian Understanding of History', in C.T. McIntire (ed.), *God, History and Historians*, pp. 61–5.

18 M.M. Thomas, *The Christian Response to the Asian Revolution* (Lucknow: Lucknow Publishing House, 1967), p. 29.

19 Ibid., p. 67, 31.

20 Ibid., p. 32.

This involves bringing to all the evidence collected—each piece being an indicator of something or of several things simultaneously—an a priori preference for 'God's activity' explanations. This can lead either to such modest and tentative conclusions that Christ's lordship would appear belittled and restricted or—when more ambitious conclusions are attempted—to two types of distortion: it can give to 'God's activity', in a particular series of events or a process of change, an importance that is unwarranted by the evidence provided; and it can give to those particular events or to that particular change an importance that is not warranted in the wider history of that time and place. Perhaps, the only way in which the historian can do justice to the divine dimension of Church History while remaining true to the demands of history as a discipline is by tracing Christian—as opposed to divine—influence upon specific events and changes in the past; by assuming a Christian understanding of providence when examining especially the unintended consequences of human actions; and by highlighting the presence of mystery in historical events—mystery which the historian's methodological rigour cannot diminish but can only deepen.

Thus, the very nature of the particular subject matter forces the historian of the Church or of Christianity either to make theological assumptions or to arrive at conclusions which have a bearing upon theological affirmations that concern not only the nature of the Church or of Christianity but also how and where God acts in history. By using methods appropriate to history as a discipline for testing the adequacy and helpfulness of theological reflection in at least those two areas, the historian enters into direct engagement with researchers in the other theological disciplines.

ASSUMPTIONS ABOUT THE HISTORY OF CHRISTIANITY IN INDIA

In turning to those assumptions which should guide the historian of Christianity in India, it is necessary to note two aspects of the preceding discussion of the working assumptions about history as an intellectual discipline and about the particular subject matter of the Church or of Christianity. On one hand, the first set of three assumptions applies to *all* historical research and, in addition, the second set of two assumptions applies to *all* historical research about the Church or Christianity; these working assumptions are thus as essential to the historian of Christianity in India as to the historian of Christianity in the United States, France, or Nigeria. On the other hand, since each of these five shared assumptions is, at the same time, an area of legitimate disagreement among historians, the historian of Christianity in India must make some very decisive choices about how to proceed at every one of these points. These choices, in turn, influence his/her potential contribution as a historian to theological research in India. Therefore, the procedure adopted here is to comment upon these five assumptions in turn and to draw some conclusions from each of them concerning the contribution of the historian to theological research in India.

First, since the historian seeks to understand past events and changes in their context, he/she must decide not only which events and changes to study but also to which context to relate those events and changes. Hence, the editorial board of the Church History Association of India (CHAI), when preparing guidelines for the authors of its multi-volume history, opted for a 'new perspective' by choosing both a new context and a new set of events and changes for the study of the history of Christianity in India. With regard to the new context, it declared that, 'The history of Christianity in India has hitherto often been treated as an eastward extension of western ecclesiastical history . . . It is now intended to write the history of Christianity in the context of Indian history'. With this in mind, it made the various regional contexts within India the basic working units into which the history was to be divided. With regard to new events and changes, the editorial board stated that the history would

> focus attention upon the Christian *people* of India; upon who they were and how they understood themselves; upon their social, religious, cultural and political encounters; upon the changes which these encounters produced in them and in their appropriation of the Christian gospel as well as in the Indian culture and society of which they themselves were a part. These elements constitute the history of

Christianity in India, and are not to be merely chapters tacked on to the end of an institutional study.[21]

These choices of events, changes and context have important implications for both the historian and the non-historian who are engaged in theological research. For the historian, it means immersing himself/herself in the general history of India and keeping abreast of the scholarship in that field. Since knowledge of the changing context is essential to good history, those who are not good historians of India cannot be good historians of Christianity in India. For the non-historians, the historians now offer both fresh information and interpretations of Christianity in its Indian context. I suspect that all too many well-intentioned efforts at contextualizing Christian theology, ethics, and liturgy have been based on very inadequate understandings of the changing internal life and context of the Church over time. Indigenization, as Brahminization, is but one example of this.

Second, if the kind of knowledge of the past which the 'new perspective' seeks to provide is to become possible, special attention will have to be paid to research method. Historians will have to ask new questions; they will have to figure out how to extract relevant evidence from mission sources written from the 'old perspective'; they will have to seek out and consult a far greater variety of non-mission and non-Christian sources than before; they will have to avoid communal bias when writing about relations between Christians and Hindus and Muslims, and so forth. Such attention to method is of great importance if the research is to be of benefit to other researchers and to the Church at large. Our past is significant because it is our heritage; we, like Church historians elsewhere, are responsible for interpreting the Christian tradition as it has developed since Biblical times; for understanding our roots as Christians and the precedents by which we have come to live—rightly or wrongly. Often, a re-examination of the historical record yields surprises of some importance, as recent studies of the role of women in the Church have begun to show.

21 'A Scheme for a Comprehensive History of Christianity in India', cyclostyled manuscript (1974), pp. 1–2.

Third, while I consider the methods and concepts of the social sciences indispensable for an understanding of the Christian people of India in their changing context, I still prefer to see the goal of research in the history of Christianity in India as self-understanding rather than as theory-building. Christians in India are a minority community with a history full of controversy. Given this situation and the consequent image which others have of Christians, self-understanding is of special importance. Is it true that our ancestors were 'rice' Christians? Is it true that they gave up their cultural heritage for whatever benefits the missionaries might provide? Is it true that they took no part in the national-ist movement but were in fact active supporters of British rule? Such accusations have been made and many educated Christians believe them even today; the number of theological statements and Church programmes based on these premises should give us pause. My own historical research had led me to conclusions very different from those generally accepted. As a result, I have come to see the role of the history of Christianity as a kind of group therapy; as helping Christians rediscover their collective past; and through that, their identity as a people; and thereby, restoring to them some of their self-respect which they have lost by believing so many half-truths about themselves.

Fourth, as has already been pointed out, the CHAI editorial board has committed itself to a view of the Church as people. In addition, it has also adopted the following ecumenical understand-ing of the Church.

> Christianity rather than any one section of the Christian Church will form the other basic framework for study. Denominational diversities will not be ignored or played down; here too, both common features of different denominational experiences in each period and region will be explored, and the growth of the ecumenical movement in India described so that these basic unities may be seen along with the diver-sities.[22]

The view of the Church as people—which requires the historian to find out who the Christian people of India were as well as what

22 Ibid.

their pre-Christian and Christian traditions have been—could make a valuable contribution to more effective preaching and ministry to them. The ecumenical working assumption about the Church could contribute to fresh theological understandings of the nature and mission of the Church.

Fifth and finally, I would argue for an implicitly, rather than explicitly, Christian view of history as the framework within which to write the history of Christianity in India. I have already addressed the question of distortion in the previous section of this essay. Here, a somewhat larger issue needs to be addressed: for whom do we write our histories of Christianity in India? Clearly, we write them for the benefit of others engaged in theological research as well as for the benefit of the Church as a whole. But is that all? I would like to see us also enter more fully into dialogue with other historians of India so that we might make our contribution to the shaping of a common Indian identity. It is sobering to discover how little space, if any, is given to Christianity in the general histories of India, even in those written on aspects of Indian history to which the contribution of Christians and Christianity has been unusually large, for example, the uplift of women and of Untouchables. If we are to make a contribution to this dialogue and to the shaping of a common Indian identity in which India's Christians are not left out, we must meet with academic standards and write in a language which other historians can understand and accept. This is why an implicitly, rather than explicitly, Christian view of history has something extra to commend it.

CHAPTER 3

The Identity of Indian Christians*

Historians are in the business of discovering, naming and shaping identity. Some do this consciously, deliberately and directly. Others make their impact on identity only indirectly or unconsciously. After all, with respect to identity, what historians choose to ignore or leave out is often as significant as what they say. The history of Indian Christians is an instructive case in point. The old mission histories focused their readers' attention upon the work of foreign missionaries and assigned only very minor and passive roles to Indian Christians. Even today, there may be references to missionaries but rarely to Indian Christians in the general histories of India. Like women, tribal people and Dalits, they are treated as non-persons or simply as part of the nameless, faceless, undifferentiated mass of Indian humanity. Such treatment makes a statement about the identity of Indian Christians.

Only in the past two or three decades have historians of Christianity in India been giving the identity of Indian Christians the scholarly attention it deserves. This essay examines how some of them have gone about the task of describing, analysing, and defining that identity. Taken together, their studies illustrate not

*This chapter was previously published in Kanichikattil Francis (ed.), *Church in Context: Essays in Honour of Mathias Mundadan CMI* (Bangalore: Dharmaram Publications, 1996), pp. 56–71. This is a revised version.

only how important, but also how complex and even controversial, the study of identity is.

MATHIAS MUNDADAN'S OVERVIEW

A good starting point for understanding the historical treatment of Indian Christian identity is A.M. Mundadan's *Indian Christians: Search for Identity and Struggle for Autonomy* published in 1984, because, as the title indicates, this book dealt with the subject of identity directly and explicitly.[1] Like all historians, Mundadan approached identity from a particular vantage point. This study was very Kerala-centric with a primary focus upon the St. Thomas (Syrian) Christians in general and especially upon those who have been in communion with Rome. That is the area of Mundadan's greatest expertise. However, the study was at the same time both national and ecumenical in scope and sympathy.

Mundadan started with St. Thomas. This starting point established the original identity of the St. Thomas Christians. Their early and foundational identity had four important components: the apostolic origin of their Church; their ecclesiastical autonomy despite their connections with the East Syrian Church; the high caste status and even civil autonomy they enjoyed within Kerala society;[2] and a unity which included a shared tradition and church life. Mundadan concluded that, prior to the sixteenth century, the St. Thomas Christians lived in two worlds at the same time: the world of India (Kerala in particular) and the ecclesiastical world of the East Syrian Church of Persia. Their identity at that time has been described as, 'Hindu in culture, Christian in Religion and Syro-Oriental in Worship'.[3]

1 A.M. Mundadan, *Indian Christians: Search for Identity and Struggle for Autonomy* (Bangalore: Dharmaram Publications, 1984).

2 Mundadan did not attribute that to the status of the groups from which the St. Thomas Christians converted; he treated it instead as a function of their high status occupations and their conformity to such general local practices as pollution and untouchability.

3 The words were actually those of Placid J. Podipara whom Mundadan quoted with his approval. A.M. Mundadan, *Indian Christians: Search for Identity and Struggle for Autonomy*, p. 22.

It was this foundational identity which the St. Thomas Christians sought to maintain in their long struggle against the Portuguese. Indeed, all four components of their identity were at stake, for the Portuguese not only challenged the apostolicity of their Church, but also sought to end their ecclesiastical autonomy and change their position within Indian society. In resisting this Portuguese onslaught, the St. Thomas Christians lost their unity in 1653. Thus, in Mundadan's presentation, their identity became linked historically with their autonomy. For those who remained in communion with Rome after 1653, the subsequent search for identity was a struggle for autonomy vis-à-vis Latin rite jurisdiction. This struggle ended in 1923 when the Syro-Malabar hierarchy was erected. Since then, they have tried to resolve an identity crisis resulting from the presence of Latin, Chaldean, and Indian elements in their rituals, laws, customs, and practices. Those who severed ties with Rome in 1653 underwent a change of rite as they became linked with the Jacobite Church of Antioch. They also became involved in a struggle with the Patriarchs of Antioch over autonomy and experienced further ecclesiastical divisions among themselves. Thus, they have had a somewhat different set of identity problems to cope with than have those who remained in communion with Rome.

When Mundadan discussed the Latin rite Catholics his concept of 'different Christian communities of India', introduced in the Foreword,[4] came into play. Mundadan analysed Latin rite Catholics in total separation from the St. Thomas Christians so that they had no apparent shared identity, nor did the identity of one have an effect upon the identity of the other. Since Latin rite Catholicism was sponsored, promoted and protected in India by the Portuguese, it presented itself as the religion of the 'Parangis', complete with foreign clergy and foreign customs. Roberto de Nobili tried to break out of this foreign mould and give Christianity a more Indian identity, but his experiment in inculturation met with such opposition that it was finally suppressed. As a result, a culturally Indian identity for Latin rite Catholics could become possible only after the development of an indigenous clergy, and

4 Ibid., p. 5.

then a transfer of ecclesiastical power from foreigners to Indians following the establishment of the hierarchy in India in 1886–87.

Up to this point, Mundadan treated the identity of Indian Christians as something worked out within the confines of the Christian Church itself. However, he took quite a different approach to the Indian Protestants' search for identity. Like Latin rite Catholicism, Indian Protestantism was begun by foreign missionaries under the umbrella of foreign colonialism and cultural penetration. However, the Protestant search for identity—led by some highly educated Indians—was an outgrowth of the Protestant mission to educate Indians at a time of rising political and cultural nationalism. The critical definition of Christianity and of Indian Christian identity as 'foreign', made by many leaders of the Indian renaissance and nationalist movement outside the Church, had a telling 'Indianizing' effect upon the educated Protestant élite's sense of identity. This led not only to movements for the transfer of power within the churches as well as for church union, but also to the development of Indian theologies and forms of spirituality among the Protestant élite. Thus, in the Protestant case, Mundadan saw Indian Christian identity being formed in response to the critique of the élite among those to whom the Church was in mission, and in significant conformity to those élite views of what constituted 'Indianness'.

It is noteworthy that Mundadan chose to use a survey history of Christianity in India from its beginnings up to the near-present to describe, analyse and define Indian Christian identity. Perhaps only such a survey could do justice to this complex subject. The other histories examined here are more limited in scope, but they do offer ways of looking at and defining Indian Christian identity which challenge the approach Mundadan took.

SUSAN BAYLY ON KERALA AND TAMIL NADU

Susan Bayly's *Saints, Goddesses and Kings*[5] represents a more anthropological approach to Indian Christian identity than does

5 Susan Bayly, *Saints, Goddesses and Kings: Muslims and Christians in South Indian Society, 1700–1900* (Cambridge: Cambridge University Press, 1989).

that employed by Mundadan. Her study was confined to the St. Thomas Christians in Kerala, the Paravas along the Coromandel Coast of Tamil Nadu, and mostly the Shanar and the Vellala Roman Catholics inland, primarily at Vadakkankulam. She set each of these three case studies within its social, political and religious milieu in order to answer her basic research question about 'what religious conversion really meant in South Indian society over the last three centuries'.[6] In particular, she looked at caste, shrines, cults, religious themes, and patronage for answers. What emerged from her study was a very different picture of Indian Christian identity from that presented by Mundadan.

The Syrian Christians were an élite seafaring community with a warrior tradition who were well integrated into 'Hindu' society prior to the beginning of the nineteenth century. 'Hindu rulers endowed and protected Syrian churches in the same way they patronized Hindu temples.'[7] The Syrian Christians' great festivals commemorating the death anniversaries of saints resembled both Muslim and Hindu festivals, while their St. Thomas cult had a 'close relationship to the martial cult traditions which played such a prominent part in both Muslim and Hindu worship in the region'.[8] They observed the same rules of ritual purity as did the high-status Nayars. The leading Syrian Christian and Nayar families were also listed as donors at each other's religious places and festivals.

This integration broke down during the nineteenth century. The religious synthesis collapsed and communal boundaries, which had not been there earlier, were erected. Several factors were

6 Ibid., p. 1.

7 Ibid., p. 251.

8 Ibid., p. 276. '...as they are recounted in Kerala, the St. Thomas legends have portrayed the apostle as a figure endowed with the same awesome characteristics as the Malayali warrior goddess. St. Thomas, too, has power over disease and other bodily afflictions, and for many centuries both the saint and his cult objects were believed to possess the power to maim and destroy. In at least one legend St. Thomas defeats a would-be temptress by turning her to stone. The account has a marked similarity to the story of the Trichy Khawjamalai pir: like this fierce avenging cult saint, the apostle has come to be regarded as a figure of vengeance and all-devouring wrath much like the goddess herself.' Ibid., p. 277.

responsible for this change. Both a decline in the sea trade and the British take-over of the military under a subsidiary alliance hurt the Syrian Christians' economic base. Then the British tried to turn the Syrians into a client community by championing their 'grievances' at the local court. This effectively drove a wedge between them and the Hindu élite. Both the internal religious revival under the influence of Protestant Evangelicals—which led to a condemnation of 'heathen idolatry'—and the mass conversion of low-caste people undermined the earlier religious synthesis. It also lowered the status of the Syrian Christians who became associated with the low-caste converts in the eyes of their Hindu neighbours.

Bayly saw the Paravas as a case of 'caste formation around a central body of Christian symbols which transformed the group's ideology but maintained them within the broader system of ranking within Tamil society'.[9] Prominent in her account was the rise of Parava notables and especially of the 'jati talaivan' (functioning like a 'little king' among the Paravas just as the metran did among the Syrian Christians) following their conversion; the development of the cults of St. Francis Xavier and the Virgin of Tuticorin; the ceremonial honours systems surrounding the Golden Car Festival for the Virgin; and the conflict between the jati talaivan and the Jesuits after their return to the area in 1837. This conflict was over the question of authority, not only in awarding ceremonial honours but also in determining who would and would not receive the sacraments. All these, Bayly indicated, were really Christian manifestations of religious themes and practices present in contemporary Hindu and Muslim religion and social practice. She drew similar parallels in her treatment both of the spread of Christianity in the Tamil hinterland—where Hindu bhakti cults prevailed—and of the nineteenth-century dispute over ceremonial honours at Vadakkankulam between the Shanars and the Vellalas. However, in these chapters, Bayly pointed out that the Shanars and the others, drawing upon the earlier success of the Paravas, saw mass conversion to Christianity as a means of enhancing their own ceremonial honour and standing vis-à-vis other local groups with whom they had been in competition.

9   Ibid., p. 378.

In fact, it is really this 'internal competition within the different social and religious groups of Tamil Nadu and Kerala',[10] rather than a distinctive religion or culture which, Bayly would say, provided the basic dynamic of the Indian Christian identity. By examining popular belief instead of formal theology, as well as cult traditions and festivals instead of rites, and by taking local society rather than foreigners as her primary reference point, Bayly drew an important conclusion about Indian Christian identity.

> Once dismissed as alien or marginal implants of European colonial rule, the manifestations of Islam and Christianity which took root in south India should now be seen as fully 'Indian' religious systems. Their underlying principles of worship and social organization derived from a complex and dynamic process of assimilation and cross-fertilization. New doctrines, texts, and cult personalities were introduced by a variety of Indian, west Asian and European teachers and churchmen, but over time these were taken over and transformed by their recipients.[11]

JOHN C.B. WEBSTER ON DALIT CHRISTIANS

My work *The Dalit Christians: A History*[12] was a social history which simply took the Indian identity of Christians for granted and directed attention instead to the kind of Indian identity Christians actually had. Given both this particular approach and this particular subject matter, I found myself forced to struggle with identity issues which had received much less attention in Mundadan's and Bayly's work.

The first of these was captured in the label, Dalit. While Mundadan had spoken of 'different Christian communities' and treated their histories in almost complete isolation from one another, and Bayly had used three not quite totally separate case studies on which to build some generalizations, the history I was writing did not allow me to follow those procedures. I had to decide, right at the outset, whether or not all Dalits, despite

10 Ibid., p. 457.
11 Ibid., p. 454.
12 John C.B. Webster, *The Dalit Christians: A History* (Delhi: ISPCK, 1992, 2nd ed. 1994).

differences in regional and jati background, did or did not share a common history and identity. If so, I could justifiably write a history of Dalit Christians; if not, I could write a history of, for example, Pulaya Christians plus Mala Christians plus Bhangi Christians. My case studies of four Dalit jatis in the opening chapter indicated that Dalits have shared not only a similar position in society but also similar histories of oppression and brokenness. The subsequent chapters showed how members of these and other separated but similar Dalit jatis were drawn together and how they interacted with one another as the modern Dalit movement developed during the course of the twentieth century. Certainly, in the eyes of others, at least from the late nineteenth century onwards, they have had a shared identity indicated by such common labels as, depressed classes, Harijans, and scheduled castes. The 1931 Census defined their distinctive shared characteristics so that they could be considered a separate category of people for political and administrative purposes. Thus, the evidence justified, indeed required, giving them a shared identity. I chose the label 'Dalit' instead of the alternatives 'because of its currency and aptness'.[13]

Imposed identity proved to be a second vital issue. In a history of Dalit Christians, it proved impossible to ignore the power of dominant castes, political majorities, the élite, and governments, at both the local and national levels, in the Church and the State, not only in defining but also in forcing an unwanted identity upon unwilling recipients. Dalit identity has always been a stigmatized identity, imposed by others, which Dalits themselves have not fully accepted and have often tried to change in a variety of ways. One such method, adopted by millions of Dalits, was conversion to Christianity. The Dalit mass conversion movements, which began during the later nineteenth century, gave the converts and their descendants a new identity.

The converts acquired a Christian identity which affirmed their dignity and status in the eyes of God despite their low social standing. In fact, both the evangelistic message presented to Dalits and the post-baptismal instruction given to those who converted sought to redefine their sense of identity in a fundamental way. They were

13 Ibid. (2nd ed.), p. x.

not inherently impure and condemned to suffer as broken people; they were beloved and precious in God's sight; they were chosen instruments of God's saving purposes; they were the ones with whom God most closely identified in the incarnation. Great efforts were made to inculcate this new sense of identity, along with the self-esteem and sense of responsibility which went with it, in the Dalit converts. Indeed, they were encouraged to replace their old jati identities with their new Christian identity, to think of themselves no longer as, for example, Chuhras or Chamars or Madigas, but as Christians.

This, however, proved to be impossible. The converts did acquire a new identity but they did not lose their old ones. There were two important reasons for this. Unlike high-caste converts, Dalits were not forced to make a total break with the past. Their biradaris did not eject them from their jatis upon baptism, but allowed them to continue as members. In fact, in those regions where two or more Dalit jatis converted in large numbers, Mangs and Mahars, Madigas and Malas, Pallars and Paraiyar, simply carried their old caste rivalries into the Church which became for them, as for the jatis which Bayly described, a new arena in which the struggle for status (and for survival) continued. Moreover, the vast majority of Dalit converts could not really have made a total break with the past anyway. They remained in their villages and cheris, in the same houses with the same neighbours, doing the same work for the same employers and patrons. Thus, in the village, they continued to be seen and treated as Dalits, even though they had changed their religion and sense of self. Thus, conversion really brought with it a dual identity, Dalit Christian, instead of replacing one with the other. Within the Church and the Christian community, where old caste values and loyalties have remained in conflict with Christian norms and values, there has been an uneasy recognition of this dual identity.

The Government of India has also played a decisive role in imposing identity upon Dalit Christians. It has given them a 'discriminated against' and 'second-class citizen' identity to go along with their stigmatized identity by ignoring the concert of forces shaping Dalit Christian life, by refusing to acknowledge their dual identity, and by defining them simply as Christians. In granting separate electorates to Christians in the Madras Presidency in 1919 and throughout India in 1935, the British put Dalit Christians in the Christian rather than the general constituency. In 1936, it declared Dalit Christians ineligible to receive Scheduled Caste benefits by virtue of their religion. This policy was continued by the Government of independent India in 1950 and was upheld by the Supreme Court in 1985, despite the religious discrimination involved. It has played a key role in driving Dalit Christians to reassert their Dalit identities as the competition in the struggle for economic security and upward mobility has intensified over the past two decades.

The third issue concerns the Dalit impact upon Indian Christian identity. Historically, the Dalit mass movements gave the Christian Church and community a new identity. Since the number of Dalits who converted was so large, in most parts of India the mass conversion movements changed the Christian community from a tiny, literate, and 'progressive' urban community into a much larger but predominantly poor, illiterate, and 'backward' rural community. In India as a whole, at least a majority of all Christians are Dalits. In some areas, the percentage would be well above ninety per cent. Thus, in most of the country, Indian Christian identity is, in fact, Dalit identity. This empirical reality has important consequences for historians. Since Dalits form the vast majority of Christians in India, and therefore occupy the centre rather than the margins of the Indian Christian community, the history of Christianity in India, its heroes and villains,[14] its major and minor actors, its truly significant issues and major distractions, must be re-visioned in order to see Indian Christian identity in its proper light.

Finally, implied in the above analysis but elaborated in the concluding chapter of the book, is the vital role which Christian theology—as presented through evangelistic or pastoral preaching and teaching—has played in forming and nurturing Indian Christian identity. This was, after all, what gave rise to the Dalit mass conversions movements and to the religious convictions which have distinguished Christian Dalits from other Dalits. It has also been,

14 For example, this would mean a significant role reversal for Roberto de Nobili.

implicitly or explicitly, very much at the centre of that uneasy relationship between Dalit and other Christians within the one body of Christ. Dalit theology is not a new thing in the history of Indian Christianity. Although not as well publicized as it is today, it has been present since the mass conversion movements began and, like other forms of Christian theology, has changed over the years. It has stood in sharp contrast to other forms of Indian Christian theology which, too, have sought to shape Indian Christian identity in different, even contradictory, ways.

FREDERICK S. DOWNS ON NORTH-EAST INDIA

In the cases cited so far, Indian Christian identity has been depicted as the identity of minority religious groups within a hierarchical social structure which they did not create. There, Indian Christian identity has not been an identity which Indian Christians have simply chosen for themselves; it has been shaped by the views of dominant groups within the wider society. The hill areas of the North-east, however, represent a contrasting case because theirs has been an alternative, tribe-based, non-hierarchical society, geographically isolated at the fringes of the predominant, caste-based hierarchical society of India. There, Christianity became the religion of entire populations within a region and helped shape that region's identity vis-à-vis the rest of India. In his histories of Christianity in North-east India,[15] Frederick S. Downs has argued that, 'For the tribals, Christianity provided a means of preserving their identities and promoting their interests in the face of powerful forces of change'[16] emanating from the plains.

15   *The Mighty Works of God: A Brief History of the Council of Baptist Churches in North East India: The Mission Period, 1836–1950* (Gauhati: Christian Literature Centre, 1971); *Christianity in North East India: Historical Perspectives* (Delhi: ISPCK, 1983); *History of Christianity in India: Volume V, Part 5: North East India in the Nineteenth and Twentieth Centuries* (Bangalore: Church History Association of India, 1992).
16   *History of Christianity in India*, vol. V, p. 7.

Because the 'primary agent of change in the North-east, the only agent with the necessary power to force change, was the British government (and its successor)',[17] Downs began with politics and the changes it brought about as the British took control of the hill areas: the erosion of the traditional socio-political structures of the hill tribes; the relatively centralized governing authority imposed upon them; pacification and the termination of such tribal customs as headhunting; the introduction of commerce and cultural contact with the plains; the threat of absorption or other forms of dominance by the larger Hindu community of the plains. He then concentrated upon the evangelization of the hitherto-isolated hill tribes in this context of change. He noted that the tribal people converted to Christianity in the largest numbers precisely in those hill areas where the British impact was the greatest and, therefore, the threat of change was most profound. Moreover, both the most successful patterns of evangelism (for example, the twentieth-century revivals) and the decentralized ecclesiastical structures which were developed for the converts as Christianity moved across tribal lines, were in keeping with the tribal way of life. Christianity not only helped integrate hitherto-separate groups within a single tribe by giving them a common organization which they had previously lacked, but it also provided a framework within which different tribes could come together and consult together on the basis of equality.

Christianity's contribution to 'the process of adjustment to a situation of traumatic change' introduced by the British penetration of a hitherto-isolated region did not stop at providing new integrating structures. The introduction of the gospel itself led to significant ideological change, especially in the ways people understood and dealt with their relationship to the spirits. Conversion to Christianity also led to a good number of lifestyle changes, affecting the institution of slavery; the consumption of intoxicants; the status of women; as well as changes in hygiene, dress and hairstyle. Christians also introduced modern medicine into the hills and provided other forms of humanitarian service.

17   Ibid., p. 144.

They developed written forms for spoken languages and a written literature in those languages. Perhaps most important of all, they provided opportunities for Western education to tribal people and thus played the major role in developing the new tribal élite. All these combined efforts enabled the hill peoples of the North-east to modernize without losing their tribal identity, and so to resist absorption into the lower levels of the wider hierarchical society of the plains people, once the isolation of the hills had come to an end.

However, despite its integrating role, not only at the intra-tribal and inter-tribal levels but also between hill and plains people, religiously as well as nationally, Christianity in the North-east has been identified as anti-national. In Downs's view, this is unjustified. The British government and the missionaries cooperated in the field of education, which missionaries controlled in some parts of the North-east, more for mutual convenience than to achieve shared objectives.[18] Since Independence, Christians have been leaders not only of separatist movements in the North-east, but also of peace movements and state governments committed to the Indian Union.[19] Downs cited other scholars to indicate that this anti-national image is counterproductive as well as inaccurate.[20] Yet this image seems to be the price paid for the close relationship between Christianity and tribal identity. As Downs pointed out in his introduction, 'it is very difficult to promote particular identities without undermining a larger regional or national identity—or at least not providing motivation for creating such larger identities when efforts began to be made to do so.'[21]

In a lecture published at about the same time as this history, Downs wrote, 'All historical writing has to have an integrating principle to make sense of the data'.[22] After describing and rejecting three alternatives, he set forth and defended his hypothesis that

18   Ibid., p. 56.
19   Ibid., p. 28.
20   Ibid., pp. 61–3.
21   Ibid., p. 7.
22   Frederick S. Downs, 'Identity: The Integrating Principle', *Bangalore Theological Forum*, vol. XXIV (March–June 1992), p. 1.

identity provides the best integrating principle for understanding the history of Christianity among the tribal people of the North-east. In the face of 'the irreversible impact of modernization, the only alternative to detribalization [was] to find a new basis for maintaining a distinctive identity.'[23] This, Christianity provided, not because the missionaries planned it that way, nor because the tribal people clearly—or even consciously—saw in Christianity a means of preventing detribalization and forging a functioning identity on a new basis.[24] Instead, this functioning identity came as an important consequence of all those other activities and attributes of Christianity described in the paragraphs above. Providing the means and the basis for that tribal identity was, in retrospect, what Downs considered to have been the most significant historical role which Christianity actually played in the North-east. Its significance made it the integrating principle of his history.

THE ROOTS OF INDIAN CHRISTIAN IDENTITY

This analysis of histories of Christianity in India might be extended to include other books and articles but, by now, two things should already be apparent. One is that Christian identity in India is not a monolithic, all-encompassing, whole which has replaced all other sources of identity among Indian Christians. There is so much diversity, even competition and conflict, among Indian Christians in historical records that the historian is hard pressed to identify much common socio-cultural or even religious substance in whatever unified identity has been shared by all Indian Christians over time. The other is that identity has been an important concern of Indian Christians down through the centuries. Historians write about it, not only because it is a matter of concern today, but also because—as these four books demonstrate in different ways—it has been important for varying reasons to the Indian Christians about whom these historians have written.

---

23   Ibid., p. 7.
24   Ibid., p. 8.

This begs the question of why their own identity has been, and remains, so important an issue to Christians in India.[25] Obviously, the collective identity of Indian Christians as a whole is of concern because it affects the identity of individual Christians in India. That observation, however, simply gives the question greater force rather than answers it. Perhaps the concern about identity has been a reflection of the subordinate position Indian Christians have occupied—to some extent within the Church itself—primarily within Indian society as a whole. Perhaps also, the aspiration behind this concern about identity has been, and continues to be, to get rid of the indignities and distortions of the past; to be who you are; to be valued as members of the body of Christ; and to be accepted within the wider society in a position of dignity and respect. One can discern, both among Indian Christians within these four accounts and among the historians who write about them, tendencies towards forms of assimilation on the one hand and towards forms of differentiation on the other, as ways of resolving (or at least easing the pain of) an identity problem that will not go away, as long as the subordination continues.[26]

The historian of Christianity in India has an important therapeutic role to play in helping Indian Christians understand the roots of their identity by analysing the changing roles played by governments, the dominant groups in Indian society, the Church and Indian Christians themselves, in shaping and defining Indian Christian identities through the ages up to the present time. This is an important and necessary role which needs to be played with great skill, honesty, empathy, and care. It is, however, a limited role, for the historian cannot resolve the identity dilemmas which Indian Christians experience, either by employing new methodologies, by discovering new facts, or by somehow simply defining those dilemmas away. In the last analysis, it is God alone, and not

---

25   I have been aided in these reflections by the essays in P.C. Chatterji (ed.), *Self-Images, Identity and Nationality* (Shimla: Indian Institute of Advanced Study, 1989).

26   My assumption here is that individuals and groups in subordinate positions are more apt to struggle with their own identity issues than are people in positions of dominance.

the historian, who grants and reveals the true identity of every individual and group of people, partially now, and more fully in God's good time. For the time being, the best we can do is try to discern in and through the particular continuities and changes in the history of Christianity in India what that identity might actually be.

CHAPTER 4

A Quest for the Historical Ditt*

Ditt is an important figure in the history of Christianity in the Punjab. Of that there can be little doubt. In the process of trying to discover more about this man, it became apparent that Ditt has been treated more as a symbol than as a person by those who have written about him. Who was the man behind the symbol and to what extent did the symbol take on a life of its own, independent of the man himself? These are the questions which have motivated this quest for the historical Ditt.

SOURCES FOR A BIOGRAPHY OF DITT

Perhaps the best place to begin this quest is Pickett's familiar *Christian Mass Movements in India* (1933) where Ditt appears right at the outset, in the very first chapter, as an illustration to help Pickett explain what he meant by the term, 'mass movement', or 'group movement' as he preferred to call it. Pickett noted that,

> The distinguishing features of Christian mass movements are a group decision favorable to Christianity and the consequent preservation of the converts' social integration. Whenever a group, larger than the family, accustomed to exercise a measure of control over the social and religious life of the individuals that compose it, accepts the

---

* This chapter was previously published in *Indian Church Historical Review*, vol. XXXVII, June 2003, pp. 53–68. This is a revised version.

Christian religion (or a large portion accept it with the encouragement of the group), the essential principle of the mass movement is manifest.[1]

Pickett then referred to Ditt as his first and primary example of this 'essential principle' at work.

The mighty Chuhra movement in the Punjab began when Ditt, the lowly first convert of a very lowly people, unlike all previous converts in the Punjab, retained his place in the group to which he had belonged, and then persuaded that group in his village to throw off the age-old bondage to animistic superstition and fear for the liberty which he had found in Christ.

The movement did not begin when Ditt was converted, but when by a valiant fight he turned group opposition, that would have expelled him, into group approval that carried all the Chuhras of his village into a confession of the Christian faith. After the decision of that first village group, Chuhras in other villages became interested, and year after year increasing numbers of them, acting together, entered the Christian fold.[2]

In his second chapter, entitled 'Historical Statement', Pickett provides a four-page account of the Chuhra movement in the Punjab in which Ditt plays the central role. Although the four paragraphs about Ditt are lengthy, they must be given in full because this has become the canonical version of Ditt's conversion and subsequent evangelistic activity.

Nattu, a Hindu of the Jat caste, son of a prosperous landowner and *lumbardar*, was converted, but disappointed the great expectations the missionaries had of him. He squandered his property and forfeited his position as prospective *lumbardar* in succession to his father. In every sense he proved to be a weak brother. Yet one day he appeared at the mission house in Sialkot accompanied by a dark, lame, little man named Ditt, whom he had taught and who declared his desire to be a Christian. The missionary examining Ditt found him well instructed and concluded that he was honest in his confession of faith, but proposed that he remain in Sialkot for a while to attend church services, receive further instruction, and permit the church to become better

1 J. Waskom Pickett, *Christian Mass Movements in India: A Study with Recommendations* (Nashville, TN: Abingdon Press, 1933), p. 22.
2 Ibid., pp. 22–3.

acquainted with him. Nattu vouched for his strict integrity, but Nattu's own status was not such as to make his commendation convincing. But Ditt pressed for immediate baptism. The missionary, the Rev. S. Martin, finally baptized him 'not because he saw his way decidedly clear to do so, but, rather, because he could see no scriptural ground for refusing.'

After his baptism Ditt asked permission to return to his village. Mr Martin hesitated. The policy favored for converts of the upper classes seemed too dangerous in this case. He feared that the poor illiterate man, lame, weak, and little-instructed, could not stand when assailed by arguments, taunts, and oppression. But seeing that Ditt was determined, Mr Martin bade him go and urged him to make a bold confession and try to win his neighbors.

Ditt had five brothers living in his village of Mirali. His own and their families numbered sixty persons. These relatives resented his conversion and declared that they would not eat, drink, or in any way associate with him as long as he professed to be a Christian. Abuse was heaped upon him, but Ditt remained faithful, refusing either to deny his faith in Christ or to cut himself off from his people. He resisted all their efforts, and he triumphed. Three months after his baptism he reappeared in Sialkot and presented his wife, his daughter and two neighbors as candidates for baptism. He had taught them what he knew; they professed their faith and their purpose to follow Christ and had walked thirty miles to be baptized. After examining them, instructing them and praying with them, Mr. Martin administered the rite, whereupon they immediately started back to their village. Six months later Ditt brought four other men who were also adjudged ready for baptism. The missionaries were by now convinced that a work of God was in progress in Ditt's village, and that it showed the way to escape from old methods of work that had seemed right but had proved wrong.

Ditt's humble occupation of buying and selling hides took him to many villages. Wherever he went he told his fellow Chuhras of Christ. Many abused him, but an increasing number heard him patiently, and before long, groups here and there began to follow his lead. In the eleventh year after Ditt's conversion more than five hundred Chuhras were received into the Church. By 1900, more than half of these lowly people in Sialkot District had been converted, and by 1915, all but a few hundred members of the caste professed the Christian faith.[3]

3 Ibid., pp. 44–5.

Pickett based his accounts on Andrew Gordon's *Our India Mission* (1886), a history of the first thirty years of the Punjab Mission of the United Presbyterian Church of North America by its founding missionary. In essence, Pickett summarized and highlighted 'the essential facts' of what Gordon had devoted seven pages to describe. However, in the process, he also changed and embellished what Gordon had written in ways that happened to suit his own missiological agenda. Ditt was not from Mirali but from Shahabdike, a village three miles from Mirali. His first two batches of converts did not come from a single village through some sort of 'group decision', as Pickett would have us believe, but from several villages around Mirali. Pickett also added things which Gordon had never mentioned. Pickett said that Ditt preached a gospel of liberty in Christ over against bondage to animistic superstition and fear, but Gordon was silent not only about Ditt's message to others but also about what he found particularly attractive or convincing about the Christian message in the first place. Pickett said Martin wanted Ditt 'to attend church services, receive further instruction, and permit the church to become better acquainted with him'; Gordon only said that Martin wanted to instruct him and test his sincerity.[4] Gordon did not say that Martin told Ditt to 'make a bold confession and try to win his neighbors', nor did he say that following Ditt's third trip to Sialkot the mission was convinced that 'a work of God was in progress in Ditt's village'. Of course, everything that Pickett added may well have been true, but he provided no clues as to from where—beyond his own historical imagination and the dictates of his theory—he had gotten these 'essential facts'.

The outline of Gordon's account was similar to that of Pickett's later summary, but Gordon included some important information not found in Pickett's summary. First of all, he provided some dates. Ditt was about thirty years old when he first visited Sialkot in June 1873 to be baptized; his two return visits with candidates for

---

4 Andrew Gordon, *Our India Mission: A Thirty Year's History of the India Mission of the United Presbyterian Church of North America, Together with Personal Reminiscences* (Philadelphia: Andrew Gordon, 1886), p. 422.

Fig. 4.1: A Photograph of Ditt
Source: Andrew Gordon, *Our India Mission*

baptism were in August 1873 and February 1874. He also provided some *verbatim* conversations Ditt had with his neighbours and relatives following his conversion. There is a group photograph (Figure 4.1) of ten mission workers, including Ditt,[5] and then a somewhat extended reference to Ditt's subsequent work as an evangelist.

> It was observed early in the history of Ditt's successful labors that whenever he detected worldly motives in persons professing religious inquiry, he refused to bring such inquirers to the missionaries. It should be further stated here, as an evidence of his remarkable dis-interestedness, that he never asked for any support from the mission. Many long journeys were performed by him on foot for the love he cherished to this good work, which grew upon him until at the end of seven years from his conversion it was observed that he had scarcely any time left for his own business, and consequently nothing to live upon. Even then he did not ask for money; but six or seven rupees a month, enough to support him in the humble way these people live, were given him as his right, thus enabling him to devote his whole time to this grand—this glorious work.

5 This photograph is located between pages 424 and 425 in ibid. The portion of it reproduced here shows Ditt seated on the ground; the others were behind him, either seated on chairs or standing. Note that he was leaning on something with his leg thrust out to the side, probably because he was lame, and, although illiterate, held a book (a Bible?) in his hand.

As is almost universally true of the *Chuhra* caste, Ditt, when converted in 1873, was unable either to read or write; nor was he successful in his attempt to learn in later years. Notwithstanding, the Lord has fulfilled to him, even in this life, the promise, 'Them that honor me I will honor.' In scores of villages throughout the Mirali region, when differences arise between Christian brethren, when advice is needed in regard to their matters of business, when marriages are contemplated, and especially when light is required in regard to matters of religion, the Christians trustingly resort to Ditt as their wise and able counsellor.[6]

Gordon's history was published in 1886, thirteen years after Ditt's conversion. Moreover, Gordon was not in India when Ditt converted, having been forced by illness to remain in the United States from 1865 to 1875. What, then, was the basis of his account? There is no reference to Ditt in the reports of the Sialkot Mission published as part of the Report of the Board of Foreign Missions in the Minutes of the Annual General Assemblies of the United Presbyterian Church, either for the years 1873 and 1874, the years on which Pickett and Gordon focused, or for the following years. The mission correspondence from India during those years, published in *The United Presbyterian*, the weekly newspaper of the United Presbyterian Church, too, made no mention of him. So far, no unpublished correspondence on the subject from the members of the Punjab Mission has come to light. The earliest statement which I have been able to find was in the annual report of the neighbouring Church of Scotland Mission in Sialkot, but this might refer to Nattu, who was a farmer, rather than to Ditt, who was not.

> . . . a remarkable movement in an outlying district in the American Mission field, to the South of Sealkote. Some time ago a farmer, who, I believe, first heard the Gospel through itinerating preaching, came to Mr Martin seeking baptism. After baptism he returned to his own home and occupation. He carried the light of the truth and God's blessing with him. During the past year upwards of fifty from this district have come seeking baptism, and as Christians have gone to their

6 Ibid., pp. 426–7.

villages and occupations bearing reproach for Christ's sake. They seek
no aid whatsoever from the Mission, and get none.[7]

Gordon's most obvious source would have been the Rev. Samuel
Martin, the missionary who baptized Ditt and was supervising the
evangelistic work of the mission in and around Sialkot at that time.
Martin may have spoken at length to Gordon about Ditt between
1875—when Gordon returned to India—and 1885, when Gordon
wrote his book. However, Martin's published correspondence
from 1873 and 1874 is of little help. On July 20, 1873 he wrote that
there had been two baptisms, one of a student in their school at
Sialkot. 'The other man baptized is a farmer from a village about
twenty miles distant. He resides in his own village.'[8] Was this
Ditt? The description does not fit him very well because, according to Gordon, Ditt was neither a farmer nor even an agricultural
labourer, but a dealer in animal hides. On the other hand, perhaps
Martin simply assumed that since Ditt was a villager, he must have
been a farmer of some sort. In August, perhaps before Ditt brought
in his first batch of candidates for baptism, Martin wrote, 'I have
little news to write.'[9] In September, his colleague in Gujranwala,
the Rev. McKee, wrote that, 'In Sealkote there have been a great
many baptisms this summer, and what is most encouraging about
the work is that men when baptized stay in their own village and
among their own friends.'[10] Six months later, he reported more
baptisms in Sialkot, all of whom 'remained in their own families
at their former employ'.[11] In August 1874, Martin was wondering
out loud whether a conversion movement was under way or not.
He was inclined to be sceptical on the basis of past experience, but

7 *Report by the Committee for the Propagation of the Gospel in Foreign
Parts Especially in India to the General Assembly of the Church of Scotland,
May 1875*, pp. 236–7.

8 'Monthly Missionary Statement', *The United Presbyterian* (25
September 1873).

9 'Foreign Missions—Monthly Statement', *The United Presbyterian*
(27 November 1873), p. 2.

10 'Foreign Missions', *The United Presbyterian* (29 January 1874),
p. 2.

11 'Foreign Missions', *The United Presbyterian* (30 July 1874), p. 2.

did consider those who had been baptized till then to have been sincere.[12] This would indicate that Pickett's assertion about the mission being convinced that 'a work of God was in progress in Ditt's village' was not correct.

The first written reference to Ditt which Martin made that I have been able to find appeared more than thirty years after Ditt's baptism. Referring to Nattu, the baptized farmer who had returned to his village, Martin wrote,

> The experiment failed in his case, yet he was made the instrument in God's hands opening the work among the lower classes. He became acquainted with some of this class in a neighboring village and taught them what little he knew. One of these, Ditt, of the village of Shahabdike, came with him to me in Sialkot. He was anxious to return to his village and as soon as he was baptized he went back. After a few weeks he returned with his family and several of his neighbors.[13]

This suggests that Nattu had not confined his evangelistic work to Ditt alone, as Gordon and Pickett implied, but had evangelized others as well, thus preparing the way for Ditt's later work.

Three features of this historical record require comment. The first is the disturbing silence about Ditt in the years 1873 and 1874. It is understandable that Ditt made no lasting impression upon Martin when they first met, but it is surprising that this should have continued when Ditt returned not just once but twice, bringing instructed converts for baptism. Such volunteer initiative was unusual and noteworthy. The second is that it was Andrew Gordon who rescued Ditt from historical obscurity and who provided what few details of his conversion and subsequent life now exist. Unlike most mission historians of his day, Gordon paid

12 This letter, dated 1 August 1874, is found in E. Josephine Martin, *A Father to the Poor* (published by the descendants of Dr and Mrs Samuel Martin in cooperation with the Board of Foreign Missions of the United Presbyterian Church of North America as a contribution to the centennial of United Presbyterian Work in India–Pakistan) with an Introduction and Comments by Robert W. Thompson, editor, p. 24.

13 S. Martin, 'Work Among the Chuhras', *Annual Report of the Board of Foreign Missions of the United Presbyterian Church of North America 1906*, p. 63.

considerable attention to the mission's converts, their stories and struggles, in addition to the customary chronicles of missionary life and 'the work'. Indeed, in the records of the Sialkot Mission for the years following the publication of Gordon's history, there are few references to Ditt. By 1898, he was an elder at Mirali[14] and he died on 16 April 1907.[15] His death was simply noted, and no obituary appeared in the reports and published correspondence of the Mission. The third is that Gordon almost certainly used memory, historical imagination, and poetic licence rather than *verbatim* reports to reconstruct the conversations which took place between Ditt and his own people following his conversion. Gordon's concern was to convey what those conversations must have been like rather than what they actually were. Both Gordon and his successors frequently used direct conversation as a literary device to heighten the dramatic quality of, and hence to involve their readers more fully in, the story they had to tell.

In subsequent United Presbyterian publications, which generally follow Gordon's account, some new information about Ditt's conversion does appear. The first was in J.W. Ballantyne's obituary of the Rev. Samuel Martin, which stated that

> Dr Martin's great work, in the providence of God, was his inaugurating and fostering the mass movement of the Chuhras towards Christianity. The story of the conversion and baptism of Ditt, of Shahabdike, is doubtless well known, yet it may not be out of place to repeat it as I remember it being told by Dr Martin himself. Ditt had come to Sialkot from his village thirty miles distant, requesting to be made a Christian. He had heard of Christ and the Christian religion, but his knowledge was meagre and vague. A place was given him on the compound and he was put under daily instruction. It soon became apparent that the man was not only sincere, but determined. But just at this point, it became necessary for Dr Martin , who had been suffering

14 Robert Stewart, *Life and Work in India: An Account of the Life, Work, Conditions, Methods, Difficulties, Results, Future Prospects and Reflex Influence of Missionary Labor in India, Especially in the Punjab Mission of the United Presbyterian Church of North America*, new ed. (Philadelphia: Pearl Publishing Co., 1899), p. 242.

15 Robert Maxwell, 'India News Letter', *The United Presbyterian* (16 June 1907), p. 15.

from fever, it being the rainy hot season, to go to the hills. But what was to become of Ditt? To leave this "Outcast" on the compound, even in the care of high-caste workers, was a doubtful course to pursue. To take him to the hills was out of the question. A decision was soon made. Dr Martin baptized Ditt and sent him home to his own village with instructions to share his knowledge with his people and bring them to him. Possibly the exigencies of the case dictated this daring course. However that may be, a less resourceful nature would hardly have ventured so radical a step in that day. By baptizing Ditt and sending him back to his own people, a mass movement was inaugurated and a new policy initiated.[16]

This account, however, is highly suspect because it is contradicted by contemporary evidence. In a letter dated 9 September 1873, Martin's colleague, the Rev. J.P. McKee, wrote not only that Martin had long been an advocate of encouraging those recently baptized to 'stay in their own village and among their own friends' but also that both he and Martin had 'remained on the plains this summer, and have had on the whole good health'.[17] In fact, Martin wrote on 22 May 1873 that he had returned from the hills three weeks earlier.[18] Moreover, as both Gordon, and then Martin in 1906, had testified, it was Ditt's decision to return to his village and not Martin's to send him back. It was Ditt, not Martin, who inaugurated the Chuhra mass conversion movement.

The history of the Punjab Mission written in 1940 by Emma Dean Anderson and Mary Jane Campbell highlighted the role which Mrs Martin had played in Ditt's baptism. While Martin wondered what he should do, 'Mrs Martin, who had a keen insight into character, said to her husband, "You will not make a mistake in baptizing him. I feel he is sincere and true."' Dr Martin no longer hesitated, and another humble man was added to the little

16 J.W. Ballantyne, 'The Rev. Samuel Martin, D.D., Annual Report of the Board of Foreign Missions of the United Presbyterian Church of North American', 1911, pp. 158–9.

17 'Foreign Missions', *The United Presbyterian* (29 January 1874), p. 2.

18 'Foreign Missions—Monthly Statement', *The United Presbyterian* (31 July 1873), p. 3.

Christian community.'[19] The source of this additional touch, added in a female narrative and omitted from earlier male narratives, may have been Kate A. Hill who went to India in 1896, became associated with the Martins, and offered this account as she had heard it from the Rev. Martin.

> No one from this caste had been baptized. There had been much discussion. Some said if a low caste man (or outcaste) be baptized, no high caste will ever come. Others said, if you want to cut down a tree begin at the roots. If caste is ever to be destroyed begin with the outcaste.
>
> So Ditt came asking for baptism. Dr Martin hesitated. Mrs Martin, with a woman's love and intuition said, "Baptize him." Dr Martin did and sent him back to his own village to live among his own people. In a few months Ditt returned with relatives and friends to be taught and to be baptized. Thus the mass movement in the Punjab began that brought thousands of low caste to Christ, and the Punjab Church was established.[20]

While projecting back to the time of Ditt's conversion—a debate which occurred only after the conversion movement was well under way[21] (and could only have occurred then)—the statement about Mrs Martin's role is not contradicted by earlier sources. Moreover, like Ballantyne's obituary, this addition to Gordon's account says more about the missionaries involved than about Ditt. Perhaps, both bear witness either to Martin's failing memory in his later years or to the poor memory of those to whom he told the story of Ditt's conversion.

The latest history of the United Presbyterian Mission, by Frederick and Margaret Stock, added further embellishments to those already mentioned. The first concerns Ditt himself, about

19 Emma Dean Anderson and Mary Jane Campbell, *In the Shadow of the Himalayas: A Historical Narrative of the Missions of the United Presbyterian Church of North American as conducted in the Punjab, India 1855–1940* (Philadelphia: The United Presbyterian Board of Foreign Missions, 1942), p. 55.

20 E. Josephine Martin, *A Father to the Poor*, pp. 5–6.

21 The earliest references to this debate in the reports of the Punjab Mission appear in 1884.

whom they wrote, 'Ditt doubted at first that the message of God's love through Jesus Christ could be for "outcastes". Being reassured on this point, he gave his heart to Christ and wished to be baptized.'[22] This is a significant addition because nowhere else do we find any statements at all about Ditt's spiritual quest, why Jesus and the Christian message appealed to him, why he became a Christian, or how he presented the gospel message to others. In this instance, the Stocks have taken a fairly common generalization about the spiritual motivation underlying Dalit conversions to Christianity at that time and applied it to Ditt himself. This conjecture on their part did provide an answer to an extremely important question about Ditt, but there is no way of knowing how valid it is in his particular case. Another of the Stocks's embellishments concerned the Martins. They asserted that, prior to baptizing Ditt, the Martins 'prayed together [and] were reminded of scriptural precedents in the Ethiopian eunuch and the Philippian jailer, both of whom were baptized immediately on request'.[23] From where did that missiologically loaded information come? At best it could have been part of United Presbyterian missionary lore in which the Stocks themselves shared; at worst, it was a missiological preference imposed upon the story of Ditt's conversion.

DITT AS SYMBOL

All the sources used in the preceding quest for the historical Ditt were produced by missionaries to express missionary concerns about subjects in which missionaries were interested to a largely Western readership. Some, like the Ballantyne obituary and the observations about Mrs Martin's influence, focus primarily upon the missionaries involved and reduce Ditt to a minor actor in the missionary drama. However, more importantly, in all of them— with the possible exception of Gordon's history—Ditt was treated more as a symbol than as a person. In fact, the subordination of

22 Frederick and Margaret Stock, *People Movements in the Punjab, with Special Reference to the United Presbyterian Church* (Pasadena: William Carey Library, 1975), p. 64.

23 Ibid., pp. 64–5

Ditt as person to Ditt as symbol has a history of its own which can be traced through the accounts cited above and is as revealing as are the bits of information about Ditt that have been uncovered so far.

It begins with the earliest references to Ditt's conversion in which he is not referred to by name but only by an occupation which was not even his own. The person was obscured; what was emphasized was the new missionary experiment in having converts return to their homes and to their people immediately following their baptism. The nameless Ditt became initially a symbol of the success of that new mission policy, while the changes in his life resulting from his conversion were not considered worth mentioning. Even in Gordon's account, which recovered the person of Ditt by providing details about his conversion and subsequent work, Ditt remained a symbol of the soundness of this new mission policy. Gordon was both a staunch advocate of the new policy and a lover of the human drama of Christian missions,[24] and so the symbol and the person competed on more or less even terms.

In Gordon's rendering, Ditt was not only a symbol of missiological 'truth', he also became the symbolic leader of the entire Chuhra mass conversion movement. The choice of Ditt was by no means as self-evident as Pickett's summary would suggest. Gordon mentioned two other similar movements which occurred near Gujranwala and Gurdaspur, quite independently of what Ditt had initiated in and around Mirali. Gordon referred to the movement around Gujranwala only in passing and did not name the initial convert there who was baptized by McKee at about the same time that Martin baptized Ditt.[25] The movement which focused upon the village of Awankha near Gurdaspur began just a few years later and had three leaders instead of one. Gordon, being posted

24 Andrew Gordon, *Our India Mission*, pp. ix–x, 423.

25 The Stocks, following Stewart (*Life and Work in India*, p. 242), implied that this was the Rev. Karim Bakhsh (*People Movements in the Punjab*, p. 67), but Gordon did not name the Chuhra convert (*Our India Mission*, p. 428). Later, Martin said that the Rev. Karm Bakhsh [note change in the English rendering of his name] was among the first Chuhra converts in the Gujranwala area. S. Martin, 'Work among the Chuhras', p. 63.

in Gurdaspur, was personally connected with that movement, and described the spiritual quests of the three in some detail. However, Ditt's movement was probably the first; it developed fairly quickly, thanks in a good part to Ditt's own efforts, and proved to be the largest of the three. Ditt—and Ditt's conversion in particular—thus made a powerful and appropriate historical symbol for the movement as a whole.

In subsequent histories, as in Pickett's account, Ditt became his conversion and his two subsequent return trips to Sialkot; he had no ministry, no accomplishments, no life worth mentioning after February 1874. The historical tradition about Ditt's conversion set by Gordon was embellished by others in ways already described, perhaps, as the earlier accounts suggest, through oral tradition within the Punjabi missionary community. For Pickett, Ditt and his conversion once again became a missiological symbol, exemplifying the nature and dynamics of mass conversion movements to Christianity. However, by altering and embellishing Gordon's account, Pickett divorced the symbol which, to him, was all-important, from what little is known of the historical realities of Ditt's life. It thus took on a life of its own, independent of Ditt himself.

The Stocks did the same thing, but in a different way. They, too, had a church growth missiological agenda to push and, in subtle ways, used the story Ditt's conversion to do just that. Their statements about Ditt's motives for conversion, drawn as they were not from the historical record about Ditt himself, but from contemporary views about Dalit conversions in general, transformed Ditt into a symbol of the typical Dalit convert who found Christ attractive because, through him, God's love reached out even to the socially despised, unloved Dalits. Perhaps, Ditt was typical in that respect; perhaps, like Chaughatta in Awankha, his religious quest and motivations were far more complex.[26] The truth of the matter is that we simply do not know. Once again, however, Ditt

---

26 Chaughatta, like Ditt, a Chuhrā, spent about twenty years travelling about visiting gurus and faqirs in a search for knowledge of God. Andrew Gordon, *Our India Mission*, pp. 440–2.

as a symbol became divorced from the known historical realities of Ditt the person.

In recent years Ditt has again become a symbol, but of a very different kind. As Punjabi Christians in India—the vast majority of whom are from Chuhra backgrounds—reaffirm their Dalit identity along with their Christian identity, Ditt has become a kind of common ancestor and identity-giver for the community as a whole. Included in this historical symbol are not only Ditt's conversion and subsequent evangelistic work, but also his caste, rural location, poverty, illiteracy, sincerity, courage and steadfastness. Ditt represents the community, its rootedness, its aspirations for a new and better life, its choice to be and to remain Christian.[27] There is, in Amritsar, a Ditt Memorial Centre which, at least symbolically, links the present-day Church in the Punjab to Ditt. In this use of Ditt as a symbol, Ditt has been treated as the person who initiated the Chuhra mass conversion movement, for the same historical reasons that are indicated in Gordon's narrative. There are as yet no embellishments, no attempts to romanticize Ditt or divorce the symbol from his person. If anything, a staunch and stark historical realism about Ditt seems to serve the Punjabi Dalit Christians well, because the crucial initial step in the transformative and liberative process envisioned for them involves facing the realities of their actual historical situation. Embellishments and symbolization, divorced from historical realities, are not considered to be in their best interests.

EVOLUTION OF THE 'DITT TRADITION'

The preceding pages have traced the evolution of what might be called the Ditt tradition. Neither his baptism nor his initial evangelistic successes was considered worth mentioning in the reports of the Mission at the time when they occurred. Only later, when

---

27 James Massey, in particular, has done much to recover Ditt as a community ancestor in his many writings. A good example of how he has used Ditt to help Punjab Dalit Christians in their continuing struggles is his *Towards Dalit Hermeneutics: Rereading the Text, the History and the Literature* (Delhi: ISPCK, 1994), chap. 2, especially pp. 44–7.

the Chuhra conversion movement was producing hundreds of converts every year and Andrew Gordon was persuaded to write an anniversary history of the Mission, did Ditt appear in the historical record. The origins of the conversion movement had to be described or explained, and Gordon presented Ditt as the person whose conversion and subsequent actions set the whole movement in motion. Since no written records about Ditt's conversion were available to Gordon, he had to rely on Martin's all too fallible memories, and perhaps those of others, for the information he did provide. Certainly much was left out of his account, most notably, Ditt's reasons for conversion, perhaps because Martin could not remember them, and Gordon either could not or did not ask Ditt himself.[28] It is impossible to determine now how much embellishment of the actual events of Ditt's conversion Gordon incorporated into his history, but Gordon's account did set some parameters for the subsequent evolution of the tradition. Nonetheless, new details, which may or may not have been accurate, were added to it over the years, and so the tradition has grown.

The story of Ditt has also become inseparable from the story of the great Chuhra mass conversion movement to Christianity in the Punjab, both because of the role he played in it and because it was the subsequent movement which, in the eyes of those who wrote about it, gave special significance to his conversion. That is why historians focus almost exclusively upon Ditt's conversion and ignore the rest of his life after February 1874, and why, behind virtually all accounts of Ditt's conversion, there is a desire to understand not Ditt himself but the conversion movement and its expansion which embraced so many converts. This is most obvious in the accounts of Gordon, Pickett, and the Stocks, all of whom built into their narratives a lot of missiological theory aimed at offering such explanations. My own account of Ditt has also been motivated by such a desire, but not by a missiological agenda. I posit Ditt as a person of influence and wide experience among his own people by the virtue of his occupation which brought him into constant contact with a wider world than his own village commu-

---

28 This contrasts sharply with his treatment of Chaughatta and others at Awankha whom he knew quite well personally.

nity. In that sense, he was already a leader prior to his conversion, and that is what made other Chuhras willing to take his testimony seriously and to follow his example.[29] In whichever way it is undertaken, a quest for the historical Ditt and the evolution of the Ditt tradition have gone hand in hand with a quest for the origins and internal dynamics of the Chuhra mass conversion movement to Christianity in nineteenth-century Punjab.

29 See John C.B. Webster, *The Dalit Christians: A History*, 2nd ed., pp. 46–7, 56.

CHAPTER 5

The Women of Amritsar through Missionary Eyes*

Historians have always used perceptions to understand both the perceived and the perceivers. But, in recent years, they have been concentrating so heavily upon the perceivers that the reader is left wondering whether the perceived are beyond the historian's reach. There is a growing body of historical literature deconstructing the perceivers' colonial constructions of India and Indians, and exposing the underlying ideological assumptions and larger interests that have shaped those constructions. Two recent books particularly germane to the subject of this particular essay illustrate this emphasis quite well. *Western Women and Imperialism*, edited by Nurpur Chaudhuri and Margaret Strobel, contained three essays dealing with some Western women's views of and various agendas for Indian women, while Anshu Malhotra's *Gender, Caste and Religious Identities* deconstructed the Punjabi Hindu and Sikh reformers' depictions of and prescriptions for the women in their lives. Both said far more about the perceivers than about the perceived.

*This chapter was previously published in Reeta Grewal and Sheena Pall (eds), *Precolonial and Colonial Punjab: Society, Economy, Politics and Culture: Essays for Indu Banga* (New Delhi: Manohar, 2005), pp. 265–88. This is a revised version.

This essay attempts to go through the perceivers to get at the perceived, not by simply accepting all their perceptions at face value, but by taking a critical look first at the perceivers and then at their perceptions, to determine whether anything of substance can be said about the perceived. Specifically, it seeks to gain some understanding of the women of Amritsar in the years between 1880 and the outset of World War I, by examining the references to them in the writings of the Church of England Zenana Missionary Society (CEZMS) missionaries who worked there during that period. The first section frames the inquiry in relationship to the two works cited above. The second section looks at the CEZMS missionaries themselves to see how their perceptions were shaped by their own aims with regard to the women of Amritsar; how they were positioned to get to know the women about whom they wrote; the kind of women with whom this brought them into contact; and which literary devices they employed in portraying those women to Western readers. The third section uses the critical lens provided in the previous section to examine the perceptions found in those missionary writings in order to discover what they reveal about the women of Amritsar themselves, and not just about the missionary perceivers. At the end, conclusions will be drawn both about the value of the critical lens employed here and about the women who have been perceived through missionary eyes.

PERCEPTUAL LENSES OF WESTERN WOMEN AND INDIAN MEN

The essays selected from *Western Women and Imperialism* focused on Western women, primarily in their role, not as observers, but as activists doing what they thought was best for Indian women. In 'Cultural Missionaries, Maternal Imperialists, Feminist Allies', Barbara Ramusack provided biographies of five British women who became concerned about the condition of Indian women: Mary Carpenter, Annette Akroyd Beveridge, Margaret Noble (Sister Nivedita), Margaret Gillespie Cousins, and Eleanor Rathborne. She then examined their patterns of association with Indian women, noting that all of them 'viewed their work for Indian women within an imperial context'—which meant trying to influence British public opinion—and made their initial personal contacts not with Indian women but with Indian men.[1] In the end, Ramusack concluded that 'these British women activists embodied a benevolent maternal imperialism', crossed boundaries of race, and provided useful skills in achieving goals set by the (élite) Indian women with whom they worked.[2]

Antoinette Burton's 'The White Woman's Burden: British Feminists and "The Indian Woman," 1865–1915' moves us closer to our particular subject. She argued that British feminists 'constructed the "Indian Woman" as a foil against which to gauge their own progress'.[3] She pointed out that liberal bourgeois feminism in Britain during that period was grounded in the idea of superiority; it was 'preoccupied with race preservation, racial purity, and racial motherhood'; it claimed racial responsibility that was 'custodial, classist, ageist and hierarchical'; and it carried a sense of special responsibility towards Indian women.[4] She examined Josephine Butler's crusade against India's Contagious Diseases Acts (1886–1915) and then some British feminist writings on Indian women for the images they projected. She concluded that,

> Although Indian women of the period were active in social reform and feminist causes of their own making, many British feminists insisted on creating them as passive colonial subjects partly in order to imagine and to realize their own feminist objectives within the context of the imperial nation into which they sought admission.[5]

The operative word in Leslie Flemming's 'A New Humanity: American Missionaries' Ideals for Women in North India,

---

1 Barbara N. Ramusack, 'Cultural Missionaries, Maternal Imperialists, Feminist Allies: British Women Activists in India, 1865–1945', in Nurpur Chaudhuri and Margaret Strobel (eds), *Western Women and Imperialism: Complicity and Resistance* (Bloomington: Indiana University Press, 1992), p. 129.

2 Ibid., pp. 133, 134.

3 Antoinette M. Burton, 'The White Woman's Burden: British Feminists and "The Indian Woman", 1865–1915', in Nurpur Chaudhuri and Margaret Strobel (eds), *Western Women and Imperialism*, p. 137.

4 Ibid., pp. 138–9.

5 Ibid., p. 151.

1870–1930' was 'ideals', for it was their ideals which shaped their encounters with Indian women; the aspects of Indian culture they chose to criticize; and the specific objectives they sought to realize through their educational, medical and evangelistic work among Indian women. These forms of work provided access, but the ideals—including the 'cult of domesticity'—came from the United States. While aiming at generally raising women's status, blurring caste distinctions, and improving women's physical well-being, they also had a vision of Christian womanhood which they applied most directly to Christian women. The Indian Christian woman was to be 'useful', first of all by carrying out an enhanced domestic role within her own household, but also by acquiring teaching and other skills of benefit to the emerging Christian community, such as the ability to lead voluntary organizations as well as to evangelize. In so doing, the missionaries 'upheld the domestic identity accorded to women in Indian culture'; enabled women to assume leadership roles which Indian culture had previously denied them; and so, 'let Indian women see *themselves* as potential agents of change'.[6]

These brief summaries of only three articles are perhaps sufficient to indicate the tremendous obstacles to accurate perception which missionary observers had to overcome. There were boundaries of race, culture and imperial power to be crossed if trust and, therefore, understanding were to be gained. There were deeply ingrained assumptions and ideologies to be exorcized if Western women were to see Indian women in their own right and on their own terms. Even the ideals and aspirations which missionary perceivers had both for themselves and for the Indian women with whom they interacted had to be set aside, lest they cloud the vision of what was. These conditions were met with only partially at best, since they require a degree of self-transcendence greater than ordinary human beings are capable of. The historian would thus seem to be forced to move from perception back to perceiver and then on to the perceived under less than ideal conditions.

6 Leslie A. Flemming, 'A New Humanity: American Missionaries' Ideals for Women in North India, 1870–1930', in Nurpur Chaudhuri and Margaret Strobel (eds), *Western Women and Imperialism*, pp. 203, 204.

Before turning to the CEZMS missionary perceivers themselves, it is important to take a careful look at Anshu Malhotra's *Gender, Caste, and Religious Identities: Restructuring Class in Colonial Punjab* for the alternative views of Punjabi women being developed by contemporary (male) Hindu and Sikh reformers. Like the essayists mentioned above, Malhotra focused on the perceivers rather than the perceived. Specifically, she examined 'the social imagination and the ideological postulations' of urban Hindus and Sikhs belonging to the mercantile and professional castes who made up 'the new élite or middle classes of Punjabi society'. It was their insecurity and desire for a self-enhancing identity which led these members of various reformist organizations to adopt 'certain postures towards women, which significantly contributed to restructuring upper caste, middle class patriarchy in this period'.[7] Malhotra's argument, developed by looking at the periodicals, tracts, pamphlets, novels, school journals, *jhagrras* and *kissas* they produced, was that 'high caste reformers of various hues in Punjab tried to protect their high born status and social privilege by controlling women's sexuality'.[8]

Thus, changes in marriage practices, such as the replacement of bride price with dowry which the reformers advocated, reflect their own obsessions with a daughter's sexuality, with ritual correctness, and with hierarchy. Their advocacy of ascetic widowhood devoted to public service, especially as a teacher, eased family financial burdens while giving the widow some independent income and self-respect. They upheld the ideology of the *pativrata* wife who was to deny her own needs and individuality for the good of the joint household. This meant not only submission to her husband but also acquiring some essential household management skills and distancing herself from the low castes. Indeed, while the reformers were worried about their wives and daughters being attracted to Christianity, their deepest fear was of the subversive power of popular culture, and particularly of the low-caste holy men and

---

7 Anshu Malhotra, *Gender, Caste, and Religious Identities: Restructuring Class in Colonial Punjab* (New Delhi: Oxford University Press, 2002), p. 31.

8 Ibid., p. 45.

religious shrines to which women turned when facing such forms of adversity as illness, barrenness, or the need for a son.[9]

Taken together, these studies provide insight into two very different perceptual lenses through which Punjabi women were being viewed during the last quarter of the nineteenth and the first quarter of the twentieth century. What gave these lenses such power among those who used them, was a shared complacent maternalism, on the one hand, and a shared insecure but ambitious determination to control, on the other. But what of the Punjabi women themselves who were being looked at through these lenses? What were they actually like? Is it possible to go beyond the ideologically shaped stereotypes or the projected hopes and fears which their observers attached to them, to see these Punjabi women, at least partially, as they were?

MISSIONARY PERCEIVERS AND LITERARY FORMS

The Church of England Zenana Missionary Society (CEZMS) was formed in 1880 to give 'a decided Church of England standpoint' to the work that was then being done by the interdenominational Indian Female Normal School Society. When these two mission societies went their separate ways, the latter transferred to the former thirty-two missionaries and sixteen mission stations, including Amritsar.[10] There the missionaries were already visiting zenanas and running several schools for girls, the most important of which was the Alexandra Girls' School, begun in 1878 as a boarding school for the daughters of the 'higher class of Native Christians'.[11] In 1879, they started a dispensary which they developed into St. Catherine's Hospital the following year. In 1884, the Amritsar Municipal Committee handed over to it responsibility

---

9 Ibid., pp. 147–9, 165–99.

10 *The Church of England Zenana Missionary Society Jubilee Souvenir 1880–1930*, p. 9.

11 Robert Clark, *The Punjab and Sindh Missions of the Church Missionary Society Giving An Account of their Foundation and Progress for Thirty-Three Years, from 1852 to 1884*, 2nd ed. (London: Church Missionary Society, 1885), p. 63.

for the city maternity hospital.[12] For the missionaries of the CEZMS, educational and medical work for women and girls was closely intertwined with zenana visitation in the city and itineration among the surrounding villages. In 1884, there were twenty women missionaries, three English assistant missionaries, as well as thirty-six Indian Christian Bible Women and teachers associated with the Amritsar Mission.[13] In addition to running zenana classes, schools, dispensaries and a hospital, they sought to address some of the special needs of the women they encountered by establishing a home for converts, a home for destitute convalescent women, a Hindu widows' industrial class, and a centre for the blind.

The aims of the CEZMS in Amritsar were clearly evangelistic. As the Society stated later in a small pamphlet introducing itself to prospective supporters in Great Britain, 'The aim of the Society is to make known the Gospel of Christ to the women and girls of India and other non-Christian lands, winning souls for Him, building them up in faith, and training them for His service'.[14] This aim, like the nature of work in which they were involved, had a major impact upon the kinds of interaction that CEZMS missionaries had with the women of Amritsar during the years under study. They approached the women as teachers, medical practitioners, as guests in the zenanas and, above all, as evangelists, and the women responded accordingly. This evangelistic aim also coloured much of what the missionaries had to say about the women of Amritsar in their annual reports and in other publications of the Society.

Given their aim and their chosen methods of work, which groups or categories of women in Amritsar did these missionaries come into contact with and write about? Zenana visitation—almost by definition—was directed towards those high-caste, and at least middle-class, Hindu and Sikh women, and comparable Muslim women, who were largely confined to their homes. Zenana visits combined the evangelistic with the educational, social and, where

12 Irene H. Barnes, *Behind the Pardah: The Story of C.E.Z.M.S. Work in India* (London: Marshall Brothers, 1897), p. 180.

13 Robert Clark, *The Punjab and Sindh Missions of the Church Missionary Society*, p. 69.

14 *Church of England Zenana Missionary Society* (1926?), p. 2.

needed, medical aims both of the mission and of the women
involved. Mission schools, whether set up in zenanas or separate
from them, catered to the same kinds of families, although the
mission did run a separate school for sweepers' children. Medical
work, on the other hand, was carried out among all classes, castes,
and communities, with much of it being done for the poor.[15] The
hospital and the dispensaries were also important locations for
interaction with widows, victims of domestic abuse and abandon-
ment, the blind and the crippled, as well as those ruined by famine.
Taken together, these would seem to represent a fairly good cross-
section of female society in Amritsar.

The mission produced two main types of source material from
which a historian might gain access to the missionaries' perceptions of Amritsar's women: the mission's annual reports and the
Society's bi-monthly magazine, *India's Women* (after 1895, *India's
Women and China's Daughters*). The former concentrated primarily upon the missionaries themselves, their work, and the institutions they ran; there is relatively little in them about the women
among whom they worked. The latter contained a variety of
articles and reports that included far more information about the
Indian women whom the CEZMS missionaries encountered while
carrying out their responsibilities than did the annual reports.
There were also occasional booklets and pamphlets which, like
the reports and articles, foreign missionaries of the Society wrote
for their Western readers in order not only to inform them about,
but also to gain their moral and financial support for, the Society's
work among Indian women.

In these publications, information about the women of Amritsar
appeared in four different literary forms. The first was the generalization. Two of the three following examples were written in
1880 by Miss S.S. Hewlett, a newly arrived medical missionary. The
zenana medical missionary, she wrote, 'comes upon scenes of long
endured pain and weakness, and long hidden sorrow'.[16] Later, she

15 'Report of the Amritsar Medical Mission,' *India's Women—The
Magazine of the Church of England Zenana Missionary Society* (July–
August 1883), p. 193.

16 'Umritsar,' ibid. (October 1880), p. 40.

went on to say that 'There are many prejudices and many superstitions and many fears in the minds of these people, which makes any attempt to doctor them a matter requiring much thought and care'.[17] The third is taken from the mission's annual report for 1909:

> There is such an eager desire to learn English in the zenanas in Amritsar that the whole staff might find sufficient work to occupy all their time and strength in this work. In every house the Bible is listened to with interest and often with earnest attention.
>
> On the other hand, to do justice to the school work, all the time might be given to that. The people are determined to have education and if we cannot supply it, others will, but without the saving influence of the Word of God.

This, she went on to note, was especially true in those homes where a family member was studying or had studied in Great Britain.[18]

All three quotations reveal much about the missionary perceivers and, indeed, offer further confirmation of many of the generalizations about Western women as perceivers of Indian women referred to in the earlier section of this essay. Ramusack's 'benevolent maternal imperialism' is evident in all three statements. Burton's sense of racial superiority and responsibility is more implicit, as are Flemming's ideals of women's physical well-being and raised status. Hewlett's two statements depicted Indian women as passive victims, whereas the later statement presented them as agents of change—a significant shift. All three statements gave Western Evangelical readers ample reason to value and support the work of the CEZMS missionaries in Amritsar. But, does this mean that the perceptions themselves were inaccurate? Does it mean that a Western doctor visiting the homes of urban, middle-class women in late-nineteenth-century Amritsar did not encounter a number of cases of long-term and debilitating but curable illness, or problems of cross-cultural communication and trust owing to differing beliefs, attitudes and customs, with regard

17 Ibid., p. 41.

18 *With the King's Heralds: A Short Report of the Work of the C.E.Z.M.S. for the Year 1909*, pp. 19–20.

to the illness and its treatment? Does it mean that Western zenana visitors and school administrators were incapable of gauging the increase or decrease in demand for their services from women and girls? What the wording of these questions implies is that the perceptions themselves were most probably accurate, but that the nineteenth-century evangelical framework within which they were conveyed might well have to be abandoned.

The second literary form frequently employed in these missionary writings was the anecdote. Miss Thom told three stories about the wife of 'a Mohammedan man of high social standing' who, she was convinced, was 'a real believer in the Lord Jesus Christ'. The most intriguing of her three anecdotes about this woman—both for what it included and what it left out—is this one:

> On another occasion she said to me, 'I was having a talk with my husband yesterday, and he said, "It seems to me you are very much inclined to become a Christian. What has drawn you so much this way?" So I answered him, "Well, one thing you will allow: whatever Christianity may be for *men*, it's a good religion for *women*." Whereupon she said, "He laughed *very* much indeed."'[19]

Miss Thom used this anecdote to support her own conviction that the woman was a real believer and thus to convince the supporters of the CEZMS that their work in Amritsar was bearing fruit. Yet, it could also be argued that, given the colonial social context in which the anecdote was set, this woman was simply telling Miss Thom what she thought Miss Thom would want to hear. However, the point that is so striking about the anecdote—the Muslim woman's observation that men and women might have different perceptions and evaluations of Christianity—was not even a minor theme in the writings of either Miss Thom or of the other CEZMS missionaries in Amritsar at that time. The insight, for which the reasons and evidence are unfortunately not given, would seem to be that of the unnamed Muslim woman herself. Whether or not she was expressing an unarticulated view of Christianity shared by other secluded women in Amritsar at that time is, on the face of it, a matter of conjecture.

19 'Amritsar', *India's Women* (July–August 1881), p. 175.

A third, but less common, literary form found in these mission sources is the short biography or character sketch. One example drawn from an accounting of ten years' work by the medical missionary, S.S. Hewlett, is illustrative of this form.

> The first baptism took place in 1880, on Easter Day. The convert was a Mussalmani; she was ignorant and poor, but possessed of fair intelligence, and she appeared very sincere in her profession of faith. It is still believed that she was in earnest at the time, but the seductive pleasures of sin were too much for her, and she fell away. Her tempter was a Eurasian, who after a short time left her in poverty and misery. At the time of her apostasy, she took away with her three children who had been baptized with their mother. These children she ultimately sold, and herself continued to lead an evil life. She was again deserted, this time by a Mohammedan, who had promised her great things; and she is now living in a state of most abject misery; helpless and ill. One of our Bible women has found her out, and tried to win her back to God, but so far she is hard and impenitent.[20]

Although this is one of the longer and more detailed of S.S. Hewlett's biographical sketches, it is, nonetheless, highly selective in what she chose to include and to omit, as well as very value-laden in the language she employed. While this sketch hardly embraced 'the whole truth' about this woman's life, and may not even highlight what in the last analysis was most important about it, the sketch does convey certain information which may be taken as reliable rather than as a fabrication or a serious distortion of facts. Moreover, as with an anecdote, a biography of this kind may provide insight but by itself cannot be the basis for generalizations about the wider female population in even just one section of Amritsar society.

The fourth literary form which these missionary authors used was the analytical description or account. The following is Miss Wauton's description which appeared in the Society's 1901 annual report of systematic Arya Samaj opposition to the CEZMS schools in Amritsar. After pointing out that the Arya Samaj sent its agents

---

20 'A Year of Labour in our Foreign Mission Field', *India's Women* (July–August 1890), p. 194.

'to preach in the streets and lanes against the "dangerous practice" of sending girls to Mission schools', she went on to say:

> Throwing down their *puggeries* before the parents, they would entreat them with tears to withdraw their daughters from Christian influence. While the fathers and brothers were often inclined to yield to these persuasions, the mothers, many of whom had themselves been in these schools, were in favour of allowing the children to continue their attendance, in spite of threats and entreaties. The young people themselves had no idea of being kept away, and often cleverly evaded their pursuers, who were watching for them in the street.[21]

What is significant about this account is that it depicted women as not merely thinking differently from the men but acting in defiance of them. Moreover, this defiance was not the act of just one or two mothers and daughters, but of a fairly large number of them, perhaps, acting in concert with one another. These do not appear to be the pativrata wives whom Malhotra's reformers wanted, but women with minds of their own who placed what they considered to be their daughters' well-being above conformity to community demands. Miss Wauton was obviously not an eyewitness to the events she described; one must presume that she got the information from the girls who came to school, or subsequently from their mothers, or from both. Either she did not know or just did not indicate what motivated the defiance she described. The writer of the annual report goes on to state, in a rather self-satisfied and probably naïve way, that

> The opponents afterwards had resort to the plan of opening rival schools. This, however, does not seem to have had much effect. Parents have learnt the difference between the teaching given and the care taken of their children at the Mission and the opposition schools; and the balance of opinion is decidedly in favour of the former.[22]

All four literary forms can be found in the one book to emerge from the CEZMS Amritsar Mission during this period, *Daughters*

---

21 *Twenty-first Annual Report of the Church of England Zenana Missionary Society for the Year Ending 31 March 1901*, p. 54.

22 Ibid., p. 55.

of the King by S.S. Hewlett. This book was written to promote support among Western readers for the evangelistic mission of the CEZMS The stories she told, as well as the generalized descriptions she offered, were all selected with that end in view. Its value here lies not only in the additional detailed information about women in Amritsar which it offers but also in the point of view it presents, as this provides an important clue to the ideological commitments of the CEZMS missionaries. Hewlett began by challenging some assumptions commonly held in the West about secluded Indian women, that is, that they lacked mental power, intellect, influence, 'civilization', or religion, and later argued that:

> It is one of the laws of nature that if any class of the community is oppressed or injured, it will sooner or later tyrannise over all the classes which have united in that oppression or injury; accordingly, if we were asked what it is which more than anything else acts as a dead weight upon progress and civilization in India, we would have to reply, *the position of the women.* Socially degraded, treated as animals of a lower order than man, excluded from society, kept in grossest ignorance, women (O strange contradiction!) yet wield the scepter in the home circle. Their influence is mighty, and all the power they possess is spent upon an ignorant and bigoted upholding and enforcing of their own religions.[23]

Specifically, Hewlett argued, Indian women were in bondage to religiously sanctioned *custom*, from which they needed to be set free.[24] Her comments on caste are particularly trenchant at this point. Caste, she said, produces an '*ossification* of the feelings' which has an 'unwomanising' effect.

> If it is terrible to see a man pass by his fellow-creature in his time of suffering, and leave him unpitied and unhelped, how much more does it shock the feelings to know that women, whose very characteristics should be love and tender kindness, should become so hardened by the requirements of caste as to utterly refuse kindness or assistance to

23 S.S. Hewlett, *Daughters of the King* (London: Church of England Zenana Missionary Society, 1886), p. 65.
24 References to bondage or slavery to custom are also found in the writings of Miss Wauton. 'Amritsar', *India's Women* (July–August 1883), p. 184; 'Plead for the Widows', ibid. (May–June 1889), p. 124.

a sister-woman in her hour of distress and anguish, or even in death? The *woman* in such beings is destroyed; the tender love, implanted by God Himself, which constrains a woman to take into her arms the suffering or weary child, or her degraded outcast sister, and minister to any and every need as long as her ministrations can avail to lengthen life or relieve pain, this love is extinguished by the cold, stern hand of caste.[25]

As this quotation suggests, Hewlett's book is hardly a detached, value-free analysis; She had an evangelistic agenda for the women of Amritsar and her language was laced with 'benevolent maternal imperialism'. Thus, while offering important insights into her own type of evangelical feminism, which was probably shared by at least some of her missionary colleagues in Amritsar,[26] her book also abounded in descriptive detail about marriage and death ceremonies, as well as about several occupations—*bihishtins, nains,* Brahminis, and sweepers—followed by women, and included numerous anecdotes which provide insights into women's lives. Thus, there is material in her book which can be a potential source of evidence about the women she described and about herself.

The foregoing analysis of the positions, work and literary productions of CEZMS missionaries in Amritsar has been designed to gain insight into them as perceivers of local Indian women. It illustrates the degree to which they and their perceptions were products of the colonial context in which they interacted with Indian women; of their own 'maternally imperialistic' cultural biases and ideological attachments; of their sense of vocation as Evangelical missionaries called to work among and for the benefit of the women and girls of Amritsar. In short, this analysis of CEZMS missionaries as perceivers has produced results very similar to

25 S.S. Hewlett, *Daughters of the King*, pp. 11–12.

26 As the previous quotation on caste indicated, Hewlett considered empathy and love to be of the very essence of womanhood. Later in her book she wrote that medical mission 'teaches the sufferers that love is a real and living thing, that those who come to their homes to help them in sickness, asking nothing in return, must be actuated by love and that God is love'. (Ibid., p. 54.) In other words, the distinctly womanly and 'womanizing' Christian witness was the witness of empathy and loving action.

those of Ramusack, Burton and Flemming. At the same time, the specific examples cited and the critical assessments made of some missionary perceptions are intended to serve as a starting point for shifting the focus of inquiry away from the perceivers towards the perceived. The assumption underlying this move is that a critical examination of specific cases, often presented in small literary units, makes less tenable those extreme forms of scepticism which would simply dismiss these missionary writings as of no value at all in developing an understanding of the women of late-nineteenth-century Amritsar. These writings—used with care that would take all their limitations into account—can still provide useful information about, and even some insight into, the lives of those women with whom the missionary writers interacted.

MISSIONARY PERCEPTIONS AND PROFESSIONAL PERSPECTIVES

The preceding section presented illustrative examples of four literary forms which CEZMS missionaries employed to assess the possibilities and limitations of each form for use as evidence concerning the lives of women in Amritsar from as early as 1880 to as late as 1909. Those examples were chosen not only because they were representative of the literary forms being evaluated, but also because each said something important about some of the women in Amritsar during that period. In this section, those examples are combined with others and arranged thematically rather than by form in an attempt to develop at least an impressionistic picture of certain aspects of the lives of women in Amritsar during that time. Since the CEZMS missionaries interacted with women as educators, evangelists, and medical practitioners, these three—at times overlapping but nonetheless distinctive—perspectives will provide the frameworks for presenting their perceptions.

Miss Smith's generalization in 1881 about the lack of interest in education found in the zenanas provides a base-point for examining the perceptions of missionary educators.

We are always glad to gain a pupil in a new house, for that assures a ready entrance to both Bible women and Lady Visitor; but there is still so much prejudice against the education of women, and their own indolence and apathy are so great, that it is often impossible to coax even one in a large household to learn to read.[27]

However, Miss Smith's generalization about pervasive apathy and indolence seems to be contradicted by current and subsequent anecdotal evidence. The following year, Miss Wauton reported about a very receptive group of Muslim women gathered in the home of one whose husband had taught her to read, and another group in the home of a Hindu woman who

> shows great determination to make the very utmost of the time dur-
> ing one visit I can pay her in a week; and I can hardly help laughing
> sometimes at the resolute way in which she turns out any one woman,
> child, or animal, whoever or whatever it may be, that causes any inter-
> ruption to the lesson—only allowing those to remain who are willing
> to sit quite still and listen to what is being read or taught. It would be
> delightful if all our houses were like this.[28]

That same year, Miss Henderson visited a Hindu home where she found 'a little congregation' of 'very respectable well-to-do' women who 'received me very cordially, and seated themselves to listen with an intelligent interest that I have not been at all accustomed to in this city'.[29] Another report in 1883 cited several examples of interest in reading and, in her book (1886), Miss Hewlett gave the testimony of a Muslim woman who, after a visit from a lady doctor, reported asking herself, '"Why do these English women know so much that we do not know? It must be because they can read!" And from that time I had a great desire in my heart for reading.' She soon persuaded her husband to get her a lady teacher from the mission.[30] Meanwhile, at the Alexandra School, Miss Dewar was reporting that, 'Taken on the average, the girls are bright, quick, and willing to learn, and quite as eager to get at the root of things as English girls of the same age generally are'.[31]

27 'Amritsar', *India's Women* (July–August 1881), p. 169.

28 'Punjab and Sindh', ibid. (May–June 1882), p. 149.

29 Ibid., p. 145.

30 'Amritsar', ibid. (May–June 1883), p. 139; S.S. Hewlett, *Daughters of the King*, pp. 126–7.

31 'Punjab and Sindh', *India's Women* (May–June 1882), p. 147.

What these missionaries seem to have been reporting is not so much a widespread as a growing interest in literacy and education among respectable, middle-class women in Amritsar during the early 1880s. This impression is strongly reinforced by their reports of opposition to their educational work from Muslim and Arya Samaj men who considered its growing popularity among women to be a threat. A brief description of male opposition and female defiance in 1900 has already been given in the earlier section of this essay. However, a more thorough and, in the short run, more effective boycott had been attempted back in 1885. Miss Wauton reported concerning the Arya Samaj:

> Knowing how the Gospel is finding its ways into homes through the influence of the women, they have aimed their blows against all female schools in the place, but more particularly against those where Christian instruction is given. Early in the year, a large house close to the doors of our central building was taken by them. A busy hum of voices told us that a school had been established; children and teachers were always swarming about, as if to make a great show of activity, and the words 'Arya Somaj' were hardly ever out of the mouths of our teachers, for, whenever any were missing from the ranks of our own scholars, we were invariably told that they had gone to the rival school.[32]

Rival schools were set up adjacent to other mission girls' schools as well, while a combination of gifts, threats and penalties were used, and Christian educators maligned, in order to persuade parents to transfer their daughters to the Arya Samaj schools. Muslim men carried out a similar boycott and succeeded in preventing visits to two houses which the missionaries had visited on a regular basis.[33] A Muslim tract circulated in the city argued, first, that 'in every religion it is taught that woman should be educated'; then, that 'the Christian teacher in our homes and their schools posed a serious threat to the Muslim religion and way of life'; and finally, that

32 'Punjab and Sindh Missions', ibid. (May–June 1886), p. 114.
33 Ibid., p. 116.

'Muslims must build their own girls' schools'.[34] Some men resisted this boycott and continued to invite zenana visitors to their homes and eventually the campaign died down. Miss Dewar commented about this joint crusade that 'Desire checked became stronger. Many ladies who were indifferent about learning hitherto became doubly anxious to read when they heard that there was a chance of losing their teacher. So, the doors, instead of closing, opened wider'.[35] As indicated earlier, women and girls defied the men by going to school during a similar agitation in 1900 and, by 1909, the demand for female education, whether in zenana or school, had exceeded the mission's capacity to meet it. Education, it would seem, was becoming increasingly important to Amritsar's middle-class women.

One educational endeavour deserves special attention because it was so different from the others. The Hindu widows' industrial class, set up to help them become economically more independent, was the mission's most significant response to 'the plight of the Hindu widow' which one woman characterized, poignantly, in this way:

'It would have been better if women had never been made,' was the remark made by one of my listeners in a Zenana; and when I remonstrated with her about this assertion, she only modified it by adding, 'Well, if they are to become widows, it would be better for them if they had never been born.'[36]

Once the class was opened, it filled up very quickly, and the municipal government contributed towards its support. Many members

34 'A Mohammedan Tract', ibid. (September–October 1885), pp. 231–3. A significant feature of this tract—a full translation of which was published in *India's Women*—is that there was no reference in it to any desire for education among Muslim women and girls. The possibility of women's initiative, however indirect, was not even suggested; the tract was one man telling other men what they should do for the women in their families.

35 'Sowing and Reaping', ibid. (May–June 1886), p. 119.

36 Miss Jackson in 'Sowing and Reaping, or Labour in the Field', ibid. (May–June 1884), p. 120. Miss Wauton wrote a more extended and generalized essay on the plight of the widow titled, 'Plead for the Widows', ibid. (May–June 1889), pp. 125–31.

of the class were children who had been betrothed or married at a very young age. During the 1900 agitation against the mission girls' schools, members of the Arya Samaj urged the widows to leave the class and even offered them a better school in return, but not one left. Miss Jackson quoted them as saying, 'Well, their words do not fill our stomachs. We have eaten your bread and found it good.'[37]

Material written from an evangelistic perspective offers a somewhat different kind of information about the women of Amritsar during this period. In the very first issue of *India's Women* is a lengthy account of the conversion of a woman named Fatima.

> B's wife will get away next Wednesday if she can, to be baptized on Thursday. The dear woman has gone straight on, never faltering or turning back; and although she trembles at what she is going to do, she counts it joy to lose all for Christ. She will come to us to be housed with Hannah the Bible-woman, near us in the compound, until the excitement is over in the city.
>
> She means to tell her husband on Wednesday what she is going to do. The chances are that he will lock her up and prevent her getting away for some time; but she thinks it more probable that he will never take her into his house again. She is a clever, lady-like woman, and has always had servants to work for her; however, she does very pretty lace-work, which is a good thing, as she will have to depend so much upon her own resources.

A week later:

> I was reading with my munshi this morning when Miss Wauton came in and told me that Fatima was in her room, and begged me to go and see her. I went, and found her lying on a mattress on the floor, looking worn out. She had had a dreadful night. She told her husband what she meant to do last night. A host of relations and friends beat her and threatened her and tore off her jewels. They cursed us and Khair-ul-Nissa, but towards morning, thinking they had effectually silenced her, the husband went to his shop, and she slipped away in a *doolie* which was waiting for her, and Bhobie, a girl who is also to be baptized to-morrow, brought her up here.[38]

37 *Twenty-First Annual Report of the Church of England Zenana Missionary Society for the Year 1901*, p. 55.

38 'Umritsar', *India's Women* (October 1880), pp. 36–37.

Instances of this kind, where a married woman left her family and was baptized by herself because of Christian conviction were very rare.[39] Fatima, baptized Nur-ul-Nissa, became a sincere and effective Bible-woman for the mission, first in Amritsar and then in Batala. She never remarried.

Somewhat more common were women—like the Muslim woman, thought that Christianity was a good religion for women—who seemed to become believers but they never left their homes or families and were never baptized. Some of the lengthier anecdotes concern another Muslim woman,[40] a Brahmin woman,[41] and a Sikh woman,[42] all three of whom were considered to be believers in Christ even though they remained unbaptized and within their family networks. S.S. Hewlett recorded this highly suggestive reply made by one such woman to a question about her reasons for praying so earnestly for Christ's coming: 'Because, if He comes, then all Hindus will be convinced, and our men will *let us believe*'.[43] Miss Dewar once reported that some Hindu women had attended Sunday morning worship in the school chapel.

> They were highly delighted with the service, and went away saying they felt very happy, and would come again. They say they do not like to go to the Mission Church because it is so public, and the men stand in crowds about the doors, but here they can come quietly without any one taking notice of them.[44]

There was at times more than a touch of wishful thinking in these anecdotes. A more sober reading of the situation in 1884 emphasized the very different motivations which the evangelist and the evangelized brought to their times together in the zenanas.

> We do not mean to imply by speaking of some interesting Zenana scholars that all are thus promising and hopeful [from an evangelistic

39 Another was Toba. *Sixth Annual Report of the Church of England Zenana Missionary Society for the Year ending 31 March 1886*, p. 33.

40 'Punjab and Sindh', *India's Women* (May–June 1882), p. 149.

41 'Amritsar', ibid. (July–August 1881), p. 174.

42 S.S. Hewlett, *Daughters of the King*, pp. 132–5.

43 Ibid., p. 25.

44 'Punjab and Sindh,' *India's Women* (May–June 1882), p. 146.

point of view]; far from it. There are many who thankfully accept the
services of the teacher, while she helps her on with Hindi, Persian, or
Urdu, or shows her how to knit comforters, socks, and gloves, but have
no desire whatever to learn of still better things. Their minds seem
a perfect blank; they know nothing of their own religion; there is no
Hinduism or Mohammedanism or Sikhism or 'ism' of any kind, in
them, except indifferentism; they appear sometimes to assent to what
we say, but in reality care nothing at all about it; they are like so many
stones in their deadness, hardness, and unconcern.[45]

Information presented from an evangelistic perspective in these
writings, like that presented from an educational perspective,
focused almost exclusively upon middle-class women and girls;
little was written about the urban poor in any detail.[46] It bears testimony to the hold which not only religiously sanctioned custom,
but also the patriarchal joint family had over women's lives. This
was most evident in the case of Fatima, the convert cited above,
who was harshly disciplined for following her own religious
convictions. At the same time, like the educational examples
mentioned earlier, these also indicate that there were middle-class
women who were trying, often selectively, to break free of these
constraints for a variety of reasons and in a variety of ways.[47]

45 'Sowing and Reaping, or Labour in the Field', ibid. (May–June
1884), p. 122. Such assessments varied in degrees of optimism and
pessimism. A more hopeful view of the 'almost Christian' state of some of
the women 'held back' by circumstances may be found four years later in
'Dawn in the East', ibid. (July–August 1888), p. 199.

46 This was not true of the rural Dalits, but they are outside the scope
of this particular inquiry.

47 A particularly angry example was that of a Muslim woman who
wanted her daughter to be educated in a Christian school, ostensibly to
learn English, because, to use the woman's own words, 'I should like her
to be acquainted with the Christian faith, and then if she chooses it of her
own accord I shall be glad, for I shall know that she will then be saved
from the wretchedness of an enforced Mohammedan marriage, which
caused me such suffering in my early years.' Twentieth Annual Report of
the Church of England Zenana Missionary Society for the Year 1900, p. 54.

The medical perspective sheds light on another aspect of women's lives in late-nineteenth-century Amritsar. In 1883 the Amritsar Medical Mission reported:

> Among all the causes of the suffering and misery endured by the women of India, few operate more powerfully than the work of those who may indeed be fitly described as 'forgers of lies, physicians of no value.' It seems impossible to estimate the amount of lifelong wretchedness and pain, and the loss of life, which may fairly be traced to the ignorant, superstitious, and often vicious practices to which women of all classes in this country blindly submit. Any one working in a Medical Mission, and therefore constantly meeting with the unfortunate victims of such practices, cannot help feeling that to win the confidence of the sufferers, to persuade them to trust to humane and reasonable treatment, and to show them the folly of being duped by 'physicians of no value,' is one of the first and most obvious duties of this branch of work among India's women. But it is a duty by no means easy, partly because the Medical Mission staff is so small, that when as many visits as possible have been paid, there must still be hundreds of sick and suffering women uncared for, and partly because the people are so prejudiced and ignorant that they often prefer the treatment of the hakim to that of the European doctor, up to the point at which it appears that there is no hope of saving the patient's life, when the medical missionary is sent for, to arrive too late to do any good, and perhaps be afterwards charged with the blame for the fatal issue.[48]

This statement reveals an obvious professional, cultural and religious bias which appears again in S.S. Hewlett's book where she provides a lengthy description of obstacles, in the form of religiously sanctioned customs and taboos, confronted by the doctor trained in Western medicine. One such case was a Hindu woman with an ailment requiring protection from the cold (so, bathing was prohibited), some medicine, and the services of a trained nurse.

> Upon this, three difficulties arose. With regard to the medicine, it could not be given, as it was impossible to make sure of any liquid being pure unless it was known to come out of the well of a Hindu of good caste. With regard to the trained nurse, the only ones who could be offered were either Christians or Mussalmanis, and their

48 'Amritsar', *India's Women* (July–August 1883), pp. 192–3.

touch would be pollution (albeit no Hindu woman of really good caste would offer herself to be trained for such work, and so difficulty meets difficulty); and when the missionary lady, making an attempt to solve the problem, said, 'But you have allowed me to touch the patient, and I am a Christian,' the husband replied (with some hesitation, for he *was* a gentleman), 'Yes, because we are helplessly obliged to let you touch her, but we shall consequently have to give her a bath the moment you are gone.' Thus the strict orders against the bath had also to be disregarded.[49]

While there is evidence of bias, this generalization and anecdote offer, at the same time, a highly plausible explanation for Malhotra's Punjabi women turning to low-caste holy men and shrines when in need of cures and healing: traditional medical practice was not getting the job done and women were seeking alternatives.

Where the medical perspective differs most from the educational and the evangelistic perspectives is in being more socially inclusive. Women from varying backgrounds and walks of life are mentioned; some of the responses of urban Dalit women to the mobile dispensaries set up in their neighbourhoods are described. However, the real centre of medical activity was St. Catherine's Hospital, used by women who were not just sick, injured, or disabled, but also abused and abandoned as 'useless'.[50] One telling example described in some detail was that of a young Afghan woman who took refuge with the medical missionaries, not to become a Christian—about which she knew nothing—but simply to escape the cruelty of her stepmother.[51] St. Catherine's was also a place where women came in desperation in times of famine[52] and to which, as death approached, they occasionally entrusted their daughters in order to save them from lives of prostitution.[53]

49 S.S. Hewlett, *Daughters of the King*, p. 13.

50 'Amritsar', *India's Women* (July–August 1884), p. 192; 'Punjab and Sindh', ibid. (July–August 1886), p. 175; 'Annual Letters Etc.', ibid. (July–August 1891), p. 189.

51 S.S. Hewlett, *Daughters of the King*, pp. 123–5.

52 'The Punjab Mission', *India's Women and China's Daughters* (May 1898), p. 110; 'The Story of Amritsar Famines', ibid. (January 1902), p. 15.

53 'A Year of Labour in our Foreign Mission Field', *India's Women* (July–August 1890), p. 195.

Many of the female converts from Amritsar, who were baptized independently of their parents or husbands, but perhaps with their children, were victims of these kinds of tragic circumstances.

FROM PERCEIVER TO PERCEIVED

This essay has been based on the assumption that the historian can use perceptions to understand both the perceivers and the perceived. However, in order to get to the perceived, one must move from the perceptions themselves, first to the perceiver—in order to understand how those perceptions have been consciously or unconsciously shaped—and only then move on to the perceived. A second important assumption is that one can separate out and utilize much of the concrete detail provided in perceptions in order to understand the perceived while, at the same time, rejecting or modifying the perceptual framework (for example, 'benevolent maternal imperialism') and concomitant value judgements (for example, about 'superstitions') through which that information was conveyed. Specific details have been generally considered here to be more reliable than more generalized and abstracted descriptions (for example, about personal encounters with widows rather than about widows in general) and, in this case, they convey the 'voice' of some of the women of Amritsar, albeit second-hand and thus somewhat filtered.

However, a historian whose eyes are on the perceived rather than just the perceiver must also decide whether to accept as empirically grounded, or modify, dismiss as ideological, or simply bypass because of the uncertainties involved, some of the central generalized statements found in these sources. For example, is it fair to characterize the secluded middle-class women of late-nineteenth-century Amritsar as being in bondage to religiously sanctioned custom and the patriarchal joint family, as the CEZMS missionaries did? Wouldn't it be fairer to modify that by saying that they were immersed in these and struggling with their pressures, thus heightening both the women's own agency and their ambivalence about their situation? Wouldn't it be still fairer to say that the first statement characterized some women; the second, others, and that it is impossible to determine what proportion of the total female population was in each category? Or would it be wisest simply to say nothing at all on the subject? Whatever choices are made in this regard and whatever the reasons for them may be, what is going to emerge from this process of inquiry is not a precise photograph but something more like an impressionistic painting of only some of the highlighted aspects of some of the lives of late-nineteenth-century women in the city of Amritsar. In short, the gains won by this method are modest but not negligible.

These gains are enhanced when this essay is read in conjunction with Malhotra's larger study. For one thing, these sources concentrate mainly on roughly the same population: the wives and daughters of men belonging to the upper castes and the middle classes, although Muslims have been included along with Hindus and Sikhs. For another, most of the detailed reports come from the 1880s when the reform bodies which Malhotra describes were in the early phases of organization. Thus, what was happening—or beginning to happen—among women, as described here, could well have influenced the kinds of male agendas and ideologies concerning women which she has described in much fuller detail. Malhotra did deal with 'the missionary threat' as a motivation for reform, especially with regard to widows and the education of girls.[54] However, because her eyes were primarily on the male perceivers of women and not on the women themselves, she did not give much credit to women for exerting the direct pressure of independent thinking, and even of defiance, upon men in order to bring about changes in the circumstances of their lives. The missionaries did notice signs of this and made what they saw part of the public record.

It seems highly probable that what Christianity represented to women in late-nineteenth-century Amritsar was options, alternatives, and choices hitherto unavailable to them. The mission first made education an option when previously it was not; later, women could choose between competing types of education under various religious auspices. The mission also opened up wage-earning options and an alternative sense of self to widows who

54 Anshu Malhotra, *Gender, Caste, and Religious Identities*, pp. 85–7, 145–7.

had previously been denied them. Christianity offered a religious option and alternative which women were invited to choose and, along with it, an alternative view of themselves as women. They not only discussed these options and alternatives in the abstract but also saw them modelled by the single Western and, usually married Indian Christian, women with whom they talked. The mission provided options in medical care as well as places of refuge for women who were disabled, abused, abandoned, or in desperate straits before other such welfare agencies existed. Of course, only a tiny proportion actually became Christian but, by providing options, alternatives, and choices, Christian educators, evangelists and medical personnel did sow some of the seeds of ferment among other women in Amritsar which would in time grow into and nurture a women's movement.

CHAPTER 6

Christian History as Indian Social History
A Review of the Literature*

Christianity has been part of Indian social history for a very long time. In Kerala and Tamil Nadu, it dates back to at least the fourth century, if not to Thomas, one of the original disciples of Jesus. After 1510, under the patronage of the Portuguese Crown, Roman Catholic Christianity spread out from Goa along the southern and western coasts, even penetrating inland in the south and to the Mughal courts in the north. The first Protestant mission was established in the Danish colony at Tranquebar in Tamil Nadu in 1706, and the second at Serampore, another Danish colony in West Bengal, in 1800. Once the British East India Company allowed missionaries into their territories in 1813 and 1833, Christianity spread throughout India from the seaports of Calcutta, Bombay, and Madras. Today, just under half of all India's twenty-four million Christians live in the southern states of Kerala, Tamil Nadu, Andhra Pradesh, Karnataka, and Goa, but the heaviest concentration of Christians is in the north-eastern states of Mizoram, Nagaland, and Meghalaya where they constitute 87 per cent, 82.6 per cent, and 70.3 per cent, respectively, of the population.

* This chapter was first published in Sabyasachi Bhattacharya (ed.), *Approaches to History: Essays in Indian Historiography* (Delhi: Primus Books, 2011), pp. 159–97. This is a revised version.

Elsewhere in India, the Christian population is relatively small.[1] Thus, in some regions of India, Christian history is much more a part of Indian social history than in others.

However, despite this long—and in some parts of India, very strong—connection, it is only very recently that Christian history has been written as part of Indian social history. This essay provides a review of only that body of literature. It omits the many histories of particular missions and churches, their personnel, work, institutions, and internal organizational matters, which shed little or no light at all on Indian social history. As indicated in Chapter 1, up to the 1960s, histories of Christianity in India were almost completely confined to matters internal to Christian missions and churches. Then Christianity became a subject of academic history and a major shift of emphasis took place in Christian historiography. For one thing, historians of India who were located in universities started using Christian source materials and writing about Christianity as a phenomenon impacting Indian history as a whole. For another, historians within the Christian community became dissatisfied with the old-style mission and institutional history and began writing its history as part of the socio-cultural history of India. The result has been a body of literature impressive in its size, scope and intellectual sophistication, which is the main subject of this chapter. For purposes of analysis, each study has been placed into one of five categories according to where its major emphasis or usefulness seems to lie. The first category consists of those studies that focus on socio-cultural change resulting from interaction between Christians and members of other communities. The second category is made up of conversion studies, and the third of studies of Christian communities as Indian communities. The fourth consists of political studies, and the fifth of general histories and reference works. The studies mentioned below are books which have been written in English; not every such book is mentioned but the sample is large enough to indicate some of the major approaches to and trends in historical writing on Christianity as Indian social history.

---

1 *Census of India 2001: The First Report of Religion Data*, pp. xxix, xxxiii.

INNOVATION, ENCOUNTER, AND CHANGE

The category with the largest bibliography is the one that focuses both on the encounter between Christians and members of other religious communities and on the changes which resulted from their interaction. In virtually every case, the Christian subjects of these histories were Protestant missionaries from overseas and, invariably, the period studied was the nineteenth century. Despite these similarities, the literature exhibits a considerable variety in specific subject matter, in the types of source material consulted, and in the frameworks of analysis. This survey begins with some early generalized studies and then moves on to the regional studies which dominate this body of literature.

Back in 1915, J.N. Farquhar, in his *Modern Religious Movements in India*, not only classified and described a large number of movements within many of India's religions, but also added sections on religious nationalism as well as on social reform and service. He mentioned several causes for this nineteenth-century 'awakening', but concluded that 'Christianity has ruled the development throughout'.[2] He listed several Christian ideas—for example, monotheism; God as the common father and all men, therefore, as brothers; the righteousness of God—which had been incorporated into these religious movements, and he added at the end that 'almost without exception, the methods of work in use in the movements have been borrowed from [Protestant] missions'.[3] In short, to Farquhar, Christianity provided the model for other religious movements.[4]

---

2 J.N. Farquhar, *Modern Religious Movements in India* (New York: Macmillan, 1915), p. 433. It is surprising that he did not include Christian views of women and womanhood in his list.

3 Ibid., p. 442.

4 Ibid., p. 434. This rather triumphalistic view of Christian influence was to be seriously undercut by Natarajan's and Heimsath's subsequent histories of Hindu social reform movements. S. Natarajan largely ignored the missions, while Heimsath included them but as one of several stimuli for social reform. S. Natarajan, *A Century of Social Reform in India*, 2nd ed. (Bombay: Asia Publishing House, 1962); Charles H. Heimsath, *Indian*

Kenneth Ingham's *Reformers in India* (1956) was confined to 1793 to 1833, the earliest period covered by Farquhar, and was more modest in its assessment of missionary influence in the area of social reform and social change. He saw this as a period of both Indian and governmental social conservatism in which Protestant missionaries were important innovators. While missionary attempts to undermine the caste system had little success, their pioneer work in education for all castes, in raising the status of women through education, in the development of languages, literature, journalism, and translation work, laid foundations on which subsequent reformers were to build. Missionaries also played major roles in making both *sati* and the pilgrim tax illegal by gathering relevant information and presenting it to the British public so that it could, in turn, bring pressure on Parliament to change the law. While Ingham referred to Indian opposition to many of the missionaries' social reform initiatives, he did not describe it in detail.[5]

Sushil Madhava Pathak's 1967 history, *American Missionaries and Hinduism*, described missionaries belonging to several Protestant denominations who worked in the Madras and Bombay Presidencies, the Punjab, the North-Western Provinces and Assam. Pathak noted at the outset that, while missionaries did influence the rise of reform movements within Hinduism, 'Hinduism in its turn changed and reformed missionary policy and activities'.[6] In his conclusion, Pathak used the word, 'contribution', to assess missionary efforts in many types of education, in medicine, in social reform, and welfare work.

While Ingham's and Pathak's work generalized about Protestant missionaries in many parts of India, the remaining studies surveyed in this section are basically regional in focus. The

---

Nationalism and Hindu Social Reform (Princeton: Princeton University Press, 1964), pp. 51–4.

5 Kenneth Ingham, *Reformers in India 1793–1833: An Account of the Work of Christian Missionaries on Behalf of Social Reform* (Cambridge: Cambridge University Press, 1956).

6 Sushil Madhava Pathak, *American Missionaries and Hinduism: A Study of their Contacts from 1813 to 1910* (New Delhi: Munshiram Manoharlal, 1967), p. xii.

first to be published were six studies devoted to missionaries and the Bengal Renaissance, which appeared in quite rapid succession. Muhammad Mohar Ali's *The Bengali Reaction to Christian Missionary Activities 1833–1857* (1965), the pioneering work, examined the reactions of two groups within Bengali society—the urban élite of Calcutta and the zamindars in the districts—in the years immediately following the deaths of both William Carey and Ram Mohan Roy. He called this the second phase of the Bengal Renaissance. Of particular interest to him were the controversies between missionaries and these two groups which were found in the press, the law courts, and in petitions to the government, all of which centred on the evangelistic work of the missionaries and the resulting conversions that upset the socio-cultural status quo. With regard to the former group, he noted that the controversy resulted in shifts in Hindu theological positions; the creation of Hindu schools as alternatives to mission schools; a series of important custody cases; a relaxation of caste discipline that allowed converts to return to the Hindu fold; and legislation (1850) allowing converts to inherit ancestral property. In the districts, where ryots were converting and facing violent persecution, he found that the missionaries were strong champions of ryot against Indian zamindar and European indigo planter interests.

By way of contrast, E. Daniel Potts concentrated upon the work of Baptist missionaries—Carey, Marshman, and Ward in particular—in the earlier period of the Bengal Renaissance and devoted only a small portion of his study to the 'Indian Response'. Judging from the Baptist records, he found the negative 'general reaction' was more often a criticism of the Indian converts—and especially those in mission employ—than of the missionaries themselves. Potts's section on the 'scholarly response' was devoted primarily to Ram Mohan Roy.[7] K.P. Sen Gupta's study of Christian missionaries in Bengal covered the same period as Potts's study but included the other Protestant missionaries in Bengal at that time. In dealing with the missionary attitude towards the Bengali people, he found

7 E. Daniel Potts, *British Baptist Missionaries in India 1793–1837: The History of Serampore and its Missions* (Cambridge: Cambridge University Press, 1967).

that descriptions written in English for readers back in Britain were far more hostile than were their Bengali publications written for Bengali readers.[8]

David Kopf recast this discussion by highlighting the conflicting British cultural policies which led to the Bengal Renaissance. The earliest was the orientalist approach which was enshrined at Fort William College and particularly in the person of William Carey, its professor of Sanskrit and Bengali. Carey and his fellow Baptists were 'popular culture orientalists' who concentrated on language-learning so as to implant Christianity and Western knowledge into the cultural soil of India. It was Macaulay and his missionary counterpart, Alexander Duff, who later adopted westernization as their cultural policy with regard to both government legislation and mission education.

> Certainly, what Duff was to the Anglicists, William Carey had been to the Orientalists. Whereas Duff promoted evangelization by accentuating the polarity between East and West, Carey promoted it through the reconciliation of apparent differences. Duff aimed at transforming Calcutta Bengalis into Scottish Presbyterians, but Carey aimed at introducing the basic principles of Christianity into the existing structure of Hindu society.[9]

What happened was that the orientalist policy came to win favour among the Bengali intelligentsia, while the westernizing policy won favour with British officialdom.

Michael Laird set his history of mission education in Bengal from 1793 to 1837 within the context of educational work in England and Scotland, as well as in Bengal. His aim was to determine not only what was distinctive about the education they pro-

---

8 Kanti Prasanna Sen Gupta, *The Christian Missionaries in Bengal 1793–1833* (Calcutta: Firma K.L. Mukhopadhyay, 1971), pp. 65–75. Despite his very negative assessment of missionary writings in English, they are Sen Gupta's most frequently cited sources in the section of his book on 'Social Conditions of Bengal in the Eighteenth Century' (pp. 21–9).

9 David Kopf, *British Orientalism and Indian Renaissance: The Dynamics of Indian Modernization 1773–1835* (Berkeley: University of California Press, 1969), p. 260.

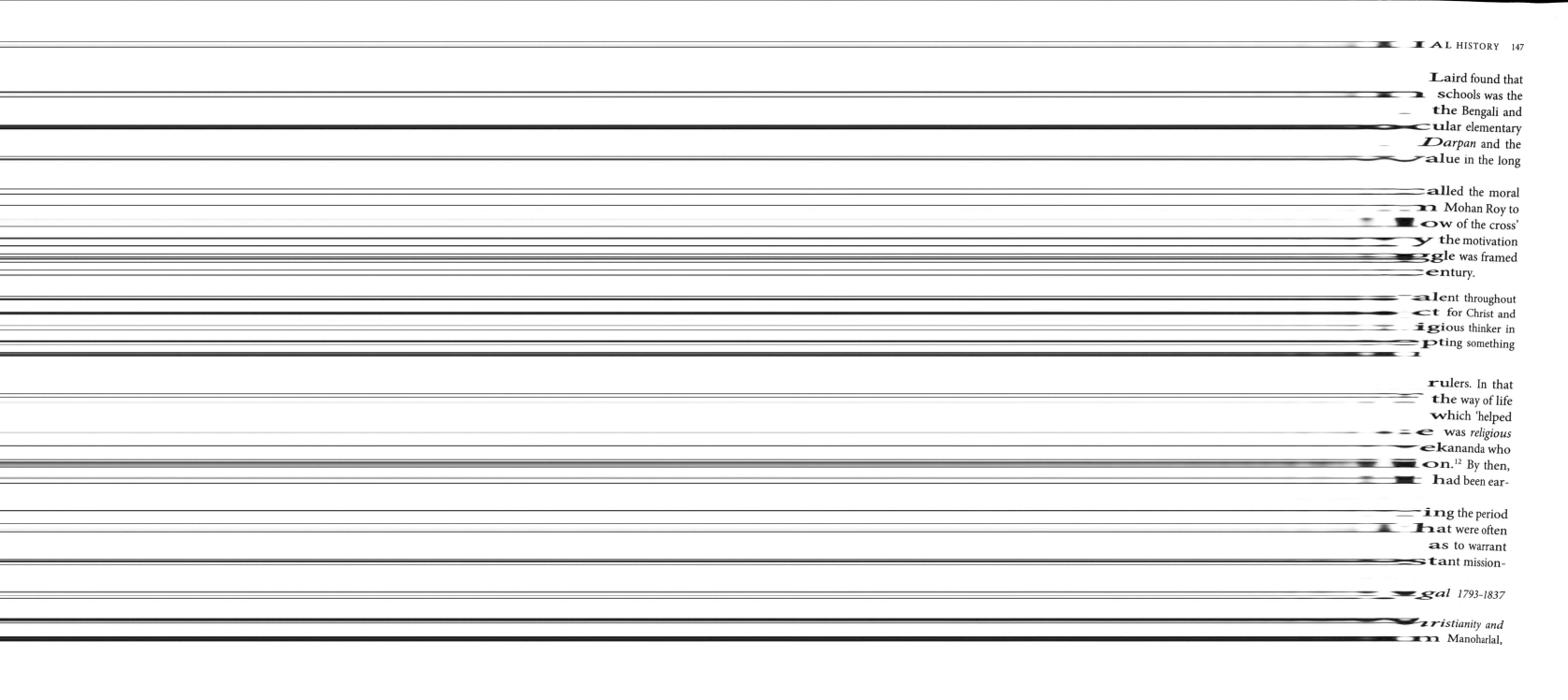

Laird found that
schools was the
the Bengali and
...cular elementary
Darpan and the
...alue in the long

...alled the moral
...n Mohan Roy to
...ow of the cross'
...y the motivation
...gle was framed
...entury.

...alent throughout
...ct for Christ and
...igious thinker in
...pting something

rulers. In that
the way of life
which 'helped
...e was *religious*
...ekananda who
...on.[12] By then,
had been ear-

...ing the period
...hat were often
as to warrant
...tant mission-

...gal *1793–1837*
...ristianity and
...m Manoharlal,

ary involvement, often in cc
agitations for social justice a
issues; early marriage and th
nautch because of its link wi
planter oppression in Bengal
Nadu; temperance; and the
made their protests known
so as to mobilize British p
pressure on the governme
attacked British as well as In
for greater gender as well a
broaden the reform agend
generally prepared to take c

A major theme of the st
explicitly but always presen
al India', a major intellectu
saw Protestant missionarie
the missionaries disagreed
best be achieved, whethe
traditional cultural forms t
and the means they used to
torians used at least three
involvement in the dyna
who focused on the mis
input–impact model to de
tion. Those who were inte
a challenge–response mo
competition and conflict,
process of modernizatio
missionaries among the n

The modernization t
of North India. My own
in Nineteenth Century N

14 Geoffrey A. Oddie,
Missionaries and Social Refo
15 John C.B. Webster,
Nineteenth Century North I

vided but also to assess its historical significance. Laird found that perhaps 'the most striking feature of the mission schools was the width of their curriculum' as compared to both the Bengali and the British schools[10] and considered their vernacular elementary schools as well as their newspapers, *Samachar Darpan* and the *Friend of India*, to be of particular educational value in the long term.

Finally, Sisir Kumar Das depicted what he called the moral struggle of the educated Bengali Hindus, from Ram Mohan Roy to Vivekananda. This struggle occurred in 'the shadow of the cross' because the missionary challenge provided not only the motivation but also much of the language in which that struggle was framed and lived out during the course of the nineteenth century.

> Bengal's response to Christianity remained ambivalent throughout the century; there was a conflict between the respect for Christ and antipathy to Christian missionary action. Every religious thinker in Bengal had to reconcile this conflict either by accepting something from Christianity or by reviving militant Hinduism.[11]

In addition, Christianity was the religion of the rulers. In that context, conversion was perceived as a rejection of the way of life of the society to which one belonged, an attitude which 'helped the growth of nationalism which in the first phase was *religious nationalism*' that found its fullest expression in Vivekananda who made patriotism a living element in Hindu religion.[12] By then, however, Christianity was no longer the challenge it had been earlier; humanism now played that role.[13]

Geoffrey A. Oddie's *Social Protest in India*, covering the period from 1850 to 1900, dealt with issues and agitations that were often nationwide, but has so much Bengali material in it as to warrant being included here. His focus was on British Protestant mission-

10 M.A. Laird, *Missionaries and Education in Bengal 1793–1837* (Oxford: Clarendon Press, 1972), p. 263.

11 Sisir Kumar Das, *The Shadow of the Cross: Christianity and Hinduism in a Colonial Situation* (New Delhi: Munshiram Manoharlal, 1973), p. 40.

12 Ibid., pp. 37, 132.

13 Ibid., p. 148.

ary involvement, often in conjunction with Indian reformers, in agitations for social justice and social reform. These included caste issues; early marriage and the age of consent; the elimination of *nautch* because of its link with prostitution; zamindari and indigo planter oppression in Bengal; land and education for Dalits in Tamil Nadu; temperance; and the end of the opium trade. Missionaries made their protests known not only in India but at home as well, so as to mobilize British public opinion to bring the necessary pressure on the government. In their reform programme, they attacked British as well as Indian interests, demonstrated a concern for greater gender as well as caste/class equality, and managed to broaden the reform agenda beyond what Indian reformers were generally prepared to take on.[14]

A major theme of the studies examined so far—at times stated explicitly but always present—was the modernization of 'traditional India', a major intellectual issue of that time. These historians saw Protestant missionaries as agents of modernization. Although the missionaries disagreed on how greater modernization might best be achieved, whether through westernization or by using traditional cultural forms to convey modern values, their religion and the means they used to impart it were modernizing. The historians used at least three different models to describe missionary involvement in the dynamics of modernization. The historians who focused on the missionaries themselves tended to use an input–impact model to describe their contribution to modernization. Those who were interested primarily in Bengali society used a challenge–response model which laid special emphasis upon competition and conflict, and hence upon Indian agency, in the process of modernization. The third model merely included the missionaries among the modernizers.

The modernization theme continued only in the first study of North India. My own *The Christian Community and Change in Nineteenth Century North India*[15] was based on three premises

14 Geoffrey A. Oddie, *Social Protest in India: British Protestant Missionaries and Social Reform 1850–1900* (New Delhi: Manohar, 1979).
15 John C.B. Webster, *The Christian Community and Change in Nineteenth Century North India* (New Delhi: Macmillan, 1976).

implicit in the challenge–response model: the Christians were a community (made up of missionaries and Indian converts); this community interacted with other communities (in religious controversy, evangelism, education, famine relief, and nationalist politics); the result of such interaction was social and cultural change. What distinguished this work from its predecessors was the role it assigned to the Christian community as such, and especially to the Indian converts, as primary agents of socio-cultural change. It was less preaching by missionaries than the converts' decisions to change their religion which challenged others to respond in ways that changed laws, customs, values, and social arrangements.

Three subsequent histories of missionaries in the North provided additional information on interaction but did not address the issue of change in fresh ways. Raj Bahadur Sharma used an input–impact model, with the major emphasis on the former, in his history of Catholic, Anglican, Presbyterian, and Methodist missions in the Meerut Division and the Dehra Dun District of the United Provinces.[16] Antony Copley used a series of biographical sketches to describe the nature of the religious conflict between Christians and members of the élite in the North as well as in Bengal and in the South during the middle of the nineteenth century.[17] Maina Chawla Singh's study of American Protestant missionary women from the 1860s to the 1940s located them within their parent culture, their male-dominated mission societies, the changing Indian context of social reform and nationalist politics, and in relation to some Indian women, now resident in Delhi, who had attended Kinnaird College for Women in Lahore or Isabella Thoburn College in Lucknow. While the missionaries themselves, as well as the institutions they created and shaped, are interesting in their own rights as missionary 'inputs', it is the alumnae testimony about the socializing 'impact' of their college experience, mostly

16 Raj Bahadur Sharma, *Christian Missions in North India 1813–1913: A Case Study of Meerut Division and Dehra Dun District* (Delhi: Mittal Publications, 1988).

17 Antony Copley, *Religions in Conflict: Ideology, Cultural Contact and Conversion in Late Colonial India* (Delhi: Oxford University Press, 1997).

during the 1940s, that constitutes this book's major contribution to India's social history.[18]

Two studies which occurred at about the same time are particularly noteworthy because they dealt with the intellectual debates between Christians and spokespersons for hitherto under-researched groups. Richard Fox Young's *Resistant Hinduism* analysed a Sanskrit apologetic for Christianity (1839) by John Muir, a 'Quasi-Evangelical' Company official, and the responses of three conservative Hindu pundits who also wrote in Sanskrit. From these responses, Young concluded that, because all three wrote from a position of 'unqualified adherence to the revealed teaching of the Veda'

> the thrust of Hindu apologetics in the period under review was to deny common ground, emphasize the *sui generis* character of Hinduism, expose Christianity as erroneous, and dissuade fellow Hindus from regarding the Khrstadharma as a serious claimant to their religious allegiance.[19]

Equally important, the pundits did recognize Christianity as an alternative dharma and therefore, by implication, religious pluralism. This Young saw as a revolutionary move out of insularity.[20]

The centrepiece of Avril Powell's *Muslims and Missionaries in Pre-Mutiny India* was the *munazara* or formal public debate, especially the munazara at Agra in 1854 between two Anglican missionaries and two Muslim scholars. Powell placed the history up to that debate within a Muslim setting, primarily in Lucknow, Agra and Delhi, and relied as much, if not more, on Muslim as on Christian sources. The big surprise in the 1854 debate was the Muslim participants' familiarity with Western scholarship on Christianity, and especially with developments in Germany in the field of Biblical criticism. The direct effects of the debate upon

18 Maina Chawla Singh, *Gender, Religion and 'Heathen Lands': American Missionary Women in South Asia (1860s–1940s)* (New York: Garland Publishing, 2000).

19 Richard Fox Young, *Resistant Hinduism: Sanskrit Sources on Anti-Christian Apologetics in Early Nineteenth-Century India* (Vienna: De Nobili Research Library, 1981), p. 135.

20 Ibid., p. 174.

Muslim participation in the 1857 revolt proved to be ambivalent, but it established a tradition of inter-faith discourse which continued through the nineteenth century.[21]

There are two studies of Western India that fall into this category. In his history of Protestant missions in Maharashtra, M.D. David treated each of the major missions separately from their early-nineteenth-century beginnings into the 1930s, but also described interaction and drew comparisons between them. In all cases, their evangelistic initiatives met with a combination of curiosity, opposition, and conversion among a small number of upper-caste Hindus and a much larger number of Dalits. The missions also had a constructive influence on three important reformers in the region: Jyotirao Phule, Shahu Maharaj of Kolhapur, and M.G. Ranade.[22] Two themes dominate the other history, David Hardiman's history of the Church Missionary Society's medical work from 1880 to 1964 among the Bhils on the Gujarat–Rajasthan border. One was modernization, exemplified in the struggle between the missionaries' Western scientific understanding of illness and its cure, and traditional Bhil understandings and practices. Most Bhils interpreted missionary medical practices (for example, injections and prayer) within their own frames of reference which saw disease and its cure as both physical and spiritual. The other theme was the colonial theme in which medical modernization came to justify the dominant role of the missionary within the hospital hierarchy in the face of Indian nationalism and even Independence.[23]

Turning to the South, Kranti Farias traced the history of Christians in South Kanara from the sixteenth into the nineteenth century before using an input–impact model to assess the impact of both Catholics and Protestants (whose social backgrounds were

21 Avril Ann Powell, *Muslims and Missionaries in Pre-Mutiny India* (Richmond: Curzon Press, 1993).

22 M.D. David, *Missions: Cross-Cultural Encounter and Change in Western India* (Delhi: ISPCK, 2001).

23 David Hardiman, *Missionaries and Their Medicine: A Christian Modernity for Tribal India* (Manchester: Manchester University Press, 2008).

quite different) upon education, social awareness, economic development, and cultural transformation. She concluded with a discussion of their involvement in the Gandhian phase of the nationalist movement.[24]

Geoffrey Oddie examined the relationship between religious institutions and movements, both Hindu and Christian, and the hierarchical social structure of the Tanjore and the Trichinopoly districts of Tamil Nadu during the nineteenth century. He began with an extended treatment of temple, sectarian and popular Hinduism in relation to inter-caste dynamics; in those chapters, Christianity entered only as a source of pressure to force the East India Company to disengage from temple management and as an attractive alternative to increasingly disillusioned educated Hindu youth. He then concentrated upon the conversion to Christianity, first of some upper-caste Hindus and then of a much larger number of Dalits. What followed amounted to a Hindu counter-attack led first by the Theosophical Society and then by the Hindu Tract Society. This slowed down but did not stop the conversions and it helped foster a greater sense of Hindu unity. Religious changes in the two districts helped create new social identities, including both the non-Brahmin and the Dalit movements.[25]

While Oddie's focus was mostly on the urban élite, Henriette Bugge's was on rural society, its cultural values and power structures. In studying two missions—one French Catholic and the other Danish Lutheran—in South Arcot District from 1840 to 1900, her point of departure was the large Dalit conversion movement of the late nineteenth century. By instituting parallel Christian festivals and processions, the Catholics succeeded in giving their converts a distinct corporate identity within the existing social hierarchy in a way that the Lutherans did not. However, the main area in which both missions made a dent in the structures and the values of rural society was by becoming, in essence, counter-patrons for their convert clients, thereby challenging the rural power structure for a

---

24 Kranti K. Farias, *The Christian Impact in South Kanara* (Mumbai: Church History Association of India, Western Branch, 1999).

25 Geoffrey A. Oddie, *Hindu and Christian in South-East India* (London: Curzon Press, 1991).

time. Indeed, the driving force behind the conversion movement seems to have been the Dalits' desire to break existing patterns of domination.[26]

Koji Kawashima returned to the theme of modernization but in a context quite different from the earlier studies described above. Travancore was a Hindu state committed to upholding dharma, to modernizing, and to being a charitable state. The rulers found Protestant missionaries, with their good schools and hospitals, to be uncomfortable allies in achieving their aims. Members of the lower castes, who sought to move up and out of the oppressed condition which the Hindu dharma had assigned to them, either converted or threatened to convert to Christianity to get what they wanted. This forced the government to bend regulations and policies in order to maintain a stable social order and prevent conversion. The culmination of government accommodation to the lower castes in the period under study was the temple entry proclamation of 1936, a major reason for which was the desire to prevent further conversions.[27]

Finally, three collections of essays on the theme of interaction deserve mention here. The first, *Hindu–Christian Dialogue: Perspectives and Encounters*,[28] while focusing primarily on the present, also includes five historical essays: two on Kerala and one each on Francis Xavier, Gandhi, and the Indian Renaissance. A pair of books, *Christians, Cultural Interactions, and India's Religious Traditions*[29] and *Christians and Missionaries in India: Cross-Cultural Communication since 1500*,[30] contain a total of twenty-four historical essays on many parts of India by scholars in a variety of academic disciplines.

26 Henriette Bugge, *Mission and Tamil Society: Social and Religious Change in South India 1840–1900* (Richmond: Curzon Press, 1994).

27 Koji Kawashima, *Missionaries and a Hindu State: Travancore 1858–1936* (Delhi: Oxford University Press, 1998).

28 (Ed.) Harold Coward (Maryknoll: Orbis Books, 1989).

29 (Ed.) Judith M. Brown and Robert Eric Frykenberg (Grand Rapids: William B. Eerdmans, 2002).

30 (Ed.) Robert Eric Frykenberg (Grand Rapids: William B. Eerdmans, 2003).

A few observations will conclude the review of this particular body of historical literature. First, the unit of study has shrunk from the broad all-India unit of Farquhar, Ingham and Pathak all the way down to one or two districts in the case of Bugge and Oddie. The most popular unit, however, has been the region. Those whose studies included more than one region have refrained from emphasizing inter-regional similarities and differences. Second, the focus, with rare exceptions, has been fixed on the missionaries—and especially the Protestant missionaries—during the nineteenth century. Abundant source materials lend themselves to this particular focus, while missionary influence inside and outside the churches reached its height in the nineteenth century, but waned thereafter. Third, virtually all the research has concentrated upon the triangle of missions, government, and the Indian élite and dominant castes in both promoting and resisting social change. The subalterns, within and outside the churches, are present in these studies, but not as primary or even important actors. Fourth, the social and cultural changes came about through competition and conflict between the missions and the Indian élite, with the government intervening—when it felt compelled to do so—to regulate, adjudicate or legislate on the matters at issue. Not only did the missions offer such a stiff challenge to existing beliefs, values, customs, and social arrangements that some sort of reform became necessary, but change also occurred within the missions as their members became better acquainted with India over time, and saw changes occur. Fifth and finally, all these studies highlight the importance of conversion—as well as the hope and fear of conversion—in stimulating and accelerating those processes of change in which Christians played an active role. Some of these studies devoted considerable space to the dynamics of conversion and conversion movements, the subject to which the next section will be devoted.

However, before proceeding, it is necessary to note that Northeast India represents a significant departure from these generalizations about religious interaction and the dynamics of socio-cultural change. This difference is reflected in the following quotation from Frederick Downs's *Christianity in North East India*.

Christian missions, and the indigenous Christian communities brought into existence through their work, played an important role in this process [of economic, social and cultural change]. In the Brahmaputra valley of Assam they were instrumental in promoting a renaissance of Assamese language and culture which preserved a distinct identity for that culture in the face of Bengali encroachment under British patronage. . . . The greatest impact has been among the tribal peoples; both those living in the plains areas and those inhabiting the hills. In turning to Christianity in increasingly large numbers, the tribal peoples have found in it a means of preserving their identities and promoting their interests in the face of powerful forces of change which threatened their autonomy.[31]

First and foremost, it was the imposition of British rule and administration upon the hill areas and, secondly, the contact with the plains people of Assam and Bengal, which British rule had brought about, that proved to be so disruptive of the hill people's society and culture. Christianity—although disruptive at the outset—through evangelism, educational, literary, medical, and generally humanitarian work, provided the hill tribes with the skills, the religious ideology, the (church) organizational structures, and the lifestyle changes they needed, both to modernize and to retain their distinctive tribal identities. Christianity was, for them, 'an agent of acculturation in a period of radical social change'.[32] These conclusions find further support in O.L. Snaitang's more detailed study of Christianity in Meghalaya.[33]

31 Frederick S. Downs, *Christianity in North East India: Historical Perspectives* (Delhi: ISPCK, 1983), p. 2.

32 Ibid., p. 280. This thesis is spelled out further in a collection of his essays, *Essays on Christianity in North-East India* (ed.) Milton S. Sangma and David R. Syiemleh (New Delhi: Indus Publishing Company, 1994). A collection of documents and essays on missionaries and the Assamese language is Maheshwar Neog (ed.), *The Resuscitation of the Assamese Language by the American Baptist Missionaries* (New Delhi: Omsons Publications, 2008).

33 O.L. Snaitang, *Christianity and Social Change in Northeast India: A Study of the Role of Christianity in Social Change Among the Khasi–Jaintia Hill Tribes of Meghalaya* (Calcutta: Firma KLM Private Ltd., 1993).

CONVERSION

The central premise on which all conversion studies have been based is that conversion is not something one person does to another person; it is something one chooses for oneself. Foreign missionary or Indian evangelists may have reached out, and even tailored their preaching, more to some sections of Indian society than to others—and mission strategies differed in that respect. But, in the last analysis, it was the potential convert who decided whether or not to receive Christian baptism. There are some studies which do discuss the criteria and the process which Christian evangelists employed in determining whether or not they would administer baptism to someone who desired it.[34] However, the heavy emphasis in the literature is upon the converts as agents: who they were; what their background circumstances were; what the processes and the motivations were that led to their conversion; and what did and did not change as a result of their baptism.

There are three volumes of historical essays devoted to the study of individual conversions and of conversion movements, not just to Christianity but to other religions as well. Geoffrey A. Oddie, the editor of the first two, raised some important historical questions about conversion in his introduction to *Religion in South Asia* (1977).[35] In his introduction to *Religious Conversion Movements in South Asia* (1997),[36] he attempted to convey what conversion has meant in the South Asian context. He saw it as a

---

34 For example, John C.B. Webster, *The Christian Community and Change in Nineteenth Century North India*, pp. 53–61; Susan Billington Harper, *In the Shadow of the Mahatma: Bishop V.S. Azariah and the Travails of Christianity in British India* (Grand Rapids: William B. Eerdmans, 2000), pp. 192–3.

35 Geoffrey A. Oddie (ed.), *Religion in South Asia: Religious Conversion and Revival Movements in South Asia in Medieval and Modern Times* (Delhi: Manohar, 1977), p. 6. Two of the eight essays deal with conversion movements to Christianity.

36 Geoffrey A. Oddie (ed.), *Religious Conversion Movements in South Asia: Continuities and Change 1800–1900* (Richmond: Curzon Press, 1997). Five of the six essays are on conversions and conversion movements to Christianity.

change of fellowship or community which involved a change of religious allegiance, going through a ritual of admission, acquiring a new 'tradition identity', a transition in belief, and an opting out as well as an opting in. He also saw an individual or collective crisis closely connected to conversion.[37] Robinson and Clarke, on the other hand, found such a characterization of conversion too constricting, for it seemed to draw questionably sharp boundary lines between religious traditions (for example, beliefs and practices do get carried over from a former to a new religion). It also ruled out many highly significant changes in religious affiliation, belief, and practice that did not require acquiring a totally new 'tradition identity' (for example, Sanskritization or sectarian revolt). So they preferred to 'imagine conversion as a fluid process of changing affiliations of religious beliefs and traditions with a range of possibilities'.[38]

In between the second and third of these collections of essays was Gauri Viswanathan's *Outside the Fold*, which also dealt with conversion to a variety of faiths. Viswanathan was critical of what she called the prevailing 'missionary-oriented focus' on conversion 'which is primarily concerned with how conversions take place, whether or not they are successful, and what further kinds of changes were triggered in the culture by way of a chain reaction from the original "transformation"'.[39] Instead, she viewed conversion as an act of cultural criticism in which prevailing national and cultural ideologies, civil law, official schema by which people are defined and classified, systems of religious belief, and political agendas are called into question. Among the case studies she chose to make this point were the conversion of Pandita Ramabai

37 Ibid., pp. 3–11.

38 Rowena Robinson and Sathianathan Clarke (eds), *Religious Conversion in India: Modes, Motivations and Meanings* (New Delhi: Oxford University Press, 2003), p. 8. Apart from the general and section introductions, four of the fourteen essays in this volume are about conversion to Christianity in Goa, Tamil Nadu, Punjab and the North-East, respectively.

39 Gauri Viswanathan, *Outside the Fold: Conversion, Modernity and Belief* (Princeton: Princeton University Press, 1998), p. 42.

to Christianity and some civil court cases involving Christian converts.

The studies which follow adopted more a narrative than a 'culture-critical' approach to the historical study of Christian conversion, although cultural criticism, alienation, resistance, and revolt did play a significant role in many of them. J.W. Gladstone's *Protestant Christianity and People's Movements in Kerala 1850–1936* 'is an attempt to show how the people—Christians and Hindus—while very often remaining within their boundaries of caste and other social and cultural segregations, participated in the struggle for their emancipation'.[40] He saw these people's movements passing through three phases: (1) mass conversion to Christianity without much organized resistance; (2) neo-Hindu movements within the Nair, the Izhava, and the Pulaya castes; and (3) a period of rising nationalism and active Hindu movements opposed to the Christian missions, ending with the temple entry proclamation of 1936. He viewed mass conversions to Christianity among Nadars, Hill Arrians, slave castes, Izhavas, and Kuravers as a struggle for emancipation paralleling similar movements by other members of those same castes seeking emancipation from social bondage.

Dick Kooiman later narrowed this focus by concentrating upon just the London Missionary Society and the nineteenth-century conversion movements among Nadars and Dalits in South Travancore. His starting assumption was that Nadars and Dalits adopted Christianity 'as part of a process of adaptation to a new situation created by western imperialism'.[41] He agreed with two missionaries writing in the late nineteenth century who saw these conversions as '"not caused by a deep conviction of sin and a strong desire to be saved", but more by the wish to better their worldly

---

40 J.W. Gladstone, *Protestant Christianity and People's Movements in Kerala: A Study of Christian Mass Movements in Relation to Neo-Hindu Socio-religious Movements in Kerala, 1850–1936* (Trivandrum: The Seminary Publications, 1984), p. 2.

41 Dick Kooiman, *Conversion and Social Equality in India: The London Missionary Society in South Travencore in the 19th Century* (Delhi: Manohar, 1989), p. 8.

conditions, to emancipate themselves from their social misery, and to be freed from the tyranny of the higher classes'.[42] In this effort, they saw the missionaries as sympathetic allies capable of helping them. In a concluding chapter, Kooiman looked at four indicators of possible cultural change among converts—caste relations, marriage customs, folk religion, and the use of the Sabbath—and found little change among them, despite missionary efforts.

In *Converting Women*, Eliza Kent noted that in colonial south India, 'conversion to Christianity appears as the movement of traditionally marginalized social groups towards new centers of power and influence' and, with Gauri Viswanathan, as entailing 'an implicit (and sometimes explicit) critique of dominant Hindu society's patriarchal or hierarchical tendencies'.[43] She treated conversion less as an inner change of belief than as a gradual process 'revealed in and aided by changes in external behavior' (for example, 'dress, diet, lifestyle, speech and comportment').[44] When seen from the point of view of the group, conversion appeared to be primarily 'about conflict, the sundering of old relationships and alienation from the shared universe of values and practices of one's old community. It appears to be less a matter of belief and more about disputes over meanings of practices, old and new'.[45] In the case of Tamil Christian women, symbolic of the community's increasing power and rising status vis-à-vis other groups, the conversion of women was shaped by what Kent called a 'discourse of respectability',

> a system of intentions, desires, practices and beliefs that organize gender and status differences in such a way that behaviors are valued positively to the extent that they exemplify restraint, containment, and orderliness, whereas behaviors are valued negatively that exemplify lack of self-control, spontaneity, and chaos.[46]

42 Ibid., p. 83.
43 Eliza F. Kent, *Converting Women: Gender and Protestant Christianity in Colonial South India* (New York: Oxford University Press, 2004), pp. 12, 239.
44 Ibid., pp. 6, 7.
45 Ibid., p. 7.
46 Ibid., p. 9.

The three groups which she found to be involved in this 'social organization of gender' around issues of Indian Christian domesticity, marriage, and sartorial style were the missionaries (women missionaries in particular), the local élite, and the upwardly mobile Indian Christians, especially Nadar Christians.[47]

The chapter devoted to late-nineteenth- and early-twentieth century Dalit conversion movements in my history of the Dalit Christians attempted to solve two questions that perplexed both missionaries and historians. One is why a conversion movement should occur within one jati, but not within other jatis placed in similar circumstances in the same district. The other concerned motivations for conversion. After examining several conversion movements, I found that they went through a series of stages—the first of which I called the leader stage. If an early convert was already a leader among his people prior to conversion, one whose judgement they trusted and whose lead they were prepared to follow, there might be a movement, otherwise not. The second stage came when that leader persuaded those in his circle of influence to join or follow him in converting. These converts, in turn, encouraged friends, relatives and acquaintances to do the same. At this stage, motivations were more psychological or spiritual, centred on a new self-image and public identity, than might be the case later. The third stage was marked by the missions becoming actively involved with furthering, rather than simply being responsive to, Dalit initiatives and inquiries. During this stage, a new dynamic came into play, the 'demonstration effect' of conversion; caste fellows could see and assess the changes which conversion had brought about in the lives of the converts (generally both lifestyle changes and inevitable persecution). When the missions reached a point where they no longer had the human resources to prepare inquirers for baptism or further 'Christianize' them afterwards, consolidation replaced growth as a mission priority. This may either terminate the movement or put it into abeyance until the mission felt capable of actively responding to it once again.[48]

47 Ibid., p. 12.

48 John C.B. Webster, *The Dalit Christians: A History*, 3rd ed. (Delhi: ISPCK, 2009), pp. 40–92. The book was originally published in 1992. This

Although Rowena Robinson's study of Christianity in Goa was more about the community than about conversion, it is included here because the pattern of conversion there was different from those described so far. The local *gauncars*, faced with heavy taxation as well as appropriation of land and labour by the Adil Shahi rulers, allied themselves with the Portuguese who used conversion as a means of gaining social allies. While, for the gauncars, conversion may have been a purely pragmatic, or even the only, choice when the Portuguese prohibited Hindu religious practices, they may also have found that the Catholicism presented to them 'could be adapted to their own social and religious needs',[49] and it was thus, for them, a genuine socio-religious choice. The servant castes then followed suit, again for their own socio-religious reasons, because Catholicism offered a more favourable identity and status than Hinduism had. In this way, whole villages, instead of members of only one caste within them, converted.

Finally, Lalsawma and Vanlalchhuanawma described yet a different pattern of conversion in Mizoram between 1906 and the 1940s. There, conversion occurred as a result of a continuing series of revivals—which the former defined as 'a vehement upsurge of public excitement into religious commitments, accompanied by diverse manifestations of emotional outbursts through songs, movements and actions'[50]—over the course of four decades. These revivals generally took place in villages and were led by local or visiting preachers, many of whom had questionable theologies and

hypothesis was based upon both the case studies presented in this book itself; in Sundararaj Manickam, *The Social Setting of Christian Conversion in South India: The Impact of the Wesleyan Methodist Missionaries on the Trichy–Tanjore Diocese with Special Reference to the Harijan Communities of the Mass Movement Area 1820–1947* (Wiesbaden: Franz Steiner Verlag, 1977), pp. 80–111; and in Geoffrey A. Oddie, 'Christian Conversions in the Telugu Country 1860–1900: A Case Study of One Protestant Indian Movement in the Godavery–Krishna Delta', *The Indian Economic and Social History Review*, vol. XII (January–March 1975), pp. 61–79.

49 Rowena Robinson, *Conversion, Continuity and Change: Lived Christianity in Southern Goa* (New Delhi: Sage Publications, 1998), p. 52.

50 Lalsawma, *Revivals the Mizo Way: Forty Years of Revival Movements in Mizoram* (Aizawl: Lalsawma, 1994), p. 7.

operated quite independently of any recognized church authority. The revivals exhibited ecstatic behaviour rooted in Mizo culture—singing, dancing, the use of the drum—which were initially considered unacceptable but were later incorporated into the regular worship life of Mizo churches. Vanlalchhuanawma saw the revivals as a Mizo reaction to the encroachment of an alien culture through the Raj and the missions and, at the same time, a major contributor to the development of a new Mizo Christianity, culture, and society in response.[51]

It is difficult to conclude this survey of conversion studies by pointing to a scholarly consensus. Historians have understood conversion in different ways and have adopted different approaches in studying it. Perhaps, one point of agreement is that conversions reveal a lot about the social contexts in which they occur and thus are well worth studying for the insights into Indian society which they provide. It is particularly important that they be studied historically with special attention not only to the social setting and location of the converts but also to the chronology, the unfolding dynamics, the meanings and ramifications of conversion, not just for the converts themselves but for the particular communities into and out of which they opted, to say nothing of the surrounding social order itself. As this brief survey indicates, these do vary from period to period, from region to region, and from social group to social group, so historical study is needed to challenge common assumptions and sweeping generalizations.[52]

51 Vanlalchhuanawma, *Christianity and Subaltern Culture: Revival Movement as a Cultural Response to Westernization in Mizoram* (Delhi: ISPCK, 2006).

52 For an excellent historical review of the political debate on conversion from the time of the Raj down through 1999, see Sebastian C.H. Kim, *In Search of Identity: Debates on Religious Conversion in India* (New Delhi: Oxford University Press, 2003). See also Sumit Sarkar's chapter on 'Christianity, Hindutva and the Question of Conversions' in his *Beyond Nationalist Frames: Relocating Postmodernism, Hindutva, History* (Delhi: Permanent Black, 2002), pp. 215–43.

CULTURAL DYNAMICS

The varying patterns of conversion described above have affected not only the social composition but also the internal dynamics of Christian communities. Thus, for example, when converts came in individually or in nuclear families from a variety of social backgrounds—as they did in the Punjab and the United Provinces until the 1880s—a new community had to be created out of diverse elements and it had to find its own way of being Christian together. However, when there were large caste-based conversion movements among jatis placed differently within the traditional hierarchy—as happened in the far South—then communities of caste could be retained within the churches, and caste rivalries occurring outside could be brought into the churches and negotiated there. In short, conversion was not such a totally transformative event, nor was Indian society so tightly compartmentalized that Christian Indians interacted only with each other and were subject only to Christian and to no other influences. (From the point of view of many nineteenth-century missionaries, that was precisely the problem!) Not only were there socio-cultural and other carryovers from former communities but the tensions, conflicts, and changes in the wider society were also reflected within Christian communities and, because of the mission archive, may well have been better documented there as a result. What made Christian communities socially different from the communities out of which their members came was, in most cases, the presence of the foreign missionary in a position of considerable decision-making power and cultural influence. This section is devoted to histories of particular communities of Christians as defined by region, or by caste, or by denomination, with an eye towards seeing what light they shed on Indian social history.

In some of these community studies the influence of historical anthropology is quite pronounced. Two are studies of present Christian communities with such strong traditions that history not only introduces but pervades the entire work. Rowena Robinson's study of southern Goa, referred to in the previous section, focused on continuities and changes in the social structure, rituals and ceremonies in one village since conversion in the sixteenth century.

Thus, for example, caste distinctions—specifically endorsed by the Portuguese—and lifestyle differences have been retained but the underlying rationale of pollution and purity is gone. 'The church remains the central arena where order, hierarchy and dominance emerge through the differing rights of different social groups'[53] and, hence, the arena where those differences are most obviously contested. Susan Visvanathan problematized the history of the Yakoba (Jacobite Syrian) Christians in a small neighbourhood of Kottayam by distinguishing between 'official history', the histories presented in the court cases of 1879–89 over the legitimacy of competing lines of ecclesiastical authority which still divide the community, and the oral accounts of that history which she heard when conducting field research in 1981–2. To this, she added histories of the neighbourhood as well as of specific family lineages and churches in it. These, and its central beliefs, rituals, ceremonies, and festivals gave the community its distinctive identity within a predominantly Hindu environment.[54]

There are two histories of missionary attitudes and policies with respect to caste which set the context for other studies. Duncan Forrester surveyed Anglo-Saxon Protestant missionary views from 1793 until just before Independence. His two concluding chapters dealt with Hindu responses to the missionary attack on caste, and Indian Christian attitudes on caste in the twentieth century.[55] Kenneth Ballhatchet did much the same for the Catholics by focusing upon caste conflict within Catholic communities in Kerala, Bombay, Madras, and Tamil Nadu between 1789 and 1914.[56] While there were exceptions on both sides, the more egalitarian Protestants saw caste as a religious institution integral to Hinduism and hence to be rooted out of the churches, whereas the more hierarchical Catholics saw it as a social institution (India's

53 Rowena Robinson, *Conversion, Continuity and Change*, p. 189.

54 Susan Visvanathan, *The Christians of Kerala: History, Belief and Ritual among the Yakoba* (Madras: Oxford University Press, 1993).

55 Duncan B. Forrester, *Caste and Christianity: Attitudes and Policies on Caste of Anglo-Saxon Protestant Missions in India* (London: Curzon Press, 1980).

56 Kenneth Ballhatchet, *Caste, Class and Catholicism in India 1789–1914* (Richmond: Curzon Press, 1998).

system of social stratification) and thus permissible. Despite these differences, both ran into difficulties when lower-caste Christians demanded greater respect and equality in the face of higher-caste Christian insistence on retaining caste distinctions.

In Part II of Susan Bayly's *Saints, Goddesses and Kings*, caste and caste conflict are at the very heart of her treatment of Christianity in what are now Kerala and southern Tamil Nadu. She began by showing how well integrated the Syrian Christians were into Kerala society at the end of the eighteenth century. Not only were they a privileged trader-warrior 'caste' worthy of serving as patrons of Hindu temples, but their own religious practices and structures paralleled those of their Hindu and Muslim neighbours. There were many and complex reasons why this arrangement disintegrated during the course of the nineteenth century, but among them were missionary attempts to 'purify' their religious life, their own deepening internal divisions and, in the end, their 'tactical' efforts to convert the low castes so as to appear progressive. Meanwhile, in neighbouring southern Tamil Nadu—where Christians had their own cults of the saints which paralleled those of other religious groups—Christian Paravas, Marawas, Shanars, Vellalas, Pallars, and Paraiyar engaged in caste-based disputes over ceremonial honours and privileges in Christian worship and festivals. So striking was this, that Bayly was led to conclude that 'religious affiliation and "conversion" have always been matters of internal competition within the different social and religious groups of Tamil Nadu and Kerala',[57] so much so that 'conversion might be thought of as the prosecution of claims to higher status by other and more militant means'.[58]

The central theme of two histories of Dalit Christians in Kerala is their struggle against caste disabilities and discrimination. George Oommen concentrated on Pulaya Christians who had joined the Anglican Church. He showed not only how they became involved in the Pulaya movement but also how many either left the Syrian Christian-dominated Anglican Church for other churches or

57 Susan Bayly, *Saints, Goddesses and Kings*, p. 457.
58 Ibid., p. 458.

created churches of their own people.[59] V.V. Thomas picked up on that theme in his history of Dalit Pentecostalism in Kerala. Most of the early Pentecostal Christians were Dalits, but when more and more Syrian Christians joined and took over the leadership of the Pentecostal churches, caste conflict between the two groups led to splits in 1930 and 1972 as well as to the growth of independent churches.[60]

While examining the social and religious life of the St. Thomas Christians in the late fifteenth and early sixteenth centuries, Mathias Mundadan saw their traditions giving them their distinctive identity. These included traditions not only about St. Thomas and their origins as a people, but also about their religious and their social life, which included their occupations, lifestyle, communal organization and privileges.[61] In a later work, *Indian Christians: Search for Identity and Struggle for Autonomy*, Mundadan returned to the Syrian Christians and carried their history forward, linking identity with ecclesiastical autonomy. In his briefer treatment of the Latin rite Catholics and the Protestants, he linked identity to autonomy vis-à-vis foreign missionary domination.

The other study on the South is Susan Harper's biography of the first Indian to become an Anglican bishop (1912), V.S. Azariah. It also concerned the Mala and the Madiga Christians in his overwhelmingly rural Dornakal Diocese in what is now Andhra Pradesh. Azariah was an ardent and effective evangelist who believed in transformation through conversion and the creation of a new community based not on caste but on the Christian gospel. Of special interest to Harper was the way Azariah engaged the culture (for example, caste, marriage customs, music) on a selective basis, where he encountered resistance, and where he won support among the thousands who converted during his episcopacy.[62]

59 George Oommen, 'The Struggle of Anglican Pulaya Christians for Social Improvement in Travancore, 1854–1966', Unpublished PhD Dissertation (University of Sydney, 1993).

60 V.V. Thomas, *Dalit Pentecostalism: Spirituality of the Empowered Poor* (Bangalore: Asian Trading Corporation, 2008).

61 A. Mathias Mundadan, *Sixteenth Century Traditions of St. Thomas Christians* (Bangalore: Dharmaram College, 1970).

62 Susan Billington Harper, *In the Shadow of the Mahatma*.

Turning to the North, Jeffrey Cox examined the fault lines of race, culture, gender, caste and class pervading the institutions and churches which Protestant missionaries created in nineteenth-century Punjab, and their attempts to overcome the resulting contradictions between 1900 and 1940.[63] Christopher Harding concentrated upon the religious transformation of rural Punjabi Dalit converts to both Catholic and Protestant Christianity during the late nineteenth and early twentieth centuries. He saw the mis-sionary–convert encounter in this process of transformation 'as one defined primarily by presentation and perception on all sides', and so he focused 'upon the particular contemporaneous inter-ests and frames of reference of Punjabi converts and of CMS and Capuchin mission personnel'.[64] He devoted separate chapters to the differing views of 'uplift' which the various parties brought to this encounter and to the way converts, especially in Christian vil-lages, sought to live in their new traditions. My own social history of Christianity in North-West India over the past two centuries paid special attention to the evolution of the Christian community within the context of the continuities and changes in the region as a whole. It described its changing social composition, its domi-nant concerns and struggles, its most serious internal divisions, as well as the impact that major events, such as Independence and Partition, had upon the community. The concluding chapter compared Christianity's history in the North-West with its history elsewhere in India.[65]

The central issue which Chad Bauman addressed in his pre-Independence history of the Satnami Christians in Chhattisgarh is 'whether and to what extent conversion to Christianity in Chhattisgarh ... entailed a process of "deculturation" or

63 Jeffrey Cox, *Imperial Fault Lines: Christianity and Colonial Power in India, 1818–1940* (Stanford: Stanford University Press, 2002).

64 Christopher Harding, *Religious Transformation in South Asia: The Meanings of Conversion in Colonial Punjab* (Oxford: Oxford University Press, 2008), p. 5.

65 John C.B. Webster, *A Social History of Christianity: North-West India since 1800* (New Delhi: Oxford University Press, 2007).

"denationalization'".[66] He used the techniques of both the historian and the anthropologist to examine the Christianization of Chhattisgarh and the 'Chhattisgarhization' of Christianity. Specifically, he devoted chapters to the Satnamis' conversion to Christianity; their myths connecting Christianity to the Satnami guru, Ghasidas; their views on medicine and on 'Christian' womanhood; as well as to some illustrative personal stories. His concluding chapter dealt with developments and key events in the post-Independence era.

Mangkhosat Kipgen had taken up the cultural theme earlier by asking why Christianity grew so rapidly in Mizoram, both quantitatively and qualitatively, as compared to elsewhere in India, including other parts of the North-east. His own answer was that it penetrated so deeply into Mizo culture through the revivals that Mizo culture shaped the way Mizos understood Christianity and worshipped God. He singled out the third revival (1919–23) as the first to give Mizos the freedom they needed to create new forms of Christian life in and through which to express their *lungleng* (devotion, love, tenderness, longing) and live out their *tlawmngaihna* (moral code) to the glory of God.[67]

There are two historical studies devoted to the status and role of women in the churches of the North-east. Frederick Downs challenged the common assumption that Christianity raised the status of women there by educating them. In looking at the status of women in Khasi–Jaintia and Mizo society before the arrival of the British and of the missionaries, he found both these societies to be in transition, moving towards becoming more patriarchal than they had been earlier. He saw Christianity both raising the status of women through education and reinforcing patriarchy by keeping church structures under complete male domination.[68] This view

66 Chad M. Bauman, *Christian Identity and Dalit Religion in Hindu India, 1868-1947* (Grand Rapids: William B. Eerdmans, 2008), p. 1.

67 Mangkhosat Kipgen, *Christianity and Mizo Culture: The Encounter between Christianity and Zo Culture in Mizoram* (Aizawl: Mizo Theological Conference, 1997).

68 Frederick S. Downs, *The Christian Impact on the Status of Women in North East India* (Shillong: North-Eastern Hill University Publications, 1996).

was reinforced by Aphuno Chase Roy's work on the impact of Christianity—and of the Baptist Church in particular—upon the status of Angami Naga women. When Christianity was introduced in 1881, it came as an agent of education and modernity. Beginning in the 1920s, it was in the churches that Angami Christian women not only became literate and educated, but also acquired new skills as evangelists, teachers, group organizers, and leaders. Moreover, through the churches, they gained entrance into public life and politics. However, since 1970, the forces of secular modernism have supplanted Christianity as a major influence in enhancing the status of women. In the churches, decision-making bodies continue to be male-dominated and women are denied ordination as clergy. She, therefore, concluded that, 'while in the larger society secular modernism is rapidly displacing all aspects of traditional culture, within the more conservative confines of the Church, the influences of the traditional Angami patriarchy continues'.[69]

Finally, mention should be made of several collections of essays on Christian communities. F. Hrangkhuma edited a volume on Christianity among diverse caste, tribal, or regional groups spread throughout India. While it was intended to answer questions about the mission of the churches, almost all the fifteen chapters are historical in nature.[70] Roger Hedlund edited a series of studies on a variety of Christian churches and movements of Indian origin. These 'independent' churches and fellowships—which have developed outside of and often in reaction to the churches of foreign missionary origin—have been growing and proliferating quite rapidly since Independence.[71] O.L. Snaitang edited a similar

69 Aphuno Chase Roy, *Women in Transition: Angami Naga Women from 1878 to the Present* (Kohima: Aphuno Chase Roy, 2004), p. 221.

70 F. Hrangkhuma (ed.), *Christianity in India: Search for Liberation and Identity* (Delhi: ISPCK, 1998).

71 Roger E. Hedlund (ed.), *Christianity is Indian: The Emergence of an Indigenous Community* (Delhi: ISPCK, 2000). Hedlund's own historical reflections on this phenomenon are found in his *Quest for Identity. India's Churches of Indigenous Origin: The 'Little Tradition' in Indian Christianity* (Delhi: ISPCK, 2000).

volume devoted to North-east India.[72] *Local Dalit Christian History* contains five case studies and an essay on methodology. A major theme running through the case studies is inter-generational social mobility.[73]

These community studies suggest that Christian communities are arenas in which some of the major cleavages in Indian society are revealed and much of its dynamics are at play. Caste is an obvious example but not the only one. There is the clash, selective appropriation, and creative syntheses of cultures between the 'West' embodied in the missionary and the 'Indian' with its many subcultures. There are struggles for status, for mobility, for influence and power, as well as just for sheer survival. Christian communities have proven to be a particularly rich field of study for historians trained in cultural anthropology, and their contribution to the field of Christian history has been considerable. These studies also render highly dubious the view of the Christian (or any other religious) community as a monolithic, homogeneous, static community with its own unchanging, self-contained subculture and belief system.

POLITICS

There are relatively few studies of Christian involvement with the nationalist, communal, and subaltern politics leading up to Independence in 1947. Several of the works cited earlier do address the subject, even at some length. For that reason, this section will refer to them while describing those books devoted primarily to Christian involvement with politics. Studies of missionary attempts to get reform legislation enacted—mentioned in an earlier section—are not included here, but studies which trace a nationalist movement against 'Missionary Raj' within the churches themselves, are included because they reveal interesting parallels with developments in the broader nationalist movement.

72 O.L. Snaitang (ed.), *Churches of Indigenous Origin in Northeast India* (Delhi: ISPCK, 2000).

73 George Oommen and John C.B. Webster (eds), *Local Dalit Christian History* (Delhi: ISPCK, 2002).

In 1979, George Thomas' *Christian Indians and Indian Nationalism 1885–1950* offered an all-India overview of this subject. At that time, the secondary literature available was quite thin, consisting of a few articles, some short biographies, and portions of institutional histories. He arranged his chapters chronologically, according to the generally accepted phases in the development of the Congress-led nationalist movement, describing Christian involvement with, and attitudes towards, the major events of each phase; Indian Christian attempts to address political and cultural nationalism theologically; and their efforts to either gain control of existing ecclesiastical decision-making bodies or to create churches of their own, independent of missionary control.[74]

A. Mathew examined Protestant missionary views and policies concerning Christian evangelism through higher education in the Madras Presidency from 1872—when mission educational aims shifted away from direct evangelism towards the dissemination of Christian ideas and principles—up to 1930. Of special interest was what Mathew called the 'mission to nationalism' espoused by liberal missionaries. This mission worked well as long as Indian nationalism remained moderate in ideology and tactics, but these same missionaries strongly opposed the more radical-militant nationalism which came to prominence in the early twentieth century. Apart from criticizing it and expressing support for constitutional reform guided by the Raj, they not only gave up on influencing the intelligentsia in favour of the masses, but also began to emphasize home rule in the churches and, under the influence of the social gospel, Christian social service to those outside.[75]

Mathew's monograph needs to be read in conjunction with several others, both because of the supporting evidence they provide and because of the lacunae they fill. For example, M.D. David showed that Indian Christians in Maharashtra withdrew from the Indian National Congress when religion-based 'extremism'

---

74 George Thomas, *Christian Indians and Indian Nationalism 1885–1950: An Interpretation in Historical and Theological Perspectives* (Frankfurt: Verlag Peter D. Lang, 1979).

75 A. Mathew, *Christian Missions, Education and Nationalism: From Dominance to Compromise 1870–1930* (Delhi: Anamika Prakashan, 1988).

came to supersede the more secular moderate politics they had endorsed.[76] D. Arthur Jayakumar has shown that the Government Memo of 1919—originally intended to control enemy nationals in India during World War I and afterwards applied to non-British missions and their employees (especially in educational institutions)—inhibited Indian Christian involvement in nationalist politics. This memo demanded the active loyalty of all members and employees as a condition of the mission's continued presence in India. Jayakumar noted that, despite this, a good number of Christians was listed among the Freedom Fighters in Tamil Nadu.[77] Daniel O'Connor's biography of C.F. Andrews, another liberal missionary, provides valuable information on Andrews's political involvement as both nationalist sympathizer and mediator with British officialdom between 1904 and 1914, when 'extremism' was in the ascendancy, as well as on North-Indian Christian political attitudes during that same period.[78]

Two regional studies present Christian involvement in politics as that of a minority community marginalized by British and Indian politicians alike. The earlier and larger work is Chandra Mallampalli's study of Christians in the public life of the Madras Presidency from 1863 to 1937. He saw this as a 'story about inclusion and exclusion from "Indian-ness," as this notion has evolved in relation to "Hindu-ness."'[79] The first section dealt with the law. Since Christianity did not have a body of personal law built into it for the courts to follow—as did Hinduism and Islam—the Madras judiciary classified Christians as culturally 'non-Hindu', despite the existence of many very similar cultural practices, and

76 M.D. David, *Missions: Cross-Cultural Encounter and Change in Western India*, pp. 372–8.

77 D. Arthur Jayakumar, *Christians and the National Movement: The Memorandum of 1919 and the National Movement with Special Reference to Protestant Christians in Tamil Nadu 1919–1939* (Calcutta: Punthic Pustak, 1999).

78 Daniel O'Connor, *Gospel, Raj and Swaraj: The Missionary Years of C.F. Andrews 1904–14* (Frankfurt: Verlag Peter Lang, 1990).

79 Chandra Mallampalli, *Christians and Public Life in Colonial South India, 1863–1937: Contending with Marginality* (London: Routledge Curzon, 2004), p. 1.

applied British law to them. The second section involved politics in which Protestants and Catholics acted quite differently. The Protestants chose to disavow communalism and Dravidianism in favor of Indian nationalism at the national level, whereas the Catholics chose to become more involved in the politics of group interests at the regional level. The third section focused on the politics of Dalit Christians where, again, Protestants and Catholics adopted different strategies. Catholic Dalits sought integration in the Church alongside 'caste Catholics', whereas Protestant Dalits tended to identify themselves more closely with other Dalits. My own history of Christianity in North-West India, where communal politics was especially pronounced, described how Christians were involved with the politics of the region from the introduction of local self-government under Lord Ripon up to and through Independence. A parallel account is also given of the struggle of the Indian Christian élite to effect a transfer of power within the churches from the foreign missionaries and their mission societies abroad.[80]

Two histories which have already been mentioned deal with Dalit Christian involvement with politics. My own history of the Dalit Christians was national in scope and set their history within the framework provided by the political history of the modern Dalit movement from the Montagu Declaration in 1917 up to the present. A full chapter, 'The Politics of Numbers', covered the period between the two world wars, in which the Dalit Christian political awakening began; then, a chapter on 'Compensatory Discrimination' dealt with their post-Independence struggles.[81] George Oommen's thesis was regional in focus. It devoted separate chapters to the way in which the Pulaya Christians in Travancore became deeply involved, first in the Pulaya movement under Ayyan Kali and then later in the Communist movement.[82]

Finally, Lalsangkima Pachuau examined the role Christianity played in the development of ethno-nationalism among the Mizos.

80 John C.B. Webster, *A Social History of Christianity*, pp. 185–90, 205–72.

81 John C.B. Webster, *The Dalit Christians: A History*.

82 George Oommen, 'The Struggle of Anglican Pulaya Christians'.

British administration broke down village autonomy and gave the Mizos a sense of commonality. Christianity—as mediated through the revivals—strengthened their bonds, and shaped their social norms and cultural values to such an extent that 'it became an important foundation of the Mizos' self-understanding' and identity consciousness.[83] Pachuau argued that there was no strong evidence to support the view that Christian missions or churches supported Mizo separatism. Instead, Christianity played a role in developing a politically active, educated Mizo élite against the autocratic chieftains with whom the British were allied. After Independence, the churches retained an independent voice during the insurgency, opposing violence on both sides, and served as mediators between the insurgents and the Government of India. What gave force to the insurgency was not Christianity *per se* but Mizo fears of assimilation, domination and oppression by Indic people who showed no respect for them or their way of life, of which Christianity was an integral part.

This body of literature is not large, but it does challenge two assumptions which often inform historical writing. One is the communal assumption that Christians in India have constituted a community with a shared political interest. While on some issue Christians have had shared interests, on most they have not. Within the community, there have been too many demonstrated cleavages based on class, caste, denomination, and gender for that assumption to stand up. The other assumption is that Christians took no part in the nationalist movement but supported their co-religionist British rulers instead. This placed them outside the 'mainstream' of twentieth-century Indian history. Of course, recent historians have moved the discussion of both nationalism and 'the mainstream' far beyond simply equating them with Congress-led politics, but, even as traditionally understood, this assumption faces too much contrary evidence to stand up. What does remain relatively unexplored, however, is the ways that members of a marginalized

83 Lalsangkima Pachuau, *Ethnic Identity and Christianity: A Socio-Historical and Missiological Study of Christianity in Northeast India with Special Reference to Mizoram* (Frankfurt: Verlag Peter Lang, 2002), p. 111.

minority community have understood what it meant to be nationalist and how they chose to put that understanding into practice.

GENERAL HISTORIES AND REFERENCE WORKS

This book began by using some early general histories of
Christianity in India to provide an insight into the trends in historical writing on Christianity in India up through the 1960s. This
section returns to general histories of Christianity in India written
since then to see what shifts in overall perspective have occurred.
This section also mentions some reference works which scholars
may find useful.

A few years before Cyril Bruce Firth wrote his textbook, *An
Introduction to Indian Church History*, P. Thomas wrote a short
history of Christianity which took a deliberately non-denominational approach so as to avoid both mission and Church history
and to focus on Christians as Indian people.[84] Aloysius Soares's
The Catholic Church in India, written in conjunction with the
Eucharistic Congress which met in India in 1964, was for the most
part an institutional history.[85] *Christianity in India: A History in
Ecumenical Perspective* (1972) was a composite history of varying
quality with no single perspective, written by historians from a
variety of Christian backgrounds.[86]

Also in 1972, the Indian edition of Stephen Neill's short history of Christianity in India appeared in anticipation of a projected
three-volume comprehensive history. However, only two of those
volumes were published, the second of which Neill had not quite
finished when he died. His history was published in the West in
1984 and 1985, clearly with Western readers in mind. The first volume began with St. Thomas and ended in 1707; the second volume
ended in 1858. Neill's aim was 'not to write mission history—in
my opinion a very dull subject—but to survey the whole history of
the Indian sub-continent in relation to the presence and growth
of a fellowship which, foreign in origins, has increasingly estab-

---

84 P. Thomas, *Christians and Christianity in India and Pakistan*.
85 Aloysius Soares, *The Catholic Church in India*.
86 H.C. Perumalil and E.R. Hambye (eds), *Christianity in India*.

lished itself as a part of Indian life'.[87] While he included chapters on Indian religions, Indian political history, and contacts between India and the West, Neill's history remained very much in the traditional mould of mission and institutional history.

In 1974, an editorial board appointed by the Church History Association of India to prepare a multi-volume history of Christianity in India developed a 'New Perspective' from which that history was to be written. Its rationale was that:

> The history of Christianity in India has hitherto often been treated as an eastward extension of western ecclesiastical history. Stress has been laid upon either its internal history or upon its 'foreign mission' dimension so that the Church is viewed as a relatively self-contained unit which acted upon and was acted upon by the society outside. In recent years a number of studies both of Christianity and of Indian society have shown that this perspective is in serious need of revision. It is now intended to write the history of Christianity in the context of Indian history.

The editorial board set forth four basic components of this new perspective, the first of which was the socio-cultural, focusing upon 'the Christian *people* of India; upon who they were and how they understood themselves; upon their social, religious, cultural and political encounters; upon the changes which those encounters produced in them, and in their appropriation of the Christian gospel, as well as in the Indian culture and society of which they themselves were a part'. The other three components were the regional (that is, using the region as the basic working unit); the national as the overall framework so that all-India developments are noted and regional diversities do not obscure national unities; and the ecumenical so that no single branch of Christianity

---

87 Stephen Neill, *A History of Christianity in India: The Beginnings to AD 1707* (Cambridge: Cambridge University Press, 1984), p. xi. The aim of the second volume shifted somewhat to depicting the history of Christianity in India 'as a not unimportant part of the gigantic drama of the confrontation between Western and Asian cultures, which had been played out in other ways in China and Japan and other Asian countries'. Stephen Neill, *A History of Christianity in India 1707–1858* (Cambridge: Cambridge University Press, 1985), p. xiii.

is privileged over the others but that the unities and the diversities within Christianity are explored.[88]

To date, three full volumes covering the history of Christianity through the end of the eighteenth century, as well as two shorter works covering Tamil Nadu and the North-east during the nineteenth and twentieth centuries, have appeared, and at least two more are in progress.[89] In the first three volumes, the region is the basic unit and inter-regional comparisons are made in the conclusions. In the other two, the chapters are arranged topically rather than chronologically. All five have been remarkably faithful to the editorial board's original guidelines, given the fact that the authors were writing the kind of history which went against the grain of most of the source materials upon which they had to rely.

Rowena Robinson's *Christians of India* is an anthropology of Christianity in India using ethnographic and historical materials organized around themes similar to those used in this essay: conversion, internal differentiation, traditions, customs and cultures. These chapters were preceded by an excellent introduction on the disciplinary roots and assumptions leading to the neglect of Christianity as a subject of study, and concluded not with broad generalizations but with many Indian 'Christianities'.[90]

88 'A Scheme for a Comprehensive History of Christianity in India' (mimeographed), pp. 1–2.

89 The five volumes published so far in *History of Christianity in India* are the following: Vol. 1, *From the Beginning up to the Middle of the Sixteenth Century* [up to 1542] (Bangalore: Theological Publications in India, 1984), by A. Mathias Mundadan. Vol. 2, *From the Middle of the Sixteenth to the End of the Seventeenth Century* [1542–1700] (Bangalore: Theological Publications in India, 1982), by Joseph Thekkedath. Vol. 3, *Eighteenth Century* (Bangalore: Church History Association of India, 1997), by E.R. Hambye. Vol. 4, Part 2, *Tamilnadu in the Nineteenth and Twentieth Centuries* (Bangalore: Church History Association of India, 1990) by Hugald Grafe. Vol. 5, Part 5, *North-East India in the Nineteenth and Twentieth Centuries* (Bangalore: Church History Association of India, 1992) by Frederick S. Downs.

90 Rowena Robinson, *Christians of India* (New Delhi: Sage Publications, 2003).

Since then, two other general histories have appeared. Two Jesuit scholars used history to introduce Christianity to Indian readers who know nothing about it. They organized their history around a series of 'springs', the first of which involved the early Christians up to the arrival of the Portuguese. The second spring was initiated by the Portuguese, the third by the Protestants, and the fourth by the Dalits and the Adivasis.[91] The most recent general history is by Robert Frykenberg. Like Neill's, his was published in the West (as part of the Oxford History of the Christian Church) primarily for Western readers. Unlike Neill, Frykenberg took an Indo-centric approach which argued forcefully that Christianity has been (and remains) an indigenous Indian phenomenon. Two major emphases of the book are especially noteworthy. It concentrated upon the South, where the majority of Christians live and where the author's own expertise lies. It also paid special attention to the foundation-laying and subsequent 'incubation' periods, when Christianity was introduced and then became part of the socio-cultural milieu of various caste or tribal communities, rather than upon later—especially twentieth-century—developments. Another significant feature is that Frykenberg frequently used detailed case studies of particular converts and conversion movements, which were followed by more summary accounts of parallel cases, to achieve both depth and balance.[92]

Finally, mention has to be made of four reference works which the historian in this field may find helpful. *The St. Thomas Christian Encyclopaedia of India* appeared in two volumes in 1973 and 1982. One volume is devoted exclusively to Kerala and the other to the rest of India.[93] M.K. Kuriakose edited a volume of 200 selected

91 Leonard Fernando and G. Gispert-Sauch, *Christianity in India: Two Thousand Years of Faith* (New Delhi: Penguin Viking, 2004).

92 Robert Eric Frykenberg, *Christianity in India: From Beginnings to the Present* (New York: Oxford University Press, 2008).

93 George Menachery (ed.), *The St. Thomas Christian Encyclopaedia of India. Volume 1: Indian Christianity by Chronological, Denominational, Geographical and Ecclesiastical Divisions* (Trichur: The St. Thomas Christian Encyclopaedia of India, 1982); George Menachery (ed.), *The St. Thomas Christian Encyclopaedia of India. Volume 2: St. Thomas, Kerala,*

documents in 1982.[94] The Centre for Studies in Civilizations has devoted a volume in its *History of Science, Philosophy and Culture in Indian Civilization* to Indian Christianity.[95] About half the essays in the volume are historical in nature. The Oxford University Press in New Delhi published *The Oxford Encyclopaedia of South Asian Christianity* edited by Roger E. Hedlund in 2011.

ASSUMPTIONS ABOUT INDIAN SOCIAL HISTORY

As this survey has shown, academic historians have approached the study of Christianity in India in diverse ways. Not only have they chosen to study different aspects of the subject, but one can also discern the influence of modernization theory, post-modernism, post-colonialism, feminism, cultural anthropology, and subalternist perspectives shaping the questions which they have posed and sought to answer. No single approach has dominated the field, although the Church History Association of India's 'New Perspective' has had a strong influence upon Christian historians in India who have come within its ambit. For them, gaining an honest appraisal of the identity of the Christian people of India is an issue of crucial importance, for much is at stake in the face of attacks by the Sangh Pariwar.

That said, there are certain assumptions about the social history of India which stand out in reviewing this particular body of historical literature. One is that India's society has been a genuinely pluralistic, rather than a homogeneous, society with a few million deviant 'others' here and there. Not only have Christians as a religious minority symbolized that diversity, but they have also included considerable diversity of caste, tribe, and culture within their own membership. A second assumption is that Indians have

---

Malabar Christianity (Trichur: The St. Thomas Christian Encyclopaedia of India, 1973).

94 M.K. Kuriakose, *History of Christianity in India: Source Materials* (Madras: The Christian Literature Society, 1982).

95 D.P. Chattopadhyaya (ed.), *History of Science, Philosophy and Culture in Indian Civilization, Volume VII Part 6: Indian Christianity* (ed) A.V. Afonso (New Delhi: Centre for Studies in Civilizations, 2009).

not lived in water-tight compartments defined solely by religion (or by any other single criterion). Only in some states in the Northeast and in a few pockets elsewhere in India have Christians wielded significant political power or owned the means of production. Elsewhere, they have been politically and economically dependent upon—and have constantly interacted with—dominant groups who did not share their religion. Culturally, they have retained many, if not most, of their inherited customs and practices. Thus, the rigid compartmentalization of Indian society, as under the British, simply flies in the face of the facts 'on the ground'.

Third and finally, it seems wisest to adopt a conflict model of society when conducting research on Indian social history. The vast majority of Christians comes from oppressed groups in Indian society—Dalits and the tribal people—for whom conflict was constantly either latent or manifest, and who saw in conversion the possibility of gaining some freedom from at least psychological, if not social, economic and political domination. Moreover, some of the major contradictions within Indian society have been reflected within the Christian churches and community: caste-based status conflicts; class conflicts between the educated urban élite and the landless labourers; identity and interest conflicts between the tribal people and others; gender conflicts between men and women; cultural conflicts between adherents of the inherited and of the new; and internal religious conflicts as between Catholics and Protestants. This is not to argue either that there has never been peace, harmony, and cooperation in India—Christian history provides ample evidence of that, too—or that conflict has been more evident in India than elsewhere in the world. However, whether grounded in a sociology of knowledge or a robust appreciation of the structural dimensions of human sinfulness, a conflict model offers a realistic and illuminating approach to the study of Indian social history.

APPENDIX 6.1

A Note on Mission Archives in India

A number of archives in India contain good quantities of mission sources. Most are located in theological colleges and seminaries where the clergy are trained. Here is a partial list which may help the researcher.

There are Syrian Christian seminaries belonging to the Orthodox, the Mar Thoma and the Roman Catholic Churches in Kottayam, and a Protestant seminary in Trivandrum which have good archives. The largest Roman Catholic holdings are at Vidyajyoti in Delhi and in the Sacred Heart College in Shembaganur (Kodaikanal) in Tamil Nadu. Other major Catholic archives are at the Xavier Centre of Historical Research at Porvorim Alto in Goa; Sadbhavana in Ranchi; Sacred Heart Theological College in Shillong; St. Xavier's College in Mumbai; and Dharmaram College in Bangalore. The offices of the various archbishops spread throughout India also have archives. The largest Protestant archival collections are at United Theological College in Bangalore and at the Brotherhood of the Ascended Christ in Delhi. Other fine collections are at Bishops College in Kolkata and Serampore College (Serampore, West Bengal); Gurukul Lutheran Theological College and the office of the Madras Diocese of the Church of South India in Chennai; and Eastern Theological College in Jorhat, Assam. Protestant materials may also be found in varying quantities at regional language theological seminaries, in Protestant colleges, and at the headquarters of the various Protestant denominations.

CHAPTER 7

Dalit Christian History
*Themes and Trends**

This chapter is designed to address two related questions: how has the field of Dalit Christian history developed since its inception and how has it been integrated into the history of Christianity in India as a whole? It presents a decade-by-decade survey of books, chapters, and independent essays on Dalit Christian history, highlighting those developments—whether of conceptualization, method, or findings—which have shaped the way it has been studied. In addition, the essay assumes that developments in this field of study cannot be separated from the profound changes which have occurred in Indian Christianity; in the situation of Dalit Christians themselves; and in the ways in which Indian history generally, as well as the history of Christianity in India, has been written. It therefore seeks to trace the major themes and trends in writing Dalit Christian history over the past century within that particular historical context. It is confined to academic works in English and gives special emphasis to developments during the last forty years when Dalit Christian history—like Dalit Christians themselves—came into greater prominence.

*Another version of this article will soon be published as 'Dalit Christian History as a Field of Study', in Tanika Sarkar, Pius Malekandathil, and Joy L.K. Pachuau (eds), *Christianity in Indian History: Issues of Culture, Power and Knowledge* (forthcoming).

Early Histories

At the end of the nineteenth century, Christianity in India—whether Protestant or Roman Catholic—was dominated by foreign missionaries.[1] Histories of Christianity were histories of their missions, their work, their personnel, their encounters, their successes and failures. The overriding aim of these missions until the end of World War I was evangelistic. Thereafter, mission and missionary priorities diversified. For some, a new priority under the influence of the social gospel placed emphasis upon educational or social work aimed at cultural and socio-economic change. However, evangelism remained the dominant priority until Independence, but close behind it was the development of self-supporting, self-governing, and self-propagating churches, often by consolidating and further 'Christianizing' the gains of the previous half-century when Christianity experienced remarkable numerical growth.

Most of this numerical growth came from large-scale conversion movements among rural Dalits during the last quarter of the nineteenth and the first third of the twentieth century. These Dalit-initiated movements posed serious problems for the missionaries. For example: 'Should we baptize them?' 'After they have met with what standards?' 'What post-baptismal religious and lifestyle changes should we insist upon?' 'How will we provide regular worship and pastoral care for them?' Nonetheless, these movements also offered reassuring evidence that the missionary endeavours of their church were now bearing significant evangelistic fruit. The stories of those conversion movements, and of the way in which the missions dealt with the issues they raised, have been described in the mission records, missionary conference reports, and denominational mission histories of the period. Julius Richter's *A History of Missions in India* (1906, English translation 1908) used this approach to Dalit Christian history by devoting

1 The Syrian Orthodox churches were the exception, but they stayed aloof from the Dalit Christians and played only a marginal role in their history.

very little space to it and using it to illustrate both missionary success and missionary challenges.[2]

Two major studies written before Independence, departed from this denominational history pattern to treat two themes of general concern in the 1930s. J. Waskom Pickett's *Christian Mass Movements In India* (1933), was written at a time when Gandhi's criticisms of Christian evangelism and its westernizing influence were putting Christians on the defensive.[3] Pickett, a Methodist missionary and later a bishop, used this survey of five mass conversion movements—three of which were Dalit—to examine the motives behind, and consequences of, mass conversion to Christianity. He preferred to call these 'group movements' rather than 'mass movements' because, in his view, their defining characteristic was not size, but a group decision to convert.[4] He saw them spreading along caste lines and, in response to Gandhi, retaining the social integration of the converts. He used history to provide background and contextual information on the conversion movements; on changes in the social and economic conditions of the converts; their motives for conversion; 'Christian attainments'; and images in the eyes of their neighbours. Pickett consolidated his data on the five movements, instead of treating them separately and then comparing them,[5] thus blurring distinctions between Dalit and other converts. He concluded with a set of encouraging

---

2 J. Richter, *A History of Missions in India*, pp. 230–4, 415–17.

3 John C.B. Webster, 'Gandhi and the Christians: Dialogue in the Nationalist Era', in H. Coward (ed.), *Hindu–Christian Dialogue: Perspectives and Encounters* (New Delhi: Motilal Banarsidass Publishers), pp. 80–99.

4 J. Waskom Pickett, *Christian Mass Movements in India*, p. 22.

5 This flaw also involved combining data on first-generation converts with that on fourth-generation Christians, as was pointed out in a review in the 15 March 1934 issue of *The Guardian*, a Christian weekly based in Madras (p. 163). I found that Pickett embellished earlier accounts of the originating conversion of the movement in the Punjab (pp. 44–5), which raises suspicions about the accuracy of the rest of his historical data. See Chapter 4.

assessments and recommendations on how to enhance this aspect of mission work.[6]

'Uplift', the other driving concern of missionaries involved with Dalits, was the subject of A.T. Fishman's *Culture Change and the Underprivileged* (1941), a doctoral thesis in race relations at Yale University. Fishman, a Baptist missionary who had been in charge of an agricultural school in rural Andhra Pradesh, used the Madiga Christians as a case study of culture change. His approach was of necessity historical, his chapters were arranged topically, and he cited personal experience[7] and anecdotal hearsay evidence, along with the customary mission and government records. He saw the missionary in his role as religious teacher, friend, and champion of the Madigas; employer of Madigas; administrator over Madigas; serving also as a transmitter of Western cultural values to a Madiga culture embedded in a village culture dominated by the privileged. To cite one example of culture change resulting from contact with the mission, Fishman argued that several decades of separate education in mission schools had helped prepare Madiga Christians psychologically for education in the integrated rural schools which the government mandated in the late 1930s.[8]

With Indian Independence, the ecclesiastical independence of many churches in India, and the gradual disappearance of the foreign missionary from India, Indian Church history emerged as an alternative to, but not as a substitute for, mission history. Church history was designed to tell the story of how Indian churches came to be the way they were. Two textbooks, published in 1961 and 1972

---

6 A more recent work of this genre is Frederick and Margaret Stock's *People Movements in the Punjab*, written from a church growth perspective rooted in Pickett's work and developed into a body of theory by Donald McGavran. Its concluding chapter provides ten 'Principles Essential for Church Planting Today'.

7 Alvin Texas Fishman, *Culture Change and the Underprivileged: A Study of the Madigas in South India under Christian Guidance* (Madras: Christian Literature Society, 1941), p. 9.

8 Ibid., pp. 48–9, 198. His approach parallels that in L.S.S. O'Malley's *Modern India and the West* (London, New York: Oxford University Press, 1941).

respectively, illustrate this kind of history. Both traced the political and structural development as well as the cultural 'Indianization' not only of the Protestant, the Catholic and the Syrian churches, but also of the ecumenical movement in India to conclude their histories. In both histories, Dalit Christian history was confined to brief treatments of Dalit conversion movements.[9]

This brief overview of the treatment of Dalit Christian history up into the 1970s sets the stage for what is to follow. Up to that point, Dalit Christian history was only a minor subplot in the much larger stories of either missions or churches, and it was virtually equated with Dalit conversion movements to Christianity. In this perspective, what Dalits contributed to Christian history was numbers, diversity, and challenges for the dominant missionaries and Christian élites. However, the period did produce two major studies of what would become continuing themes of Dalit Christian history—conversion and cultural change—along with considerable source materials for future historians to work with.

THE 1970S

In the 1970s, Dalit Christian history began to appear in books and articles more frequently than before. Three important changes that had occurred since Independence created the conditions which made such a development possible. One was that the Indian academic community took an increased interest in the Indian history of Christianity. Not only did doctoral theses on the subject begin to appear from Indian university history departments but the theological seminaries also began to encourage more advanced research in the field by introducing Master of Theology and, then, doctoral degree programmes. The Church History Association of India was revitalized and, in 1967, began publishing the *Indian Church History Review*, which included many of the early articles

9 Cyril Bruce Firth, *An Introduction to Indian Church History*, pp. 194–8. Achilles Meersman, 'The Catholic Church in India since the Mid-Nineteenth Century', in H.C. Perumalil and E.R. Hambye (eds), *Christianity in India*, p. 253; T.V. Philip, 'Protestant Christianity in India since 1858', in ibid., pp. 271–2.

on Dalit Christian history. Thus, the history of Christianity in India became a subject of broader academic (and not just 'churchly') interest shaped by the standards and changing ethos of the academy.

With increased academic interest came a re-examination of, and diversity in, the perspectives from which the history of Christianity in India was to be written. When the Church History Association of India decided to publish a multi-volume history of Christianity in India, the 'New Perspective' of its editorial board reflected the more widespread interest of that time in modernization, social change, and social history. It explicitly rejected both the mission history and church history perspectives and opted for a socio-cultural approach instead. While this 'New Perspective' was in keeping with the concurrent search for Indian roots in developing new Christian theological formulations, it was not binding on everyone carrying out research on the history of Christianity. However, it did have a fairly immediate impact on the kind of research being conducted at least through the theological seminaries in India.

The third development during the 1970s was a noticeable rise in assertiveness among some Dalit church leaders. They made the plight of Dalit Christians an issue of concern within both the churches and the wider public arena, by pointing to instances of blatant discrimination against Dalit Christians not only in society at large—which treated them no differently from other Dalits—but also in the churches and the Christian community. They also charged the Government of India with religious discrimination in the Presidential Order (Scheduled Castes) 1950, which granted Scheduled Caste benefits to Hindu (and later, to Sikh and Buddhist) Dalits but not to them.[10] This controversy, and the court cases which followed, was to stimulate social science and historical research on the changing situation of Dalit Christians, vis-à-vis, both other Dalits and other Christians in various parts of India.

One notices in the 1970s a considerable increase in the amount of Dalit Christian history being written, whether as portions of

10 A description is provided in John C.B. Webster, *The Dalit Christians: A History*, 3rd ed. (Delhi: ISPCK, 2007), pp. 235–8.

larger studies or as important subjects in their own right. Virtually all of it concentrated upon Protestants during the nineteenth century and focused upon large-scale Dalit conversion movements to Christianity. Most of it also continued to use a mission history framework, but devoted far more space to Dalit Christians than had earlier works. For example, between 1970 and 1983, James P. Alter wrote a series of articles in the *Indian Church History Review* on Anglicans in Meerut, Presbyterians in Farrukhabad, and Methodists in Moradabad, which were later revised and appeared together in a book.[11] In them, he traced the history of these missions from their inception in the early- to mid-nineteenth century up to World War I. All three missions experienced Dalit conversion movements which Alter described in some detail. In his portraits of the rural Dalit Christian communities created by those movements, he addressed the question not only of how sharp a break converts made from their former caste *biradaris*, customs and religious beliefs, but also how the missions had to adjust their educational and medical work to deal with this rural Dalit presence in their churches.

In another mission history, Sundararaj Manickam, a Dalit Christian who became Head of the History Department at Madurai Kamraj University, used an input–impact framework while studying Methodist missionaries in the Tanjore–Trichinopoly area of the Madras Presidency. Missionary inputs were primarily evangelistic, educational, and medical. Their impact—especially upon Dalit communities—was assessed with reference to the creation of a Christian church and community, leadership development, education, community development, and social reform. Manickam took on the critics of Christian evangelism and Dalit motives for conversion in a lengthy chapter on the Dalit mass movements that focused upon the converts themselves; their reasons for conversion; the dynamics of their conversion movements; the forms of opposition they faced; and, in the end, the kind of responses they

11 These appeared in the December 1970, December 1975, June 1976, December 1976, December 1982, and June 1983 issues. The book is *In the Doab and Rohilkhand: North Indian Christianity 1815–1915*, revised and completed by John Alter (Delhi: ISPCK, 1986).

evoked from the Methodists. Because the converts from these movements were Adi Dravidas as well as Madharis, Manickam addressed the issue of inter-caste relations among Dalit Christians as one of the carry-overs from their past.[12]

Another important contributor to Dalit Christian history at this stage was Geoffrey A. Oddie of the University of Sydney. He wrote an early essay on Protestant missionary attitudes towards caste inside as well as outside the churches which impacted the laws (for example, concerning the use of public wells and roads) affecting Dalit Christian lives,[13] and later carried out a more detailed study of a late-nineteenth-century missionary agitation in the Madras Presidency to gain land and educational opportunities for Dalits.[14] However, his most direct contribution to Dalit Christian history was an essay on a Dalit conversion movement among the Malas and then the Madigas in Andhra Pradesh. He described the course and the main features of this movement, explaining how it spread (noting that it tended to do so from the economically independent Dalits to those who were less so), the forms of opposition it faced, and the reasons why so many chose to convert.[15]

While Alter and Manickam placed their Dalit conversion movements within a larger narrative of the development of the Christian community, and Oddie was more interested in large-scale conversion movements as such, all three approached Dalit conversion movements in similar ways. They combined narrative accounts of the origins and the spread of these movements with

12 Sundararaj Manickam, *The Social Setting of Christian Conversion in South India*, pp. 92, 192–7.

13 'Protestant Missions, Caste and Social Change in India', *Indian Economic and Social History Review*, vol. VI (September 1969), pp. 259–91. Duncan B. Forrester's 'Indian Christian Attitudes to Caste in the Twentieth Century', *Indian Church History Review*, vol. IX (June 1975), pp. 3–22 has a similar relevance.

14 *Social Protest in India: British Protestant Missionaries and Social Reforms, 1850–1900* (New Delhi: Manohar, 1979), pp. 128–46. See also Raj Sekhar Basu, '"Rights over Wastelands" and New Narratives of the Paraiyan Past (1860–1900)', *Studies in History*, 24:2 (2008), pp. 265–93.

15 Geoffrey A. Oddie, 'Christian Conversions in the Telugu Country 1860–1900'.

analyses of motives and reasons for conversion; the obstacles faced; the continuities with and the changes from the pre-conversion past; as well as missionary responses to the challenges these conversion movements posed. Two other studies from the 1970s took different approaches. J.W. Gladstone simply used the agitation of London Missionary Society missionaries for the social liberation of the lower castes—and especially for the 1855 proclamation setting the slave castes free—as the context for the subsequent Dalit conversion movement in South Travancore.[16] Duncan Forrester noted that, after 1860, Dalit mass conversion was a widespread phenomenon in India, and he sought to figure out why this was so. This led him to ask the following questions: 'Why was there such an upsurge of discontent among the depressed classes from the middle of the nineteenth century onwards?' 'Why this restlessness so largely sought a religious form of expression, or why it flowed towards Christianity in particular, and initially towards the Protestant form of Christianity?'[17] He sought answers primarily in the dislocations caused by the Western impact upon rural society which allowed Dalit aspirations to surface; in the fact that those aspirations were not just economic;[18] in the fact that Protestant missionaries were very anti-caste; and in the fact that the Protestants were the first to respond to Dalit aspirations. He cited a number of diverse examples, not all Dalit, to develop his answers.

These forays into Dalit Christian history were made by Christian historians interested in Christian history, some of whom were seeking a readership wider than the Christian community

16 J.W. Gladstone, '19th Century Mass Movement in South Travancore—A Result of Social Liberation', *Indian Church History Review*, vol. X (June 1976), p. 60.

17 Duncan B. Forrester, 'The Depressed Classes and Conversion to Christianity, 1860–1960', in Geoffrey A. Oddie (ed.), *Religion in South Asia*, pp. 40–1. This was later incorporated, in a revised form as a chapter in his *Caste and Christianity*, pp. 69–96.

18 'The search for material improvement or enhancement of status is seldom, if ever, the sole or even the dominant motive in a mass movement. Dignity, self-respect, patrons who will treat one as an equal, and the ability to choose one's own destiny—all these are powerful incentives to conversion'. Ibid., pp. 42–3.

itself. Clearly, group conversions and their immediate aftermath—which constituted the origins of Dalit Christian history—were the dominant theme in Dalit Christian history writing at this stage. These histories provided some short, discreet, well-researched case studies from both north and south India, and a fresh overview. In them, Pickett's main assumptions—that these were movements characterized by group decisions which spread along caste lines and retained the converts' social integration—were often cited and retained, but his classification of the diverse motivations for conversion as spiritual, secular, social, and natal[19] was dropped. Historians of the 1980s and beyond were now in a better position than before to understand, compare, and make generalizations about the large-scale rural Dalit conversion movements of the late nineteenth and early twentieth centuries.

THE 1980S

Dalit Christian assertiveness continued to increase during the 1980s. Two events were of particular importance in framing the ways in which Dalit Christian history came to be written. One was the Soosai case which went all the way to the Supreme Court. Soosai, a Catholic Adi Dravida cobbler in Madras, was denied access to a welfare scheme on the grounds that, as a Christian, he was not deemed to belong to a scheduled caste. In deciding the case, the Supreme Court declared,

> To establish that paragraph 3 of the Constitution (Scheduled Castes) Order, 1950, discriminates against Christian members of the enumerated castes, it must be shown that they suffer from a comparable depth of social and economic disabilities and cultural and educational backwardness and similar levels of degradation within the Christian community necessitating intervention by the State under the provisions of the Constitution. It is not sufficient to show that the same caste continues after conversion. It is necessary to establish further that the disabilities and handicaps suffered from such caste membership in the

19 J. Waskom Pickett, *Christian Mass Movements in India*, p. 164.

social order of its origin—Hinduism—continue in their oppressive severity in the new environment of a different religious community.[20]

The other event was the development of Dalit liberation theology during the course of the decade. A conference in December 1986 marked its official arrival on the theological scene,[21] and its influence was to increase during the coming decades. Like other liberation theologies, Dalit theology adopted a conflict model of society, but treated caste as the major divide between oppressor and oppressed in Indian society. These two events encouraged the setting of Dalit Christian history within a liberation framework and making comparisons between Christian and Scheduled Caste Dalits an integral part of that history.

In the 1980s, conversion studies continued to hold a prominent place in Dalit Christian history, but one finds some forays not only into political history but also into the key issues of social mobility and of caste in the churches. The twentieth century also received more attention than previously. While the history of Dalit Christians continued to be placed within mission and church history frameworks, it was beginning to be studied as important in its own right.

Two major conversion studies added significantly to understanding that aspect of Dalit Christian history. J.W. Gladstone's *Protestant Christianity and People's Movements in Kerala* (1984) not only added Travancore to the regions under study but also took a somewhat different approach to Dalit conversion movements. He set large-scale Dalit conversions to Christianity alongside other oppressed people's movements which were also aimed at social emancipation and saw these movements going through three phases. In the first phase, conversion movements to Christianity progressed without competition, but not without opposition. In the second, there came the rise of neo-Hindu social

20 Jose Kananaikil (ed.), *Scheduled Castes in Search of Justice, Part II: The Verdict of the Supreme Court* (New Delhi: Indian Social Institute, 1986), p. 49.

21 The papers were published in M.E. Prabhakar (ed.), *Towards a Dalit Theology* (Delhi: ISPCK, 1988).

and religious movements which, like the conversion movements, developed within the boundaries of caste. The third saw more organized and active Hindu, as well as nationalist, opposition to the missionaries' evangelistic work, culminating in the temple entry proclamation of 1936 which brought the conversion movements to an end. Gladstone placed special emphasis upon Dalit initiative and agency in these movements as well as upon the opposition they faced, not just from caste Hindus but also from Syrian Christians. Dick Kooiman, who studied conversion movements in South Travancore, was basically in agreement with Gladstone in considering those movements to be aimed at socio-economic improvement, but with the caveat that there was so much moving back and forth across religious boundaries that 'change of religion often amounted to a change of emphasis from one trend to another within a larger religious complex'.[22] Lancy Lobo was in basic agreement that the desire for both aspects of social emancipation was what motivated the Vankars in central Gujarat who became Catholics in the early twentieth century well after the famine years.[23]

The main interest of Kooiman and Lobo, however, was in the relationship between conversion to Christianity and social mobility or social equality—an emerging theme in the 1980s. Kooiman's basic question was not so much about continuities and discontinuities with the pre-conversion past, but with whether—and to what extent—low-caste converts to Christianity gained the social mobility and equality which they were seeking through conversion. He therefore examined education, employment, the fight against civil disabilities, and cultural change during the course of the nineteenth century. When drawing conclusions, Kooiman distinguished between the Shanar and the 'slave caste' converts more in the economic than in the cultural sphere. The former were better positioned to take advantage of the new economic opportunities

22 Dick Kooiman, *Conversion and Social Equality in India. The London Missionary Society in South Travancore in the 19th Century*, p. 82.

23 Lancy Lobo, 'Conversion, Emigration and Social Mobility of an Ex-Scheduled Caste from Central Gujarat', *Social Action*, vol. 39 (October–December 1989), pp. 423–37.

which were opening up under colonial rule and the cash economy, although many of the latter migrated to coffee plantations and even to Ceylon for the higher wages being offered there. In the area of cultural change, Kooiman used 'caste relations, marriage customs, folk religion, and the use of the Sabbath day' as indicators to discover the extent to which 'the customs of the south Travancore Christians were determined by their old or their new faith'.[24] He concluded that their traditional values were the more influential of the two. Lobo found that those Catholic converts who migrated to Mumbai did not get the social emancipation they sought; most continued in the same occupations as other urban Dalits and ran into caste discrimination within the churches.[25]

Both Gladstone and Kooiman devoted space in their histories to an issue which attracted considerable attention in the 1980s: caste in the Christian churches and community, especially in Kerala and Tamil Nadu. With regard to Kerala, however, they were preceded by Forrester who saw the Syrian Christians functioning as a caste, not in their theological convictions, but in the operative norms on which their behaviour was based. When faced with the egalitarian challenges posed by conversions from lower castes, including the slave castes, they were adamant in preferring to retain a high status image rather than mixing fully and freely with these fellow Christians. This priority persisted, despite some individual attitude changes, up to the time of writing (1980) in Catholic, Syrian Orthodox, and Protestant churches.[26] In his treatment of this subject, Gladstone focused on the triangle of missionaries, Syrian Christians, and Dalit Christians, with the missionaries favouring the Syrians over the Dalit majority until, finally in 1907, many of the Dalits rebelled and joined the Salvation Army

---

24 Dick Kooiman, *Conversion and Social Equality in India*, p. 171.

25 Lancy Lobo, 'Conversion, Emigration and Social Mobility of an Ex-Scheduled Caste from Central Gujarat'.

26 Duncan B. Forrester, *Caste and Christianity*, pp. 97–117. For a more detailed account of the Syrian Christians and caste, see Susan Bayly, *Saints, Goddesses and Kings: Muslims and Christians in South Indian Society, 1700–1900*, pp. 241–320.

as well as the Plymouth Brethren.[27] According to Kooiman, in the London Missionary Society area of South Travancore caste feeling was equally high, with Christians of all jatis discriminating, but the Nadars, rather than the Syrian Christians, came to dominate. The result, however, was no different. Many Paraya and Pulaya Christians left the London Missionary Society churches for the Salvation Army around the turn of the century.[28]

With regard to Tamil Nadu, there were two case studies covering the nineteenth-century history of this issue in two areas where Dalits constituted a significant portion of the Christian population. Like Kooiman, Oddie sought to find out whether Christians in the Kaveri Delta 'continued to follow Hindu tradition and social customs, or were developing a social system and style of life recognizably different from Hindus',[29] by examining marriage practices in particular. He found that, despite differing histories with the issue during the course of the century, caste practices continued into the new century among Catholics, Lutherans, Anglicans, and Methodists alike. Immanuel David found that the Reformed Church missionaries in North and South Arcot districts took a hard line against caste distinctions and practices in their churches, but he could not determine how successful this policy was in achieving its aims.[30] In nearby Mysore, also during the nineteenth century, Henry Wilson found Wesleyan missionaries seeking to develop a church in which caste distinctions were absent. This worked well when individuals or nuclear families converted. However, when

27 J.W. Gladstone, *Protestant Christianity and People's Movements in Kerala*, pp. 123–38.

28 Dick Kooiman, *Conversion and Social Equality in India*, pp. 172–8.

29 Geoffrey A. Oddie, 'Christianity in the Indian Crucible: Continuity and Change in the Kaveri Delta, 1850–1900', *Indian Church History Review*, vol. XV (June 1981), p. 48. He later attributed the Dalit conversions and continued existence as Christians in the region only to the Dalit desire for patrons to protect themselves in uncertain times but also to their growing awareness of their own rights and worth. *Hindu and Christian in South-East India*, pp. 153–69.

30 Immanuel David, *Reformed Church in America Missionaries in South India, 1839–1938: An Analytical Study* (Bangalore: Asian Trading Corporation, 1986), pp. 111–18.

larger numbers of low-caste people came in, they faced constant caste quarrels, not just between Dalits and non-Dalits, but between members of different Dalit jatis as well.[31]

The other theme to emerge in the 1980s was Dalit Christian involvement in politics, mostly as victims but also as actors. Both Susan Billington Harper and I wrote lengthy essays on Christian involvement in the political debates concerning the Dalits from Gandhi's 1932 fast in opposition to the Communal Award until the end of the 1930s. By then, the institution of separate electorates had politicized conversion by making a change of religion a change of political constituency as well. Her essay focused on the controversy between Gandhi and Bishop V.S. Azariah of Dornakal over Christian evangelism among the Dalits. Both had allied in opposition to separate electorates but their alliance was undercut, first, by Ambedkar's declaration (1935), and then by the Izhavas threat to convert (1936), as well as by the National Christian Council's 1935 commitment to a five-year evangelistic campaign among the Dalits.[32] My essay dealt with the national debate as recorded not only in the Christian press but also in *The Indian Social Reformer* and in *Harijan*, and its immediate impact upon Dalit Christians.[33] While both essays described the controversy among the élite with only marginal Dalit Christian input, their impact upon the Dalit Christians' immediate and future prospects of receiving Scheduled Caste benefits, was considerable. Dr Jose Kananaikil of the Indian Social Institute not only wrote a short history of the Dalit Christians which placed special emphasis upon their Scheduled Caste status, particularly in the post-Independence period, but also edited a

31 H.S. Wilson, 'Involvement of the Wesleyan Kanarese Mission in the Mysore Territory in the Nineteenth Century', *Indian Church History Review*, vol. XX (June 1986), pp. 60–4.

32 Susan Billington Harper, 'The Politics of Conversion: The Azariah–Gandhi Controversy over Christian Mission to the Depressed Classes in the 1930s', *Indo-British Review*, XV:1 (n.d.), pp. 147–75.

33 John C.B. Webster, 'Christians and the Depressed Classes in the 1930s', in D.N. Panigrahi (ed.), *Economy, Society and Politics in Modern India* (New Delhi: Vikas, 1985), pp. 313–44.

series of booklets documenting three key government decisions in their struggle for justice.[34]

By the end of the decade, Dalit Christian history was emerging from a kind of Christian intellectual ghetto and engaging a wider readership on cultural and political issues of broader national concern. Gladstone, Harper and I made initial attempts to connect Dalit Christian history to Dalit history, a field which, itself, was only in its very early stages. In addition, Dalit Christian history was getting more directly connected to some of the central issues in the current Dalit Christian struggle, as was evident in Kananaikil's work and my own.

THE 1990S

Politically, the 1990s began on an optimistic note with a huge rally in New Delhi aimed at getting the government to grant Scheduled Caste status to Dalit Christians. This was followed by a series of smaller rallies and demonstrations on the same issue throughout most of the decade, but the government failed to make the desired change. The decade ended with the Bharatiya Janata Party in power and more acts of anti-Christian violence being committed than India had experienced in the entire fifty years since Independence. Meanwhile, Indian historians had already written monographs on Dalit history which provided both models and invaluable contextual information for those writing about Christian Dalits.[35]

34 Jose Kananaikil, *Christians of Scheduled Caste Origin* (New Delhi: Indian Social Institute, 1983); Jose Kananaikil, *Scheduled Castes in Search of Justice. Part I: Knocking at the Door of the Lok Sabha; Part II: The Verdict of the Supreme Court; Part III: Constitution (Scheduled Castes) Orders (Amendment) Bill, 1990* (New Delhi: Indian Social Institute, 1986, 1986, 1993).

35 Surveys of this literature are to be found in John C.B. Webster, 'Understanding the Modern Dalit Movement', *Sociological Bulletin*, vol. 45 (September 1996), pp. 189–204; and 'Towards Understanding the Modern Dalit Movement', *The Fourth World*, vol. 7 (April 1998), pp. 13–36; Yagati Chinna Rao, 'Dalits and History Writing in India: Some Historiographical Trends and Questions', in Sabyasachi Bhattacharya (ed.), *Approaches to History: Essays in Indian Historiography*, pp. 323–43.

Most of the studies cited so far had used the denominational mission as the basic unit of study. This decade began with three general histories which both built upon the earlier studies already described and contained fresh research on Dalit Christian history. The first of these was Hugald Grafe's more ecumenical history of Christianity in Tamil Nadu in the nineteenth and twentieth centuries which was part of the Church History Association of India's multi-volume history of Christianity in India written from its 'New Perspective' described earlier. Grafe arranged his chapters topically. Dalit Christians appear in those devoted to the Christian people and to the induction of social change. The first dealt with motives for conversion, in which Dalit motivations were not differentiated from the motives of other rural converts who came in large numbers, and caste conflict, which covered much the same ground as Oddie and Forrester, but also described Dalit-initiated, twentieth-century caste conflicts in Catholic churches. The chapter on social change devoted an entire section to the uplift of the depressed classes. These uplift measures included agitation for land, opening up educational opportunities to Dalits, and attempts to end caste pride within the Christian churches.[36] In a thesis cited by Grafe and later published as a book, Franklyn Balasundaram set the work of the London Missionary Society among the Dalits in Tamil Nadu from 1919 to 1939 in the context of a developing Dalit movement and the 'Dalit uplift' efforts of other agencies. His account of London Missionary Society's 'uplift' efforts included educational, medical, rural reconstruction, and women's work among Dalits generally, as well as efforts to develop leadership and self-reliance among Dalit Christians.[37]

The second general history was my *The Dalit Christians: A History*[38] which used all of India as its unit of study and was set in

36 Hugald Grafe, *History of Christianity in India: Volume 4, Part 2: Tamilnadu in the Nineteenth and Twentieth Centuries.*

37 Franklyn J. Balasundaram, *Dalits and Christian Mission in the Tamil Country: The Dalit Movement and Protestant Christians in the Tamil Speaking Districts of Madras Presidency 1919–1939 with Special Reference to London Missionary Society Area in Salem, Attur, Coimbatore and Erode* (Bangalore: Asian Trading Corporation, 1997).

38 Delhi: ISPCK, 1992.

the context of the history of the modern Dalit movement. This I saw passing through three phases, the first of which began in the late nineteenth century and included the mass movements. I challenged Pickett's definition of these movements as *characterized by*—I preferred to say 'as *including*'—group decisions to convert. I saw those conversion movements initiated and sustained by Dalit agency passing through several stages with different motivations operative at each stage. By the beginning of the twentieth century they had succeeded in making the Dalit issue a public issue which could no longer be ignored, especially after communal electorates were introduced in 1909.[39] The Montagu Declaration of 1917 ushered in a new phase of the Dalit movement which was mostly political and focused on the issue of representation. Thanks to the rigid categories which the British used for classifying Indians, Dalit Christians were placed in the Christian rather than the Scheduled Caste constituency, without really being consulted. This kind of inflexible communal thinking carried over into the third phase initiated, first, by the 1950 Constitution with its provisions for compensatory discrimination and, then, by the Presidential Order which limited Scheduled Caste status to Hindus. This led me to set the post-Independence history of the Dalit Christians alongside that of the Dalit beneficiaries of compensatory discrimination with regard to social change, political action and, in the case of the Christians, caste in the churches. A concluding chapter described how the Dalit presence changed the ways in which the Christian gospel came to be articulated in each of these phases.[40]

39 The last two points, I spelled out in some detail with reference to the Punjab in 'Large-Scale Conversions to Christianity in Late Nineteenth Century Punjab as an Early Dalit Movement', in Chetan Singh (ed.), *Social Transformation in North-Western India during the Twentieth Century* (New Delhi: Manohar, 2010), pp. 343–58.

40 Later in the decade, I traced the history of the village catechist-teacher as a leader and sustainer of the Dalit conversion movement in the Punjab from its inception until after Independence. 'Leadership in a Rural Dalit Conversion Movement', in Joseph T. O'Connell (ed.), *Organizational and Institutional Aspects of Indian Religious Movements* (Delhi: Manohar, 1999) pp. 96–112.

A third general history was James Massey's *Dalits in India*, the major thrust of which was given in the subtitle: *Religion as a Source of Bondage or Liberation, with Special Reference to Christians.*[41] Massey, a well-known Dalit Christian activist, defined the problem which Dalit Christians faced in the following terms:

> As we have seen, by the Constitution (Scheduled Castes) Order, 1950, the Christian Dalits on the basis of religion have been deprived of their basic human rights including the constitutional fundamental rights, which the Constitution gives to other Dalits who profess Hinduism, Sikhism, or Buddhism. Not only are they deprived of their basic rights of equality in Indian society, they are also equally deprived of their rights within the Christian Church or society.[42]

Massey used history to explain why 'Dalits continue to suffer oppression even after joining a very egalitarian religion like Christianity',[43]—a very important question in the light of the Soosai case mentioned earlier. His own outline history of and commentary on the Dalit Christian past concentrated almost exclusively upon missionary policies and practices which he saw as primarily responsible for the Dalit Christians' failure to gain 'their equal human dignity or basic rights'.[44] This was compounded by the government's failure to give Christian Dalits, because of their religion, the 'full fundamental and protection rights' granted under the Constitution to other Dalits.[45] Dalit Christian history was, in this view, almost completely a history of deliberate and unconscious victimization. Massey concluded with some strategic proposals to turn that situation around.

This decade also witnessed the first major histories of Roman Catholic Dalits, all of which made use of the comparative method, albeit in different ways. David Mosse adopted a historical anthropological approach to the issue of long-term social mobility among Catholic, Protestant, and Hindu Dalits belonging to several castes

---

41 James Massey, *Dalts in India: Religion as a Source of Bondage or Liberation, with Special Reference to Christians* (Delhi: Manohar, 1995).

42 Ibid., p. 81.

43 Ibid., p. 84.

44 Ibid., p. 113.

45 Ibid., p. 144.

in one Tamil village. However, his main focus was upon the Pallar Catholics who, along with their Maravar overlords, had converted back in the seventeenth century and since then were the most mobile Dalit group in the village. They gained a greater degree of economic independence than had other Dalits there. Not only were they making lifestyle changes in dress and diet but they were also either withdrawing from or redefining those service tasks in the economic and festival life of the village which expressed caste inferiority. In addition, they took advantage of opportunities for occupational mobility which the missionaries opened up to them; they claimed equal caste honours and privileges within the Church and at Christian festivals until these were granted. Following Independence, they organized agitations against untouchability and some even joined the more egalitarian Pentecostal church. All these strategies seemed aimed at emphasizing a separate and distinct identity 'not dependent upon established social relationships'.[46]

Henriette Bugge drew upon Mosse's earlier work elsewhere in her *Mission and Tamil Society*. She set her chapter on the late-nineteenth-century Dalit mass movements in South Arcot district within the context of changing power relationships in rural society, and compared the conversion movements with which the Danish [Lutheran] Missionary Society and (Roman Catholic) Paris Foreign Missionary Society were involved. She found that, in the former case, mass conversions had taken place in those villages where relations between the dominant castes and the Dalits were most polarized. In the latter case, the missionaries established a custom of temporal assistance to inquirers and converts as compensation for lost daily wages even before the 1877–8 famine. In both cases, converts sought new patrons who would be more benevolent and reliable than their village patrons. Bugge concluded that, because the Catholics 'went a long way towards providing the converts with a new corporate identity without disengaging them from their social background' (which the Lutherans did not), 'the

46 David Mosse, 'Idioms of Subordination and Styles of Protest among Christian and Hindu Harijan Castes in Tamil Nadu', *Contributions to Indian Sociology*, 28:1 (n.s.) (1994), p. 101.

Roman Catholic policy of accommodation in the long run was better suited to support changes within the system than the Protestant
policy of unquestioning rejection of the caste system'.[47] That is one
side of the story. The other is provided by Kenneth Ballhatchet's
survey of nineteenth-century Roman Catholic attitudes towards
caste in which he compared Carmelites in Kerala, Carmelites in
Bombay, Capuchins and Irish missionaries in Madras, as well as
French Jesuits in Tamil Nadu. He found that, while the general
tendency was to avoid offending high-caste Catholics, the Irish in
Madras were an exception. Indeed, it was in Madras and Tamil
Nadu, where serious caste discrimination was built into the very
architecture and ceremonial life of the churches, that caste conflicts
among Christians, in which Dalits were involved in conjunction
with the Paravas and the Shanars, were most prevalent.[48] Oddie,
in a short essay on the link between conversion and social mobility, concluded on the basis of his own and the other Tamil Nadu
studies mentioned so far, that conversion led to little or no social
mobility for Dalit converts who remained in their villages, but did
lead to some mobility among those who migrated to urban areas
and took on caste-neutral occupations there.[49]

Like Mosse and Bugge, Gunnel Cederlof focused on the impact
which Dalit kinship-based conversion movements had upon social
relationships within village communities. *Bonds Lost* is a study of
'the major characteristics of the relationship between the Goundar
and Madhari communities, on the one hand, with regard to the
division of labour and the control over and distribution of the
resources of agricultural production and, on the other, with regard

---

47 Henriette Bugge, *Mission and Tamil Society*, p. 178. See also her
'The French Mission and Mass Movements', in Geoffrey A. Oddie (ed.),
*Religious Conversion Movements in South Asia: Continuities and Change,
1800–1900*, pp. 97–108.

48 Kenneth Ballhatchet, *Caste, Class and Catholicism in India 1789–
1914*, pp. 104–40.

49 Geoffrey A. Oddie, 'Christianity and Social Mobility in South India
1840–1920: A Continuing Debate', *South Asia*, vol. XIX (Special Issue
1996), pp. 143–59.

to local power relations'.[50] Hence, her questions about Madhari (and Paraiyar) conversions were what they meant and how they affected those relationships within the village communities of Coimbatore district. For her, the most important of these questions was, 'Did the presence of mission representatives in the village make a difference to the relationship between the Goundar and Madhari communities?'[51] This, she sought to answer, first, by finding out how well the representatives of the missions became integrated into the social life and relationships of the village. She then asked whether their presence and the Madhari decisions to convert in large numbers reinforced or threatened prevailing Goundar–Madhari relationships. Finally she asked, 'whether expressed in themes or practices, did the ideology of the mission present a viable alternative to an ideology that ascribed the lowest position in the social hierarchy to the Madhari, as well as their identity as leather-workers and agricultural labourers?'[52] Each of these main questions had its own subset of questions and her findings—while not easily summarized—do tend to reinforce those of earlier studies. Even though the presence in the village of a church with its alternative ideology, rituals, and outside relationships did not in fact change Goundar–Madhari relationships much, the Goundars did perceive it as a threat. Cederlof concluded by saying that 'the Madhari who chose to convert found an additional place outside the village and its hierarchical relationships to anchor themselves in. The identity ascribed to them by local society had to carry a new component' (that is, the Christian).[53]

Two scholars who published several essays on Dalit Christian history during this period were George Oommen and Saurabh

50 Gunnel Cederlof, *Bonds Lost: Subordination, Conflict and Mobilisation in Rural South India c. 1900–1970* (Delhi: Manohar, 1997), p. 5.

51 Ibid., p. 164.

52 Ibid., p. 166.

53 Ibid., pp. 226–7. In a later essay, she compared Paraiyar and Madhari conversion movements and attributed the differences between them to the fact that the latter were more locked into the village economy and thus less mobile than the former. Paraiyar conversions seemed to be driven by a desire for social mobility, whereas the Madhari, whose

Dube. Oommen wrote his doctoral dissertation on the Anglican Pulayas in Kerala under Oddie's supervision. His first essay dealt with the impact which the Communist movement had upon them as well as with the way they responded to it during the 1940s and 1950s. Contact began with Pulaya Anglican participation in the Travancore Agricultural Labour Union, and moved from there to involvement in Communist agitations and then to viewing the Communist Party of India as 'their party', championing their interests and including some of 'their' people in leadership positions. In the 1959 'liberation struggle', Pulaya Anglicans remained very loyal to their church but sided with the Communists rather than with their Syrian Christian co-religionists.[54] Oommen's other two essays dealt with Pulaya conversions. He opened one by stating that previous historians had not given adequate attention to the 'elements of protest and remonstrance' in Dalit conversion movements.[55] He then proceeded to show how, both among Pulayas in general and in their conversion movement, there was widespread resistance to and protest against landlord oppression, to which Anglican missionaries responded. His other essay focused on 'the nature of gospel communication and the role of ideas during and in the follow-up of the Dalit conversion movements in central Kerala'.[56] He found that the communication of Christian teachings

conversion faced stiffer Goundar opposition, sought a new identity 'derived from outside and beyond village control'. 'Social Mobilization among People Competing at the Bottom Level of Society: The Presence of Missions in Rural South India, ca 1900–1950', in Robert Eric Frykenberg (ed.), *Christians and Missionaries in India*, p. 351.

54 George Oommen, 'Communist Influence on Dalit Christians— The Kerala Experience', *Bangalore Theological Forum*, XXVI: 3 and 4 (September and December 1994), pp. 43–62; reprinted in Francis Kanichikattil (ed.), *Church in Context: Essays in Honour of Mathias Mundadan*, pp. 31–55.

55 George Oommen, 'Dalit Conversion and Social Protest in Travancore 1854–1890', *Bangalore Theological Forum*, vol. XXVIII (September–December 1996), p. 69.

56 George Oommen, 'Strength of Tradition and Weakness of Communication: Central Kerala Dalit Conversion', in Geoffrey A. Oddie (ed.), *Religious Conversion Movements in South Asia*, p. 79.

during the (often two-year) 'probation' period prior to baptism was weak. In addition to facing language or translation barriers, Christian teaching did not fit into prior Pulaya systems of religious belief and practice which continued after baptism. Pulayas liked the idea of a god of love and equality who was more powerful than the evil spirits, but Oommen concluded that 'sociological rather than cosmological factors were of primary importance in the conversion process'.[57]

Saurabh Dube's study of the encounter between the missionaries of the German Evangelical Mission Society and the (Dalit) Satnamis of Chhattisgarh was a study in missionary colonialism set in the Christian settlement of Bisrampur, where the missionary functioned as landlord, pastor, and bearer of 'civilization'. Dube attributed the conversion of Satnamis to Christianity less to an affinity of beliefs (one God, no idolatry, no caste) than to the power of kinship and a desire to share the benefits of the settlement's benevolent and paternalistic economy. Most of his essay was devoted to a Christian rebellion against missionary decisions in which he explored the very contrary, culturally conditioned, ways of thinking which the protagonists displayed.[58] Dube later covered the same initial ground in sections of his history of the Satnamis and added a section on the Christian apologetic used to explain how Christ fulfilled what Ghasidas, the original Satnami guru, and Satnam Panth were really all about.[59]

Three other works from this decade deserve mention here. M.E. Prabhakar set the life and work of the great Telugu poet, Samrat Gurram Joshua (1895–1971) in the context of both Joshua's Dalit background and his Christian faith. Prabhakar concluded with some reflections on the light which Joshua sheds on current

57 Ibid., p. 93.

58 Saurabh Dube, 'Paternalism and Freedom: The Evangelical Encounter in Colonial Chhattisgarh, Central India', *Modern Asian Studies*, 29:1 (1995), pp. 171–201.

59 Saurabh Dube, *Untouchable Pasts: Religion, Identity, and Power among a Central Indian Community, 1780–1950* (Albany: State University of New York Press, 1998), pp. 70–7, 193–204, 211–3.

Dalit Christian issues.[60] Samuel Jayakumar's study of Anglican approaches to conversion in Tinnevelly was marred by a running polemic against Dalit liberation theologians and by a questionable inclusion of Nadars among the Dalits. Nevertheless, it contains useful information on conversion, caste conflict, and their impact upon Dalit Christian consciousness in that part of Tamil Nadu.[61] Finally, F. Hrangkhuma edited a volume of essays—the major thrust of which was more missiological than historical—on conversion movements among a number of selected caste and tribal groups. Only two essays on Dalits, one on Dalits in North India by James Massey and the other on Mahars in Maharashtra by Atul Y. Aghamkar, provide introductory histories.[62]

By the end of the twentieth century, Dalit Christian history had become a well-established field of study. It had made its way into the curriculum as an elective subject with a widely used textbook in at least the Protestant theological seminaries in India. Research in the field had not only broadened well beyond its nineteenth-century Protestant-missionary base, but it also included more themes than conversion movements and the initial continuities and changes in the lives of the converts. It moved more and more out of the domain of exclusively Christian history, and its connections with Dalit history increased significantly. While Kerala and Tamil Nadu were the best-covered regions, the research of the decade included other parts of India as well. The major innovation of the decade—pioneered by David Mosse and followed by Dube and Cederlof—was bringing the discipline of historical anthropology

60 M.E. Prabhakar, 'In Search of Roots—Dalit Aspirations and the Christian Dalit Question: Perceptions of the Telugu Poet Laureate, Joshua', *Religion and Society*, XLI:1 (March 1994), pp. 2–20. See also his 'The Dalit Poetry of Poet Laureate, Joshua', in Joseph Patmury (ed.), *Doing Theology with the Poetic Traditions of India: Focus on Dalit and Tribal Poems* (Bangalore: PTCA/*The Sathri Journal*, 1996), pp. 3–20.

61 Samuel Jayakumar, *Dalit Consciousness and Christian Conversion: Historical Resources for a Contemporary Debate* (Oxford: Regnum International; Delhi: ISPCK, 1999).

62 F. Hrangkhuma (ed.), *Christianity in India: Search for Liberation and Identity* (Delhi: ISPCK, 1998).

to bear upon Dalit Christian history. Some of the main 'schools' of historical inquiry which rose to prominence during this decade—subaltern, feminist, and post-colonial scholarship—had little or no influence at all.

SINCE 2000

Publication in the field of Dalit Christian history continued to increase and diversify during the first decade of the twenty-first century. Up to this time, conversion movements had received the most attention. That is where the roots of Dalit Christian history lay, and the motivations behind those conversion movements have long been a matter of public controversy. Drawing upon case studies of different caste groups in different regions of India converting to differing forms of Christianity, these historians had more or less been unanimous in recognizing the oppressive situation in which Dalits were living. They had studied the mixed motivations which undergirded these movements: seeking new identities with new dignity; new patrons who were more benevolent and could function as a counter to their village patrons; social protest; and improved chances for mere survival. Less attention was paid to the inner dynamics of the movements, and less consensus was achieved as a result. Historians concurred in seeing strong continuities with the pre-conversion past among converts, but not always on the nature of those continuities (caste rivalry and conflict being a case in point). The changes resulting from conversion were more ambiguous, and it is difficult to find a scholarly concord there, whether one looks at Dalit Christian culture or at their politics. However, as this brief summary makes clear, historians have been moving missionaries, mission policies, and programmes from the foreground to the background of their studies and foregrounding the Dalit Christians themselves instead.

In turning to the publications of the twenty-first century, the basic question is, therefore: Has the field of study advanced from this point in any way (and if so, in what ways and by what means), or has it simply broadened? In seeking to answer that question, emphasis will be placed on what is new in either research design or findings, and the literature will be surveyed by region rather than thematically. However, there is one interregional study which deserves to be considered at the outset. *Local Dalit Christian History* contains five case studies, each of which was devoted to one particular congregation or cluster of congregations: some rural churches in Tamil Nadu by P. Dayanandan; a congregation in Karnataka by Godwin Shiri; another in Kerala by George Oommen; one in Gujarat by Raj Kumar Hans and Siddhi Macwan, and one in Delhi by Monodeep Daniel. The introduction locates this project in the historiography of Christianity in India and singles out four themes which pervade the case studies: memory, identity, mobility, and fragility. The book also includes an essay on the methodological issues which the authors encountered in the course of their research.[63]

Tamil Nadu was the most heavily researched region during this decade. In an overview rather than a specific case study, Sathianathan Clarke, a theologian, drew upon social analysis similar to that of Cederlof in conceptualizing Dalit conversions in Tamil Nadu in these terms: 'Religious conversion to another symbolic world vision, in this case Christianity, was an effort at community-initiated bailing out from the constructs of the Brahmanic symbolic world vision and contracting of newer pictures of the world.'[64] He also saw Dalit conversion to 'the Christian symbolic world vision' as ambiguous because it did not 'eventuate into a real world of equality, freedom and dignity', but did provide theological and historical resources 'that could be used to construct an alternative world'.[65]

J.G. Jacob Sundarsingh traced the rise of the Paraiyar within the Lutheran churches in Tamil Nadu from being victims of caste discrimination to acquiring key positions of power in denominational power structures after Independence. He also assessed their

63 George Oommen and John C.B. Webster (eds), *Local Dalit Christian History.*

64 Sathianathan Clarke, 'Conversion to Christianity in Tamil Nadu: Conscious and Constitutive Community Mobilisation towards a Different Symbolic World Vision', in Rowena Robinson and Sathianathan Clarke (eds), *Religious Conversion in India*, pp. 335–6.

65 Ibid., p. 346.

contributions, first, to the Lutheran ministry as (largely invisible) catechists, evangelists and Bible women, and then to church finances as well as its 'Indianness'. Despite these contributions, the aspirations of the vast majority for freedom, equality and prosperity remain frustrated.[66] J. Dorairaj continued the story of Dalit Christians in the Trichy–Tanjore Diocese of the Church of South India where Sundararaj Manickam had left off. Of particular interest in this post-Independence and post-mission history, is its account of the conflict between the diocesan authorities and a large body of Madhari Christians between 1970 and 1973.[67]

With regard to politics, Chandra Mallampalli devoted a chapter of his *Christians and Public Life in Colonial South India 1863–1937* to the debate over Dalit conversions involving Gandhi, Ambedkar, Periyar, and the Self-Respect Movement between 1925 and 1937, and another to Dalit Christians between 1917 and 1937. He pointed out that the Catholic and the Protestant élite disagreed about the 'political character of the Christian community'.

> South Indian Catholics wanted to preserve the uniqueness of their culture and institutions and regarded the policy of separate electorates as the best means for doing so. Protestant notables, by contrast, repudiated any and all forms of 'Christian communalism' and tried more deliberately to blend with national culture.[68]

Similarly, Catholic Dalits sought to become more integrated into their Church and community, whereas Protestant Dalits tended to assert their autonomy vis-à-vis the Protestant élite, and ally themselves more closely with the wider Dalit movement. Both faced considerable caste conflict within their respective churches throughout this period. David Mosse showed some of the later consequences of this Catholic position while examining Catholic Dalit activism since the 1980s. This was led by Dalit priests who

66 J.G. Jacob Sundarsingh, 'The "Outcastes" and the Lutheran Church in Tamil Nadu: Towards an Alternative Historiography', *The Sathri Journal*, 2:1 (May 2008), pp. 90–136.

67 J. Dorairaj, *Springs of Hope: Dalit History* (Madurai: Tamil Nadu Theological Seminary, 2009), pp. 293–314.

68 Chandra Mallampalli, *Christians and Public Life in Colonial South India, 1863–1937*, p. 171.

had personally experienced caste prejudice during and following their training, and so focused their resentment—as did other
Catholic Dalits—primarily on the 'institutionalized caste discrimination within the churches' rather than on caste Hindu society.[69]
The Church responded by identifying itself as 'a Dalit Church' and
making Dalits a priority, a policy which garnered Dalit sympathy
in the face of Hindutva attacks. This, in turn, helped to broaden the
Catholic Dalit activist agenda.

Two works on Kerala have appeared during this decade. George
Oommen looked at 'the role of Pulaya Christians' caste consciousness at work' in their involvement with the Pulaya Self-assertion
and the Communist movements 'to assess the relationship between
Christianization and Dalitization' in their consciousness.[70] The
experience of caste discrimination at the hands of Syrian Christians
led to involvement with the former movement and an enhanced
sense of caste solidarity as a result. 'Continued caste segregation
within the Church combined with the oppression outside the
Church had drawn them closer to the Communist Movement',[71]
as described in his earlier essay. Both experiences point to increasing Dalitization among Pulaya Christians. The other work was a
history of Dalit Pentecostalism in Kerala by Oommen's student,
V.V. Thomas. Dalit Christians were attracted to Pentecostalism as
a way out of the casteism of the older churches and because they
valued the more active, participatory worship of the Pentecostal
churches. There were two splits in Kerala Pentecostalism, largely
over caste issues, one in 1930 and the other in 1972. The continued
attraction of the now-independent Dalit Pentecostal churches lies
in their freedom from caste prejudice, as well as a style of worship

69 David Mosse, 'The Catholic Church and Dalit Christian Activism
in Contemporary Tamil Nadu', in Rowena Robinson and Joseph Marianus
Kujur (eds), Margins of Faith: Dalit and Tribal Christianity in India (New
Delhi: Sage Publications, 2010), p. 242.

70 George Oommen, 'Christianization or Dalitization: The Twentieth
Century Experience of Dalit Christians in Kerala', Indian Church History
Review, XXXVII:1 (June 2003), p. 2.

71 Ibid., p. 19.

and governance more congenial to Dalits than the formalized style of the churches they left behind.[72]

Two scholars have made significant contributions to Dalit Christian history in Andhra Pradesh during this period. Susan Billington Harper's biography of V.S. Azariah, Anglican bishop of the Dornakal Diocese from 1912 until his death in 1945, reads like a mission history in the chapters most directly concerned with Dalit Christians. She traced the history of the mass conversions of the Malas and the Madigas within the diocese, and described Azariah's policies with regard to evangelism; the Christian nurture of converts; the building up of the church among them; and his decisions about what was to be retained in the local culture and what was to be given up upon conversion. Azariah was less successful in persuading them to renounce their caste identities, markers, and rivalries, as well as many of their marriage customs, than in giving up drinking alcohol and eating carrion (some also chose to give up eating beef and pork as well). This choice suggests that they utilized indigenous more than Western modes of upward social mobility.[73] James Elisha Tanneti retold the familiar story of the Madiga conversion movement around Ongole, but with a new twist. He was less interested in what Christianity, Clough, and other Baptist missionaries had done to or for the Madigas than in 'what Madiga Christians did with the gospel and Christian missionaries'.[74] He argued that they gave Christianity a (hitherto-absent) social dimension in keeping with their own emancipatory ambitions and, in continuity with their own religious past, gave

72 V.V. Thomas, *Dalit Pentecostalism: Spirituality of the Empowered Poor* (Bangalore: Asian Trading Corporation, 2008).

73 Susan Billington Harper, *In the Shadow of the Mahatma*, chaps. 6, 8. See also her 'The Dornakal Church on the Cultural Frontier', in Judith M. Brown and Robert Eric Frykenberg (eds), *Christians, Cultural Interactions and India's Religious Traditions* (Grand Rapids: William B. Eerdsman, 2002), pp. 183–211.

74 James Elisha Tanneti, 'Madiga Christians and the Subversive Gospel', in C.I. David Joy (ed.), *Transforming Praxis: God, Community, and Church: Essays in Honour of Dr I. John Mohan Razu* (Bangalore: United Theological College, 2008), p. 134.

women a larger role in their collective religious life than the missionaries had wished to concede.

The other region to receive considerable scholarly attention was North-West India. I wrote two articles on Dalit Christians in the Punjab and one on them in Delhi. The first concentrated on cultural interaction between Chuhra inquirers or converts and missionaries over the course of at least two generations. My emphasis was as much upon the inner psychological aspects of culture as upon its more outward behavioural forms. While the interaction of the first generation of converts had a rural focus, that of the second generation included schools and urban churches as well.[75] The next essay sought to discover what had changed in the lives of Chuhra Christians as a result of conversion. It compared converts under the auspices of two very different missions—the Sialkot Mission of the United Presbyterian Church of North America and the Punjab Mission of the Church Missionary Society—up to World War I, and then, looked at later studies to see what had been the long-term effects of conversion. Like the previous essay, it was based on the assumption that meaningful change—whether psychological, cultural or socio-economic—may take more than one generation to become obvious, as the second generation could add to, retain, or lose what the first generation had gained by converting.[76] The other essay compared the differences between the Baptist and the Anglican missionaries in Delhi over evolving a 'popular Christianity' among their Chamar converts from 1858 to about 1890. While the former—under the leadership of James Smith—sought to develop a church on the guru-panth model of the Chamars, the latter—under Robert Winter and the Cambridge

---

75 John C.B. Webster, 'Dalits and Christianity in Colonial Punjab: Cultural Interactions', in Judith M. Brown and Robert Eric Frykenberg (eds), *Christians, Cultural Interactions and India's Religious Traditions*, pp. 92–118.

76 John C.B. Webster, 'Christian Conversion in the Punjab: What has Changed?' in Rowena Robinson and Sathianathan Clarke (eds), *Religious Conversion in India*, pp. 351–80.

Mission to Delhi—sought to introduce the Chamar Christians to a more 'churchly' model of Christianity.[77]

While, in *Imperial Fault Lines*, Jeffrey Cox was interested primarily in Protestant missionaries in the Punjab, his chapter on 'Village Christians/Songs of Deliverance' contributed to understanding Dalit Christian history there at two key points. He rejected the categories of 'indigenous', 'foreign', and 'hybrid' as accurate descriptions of village [Dalit] Christianity; it was unique and, in it, hymnody played a key role.[78] He also argued it was missionary élitism and authoritarianism that had reduced Christianity to irrelevance among the originally receptive Chamars in urban Delhi.[79] Christopher Harding sought to understand what 'conversion' and 'religious transformation' actually meant in the context of the rural Punjab mass movement.[80] This led him to look at the varying views of 'uplift' operative in the Punjab—especially among the Chuhras— and the CMS and Belgian Capuchin missionaries, the two mission societies that provided his case studies. He then examined the roles of Punjabi converts and mission employees as communicators of Christianity, as well as what rural Christianity—including patterns of authority, education and medical care—came to look like. The book ends with a chapter on the converts' and missionaries' visions of the future in two Christian villages which these two missions created. My own social history of Christianity in North-West India made two contributions to Dalit Christian history not already mentioned. It told their story from the beginnings of the Chamar conversions in Delhi and then the much larger Chuhra conversion

77 John C.B. Webster, 'Missionary Strategy and the Development of the Christian Community: Delhi, 1859–1884', in Selva J. Raj and Corinne C. Dempsey (eds), *Popular Christianity in India: Riting Between the Lines* (Albany: State University of New York Press, 2002), pp. 211–32.

78 Jeffrey Cox, *Imperial Fault Lines: Christianity and Colonial Power in India, 1818–1940*, p. 152.

79 Ibid., p. 144. On this same problem, see P. Dayanandan, 'Dalit Christians of Chengalpattu Area and the Church of Scotland', in George Oommen and John C.B. Webster (eds), *Local Dalit Christian History*, pp. 18–64.

80 Christopher Harding, *Religious Transformation in South Asia*, p. 3

movements in the Punjab up into the present century. It also tried to integrate their story into the larger history of Christianity there over a period of two centuries. It did this, not by treating them separately—as Grafe had done with Tamil Nadu—but by keeping the social base and demographics of the Christian community constantly in the foreground, and by employing a conflict model which highlighted the differences between the community's urban educated élite and rural Dalit poor, as social base, demographics, differences, and conflicting interests played crucial roles in their history.[81]

The other major work from this decade was Chad M. Bauman's history of the Satnami Christians in Chhattisgarh. Researching and writing in the context of increased Hindutva attacks upon Christianity as 'foreign' and 'denationalizing', Bauman investigated Satnami–Christian interactions and found that 'the Christianization of Chhattisgarh—limited as it was—also entailed the *Chhattisgarhization* of Christianity'.[82] He labelled his work 'a historical ethnology of a religious community'; an '*episodic* history, a series of snapshots rather than an unbroken catalog of events and occurrences'; and 'a work of subaltern history'[83] based on the works of other scholars, written records, and oral history. After providing the Chhattisgarh context, he dealt with conversion, myths connecting the Christians with their Satnami past, medicine, women (the fullest historical treatment of Dalit Christian women produced so far), some individual biographies and some post-Independence developments.

Other regions of India received briefer and less original treatments,[84] but the studies cited above represent some of the

81 John C.B. Webster, *A Social History of Christianity: North-West India since 1800* (New Delhi: Oxford University Press, 2007).

82 Chad M. Bauman, *Christian Identity and Dalit Religion in Hindu India, 1868–1947* (Grand Rapids: William B. Eerdmans, 2008), p. 6.

83 Ibid., pp. 20, 21, 22.

84 For example, Maharashtra. M.D. David did provide data on Dalit Christians within a [Protestant] mission history framework and Camil Parkhe provided some information on Dalit [mostly Catholic] Christian agitations for reservations there. M.D. David, *Missions: Cross-Cultural*

major advances in the field since 2000. There were no new or dramatic findings on Dalit conversions; newer studies seemed to confirm, in their own way, the findings of earlier ones. The same could be said for studies of what the missions did to further emancipate Dalits. The denomination and the region continued to be the basic unit of study for most histories, although there were exceptions. Innovations were most noticeable in the analysis of Dalit Christian communities and Dalit Christian politics. As a comparative approach become more popular, the diversities among Dalit Christian communities—whether based on caste or denomination or region—became more apparent. New ways of integrating Dalit Christian history into the larger histories either of Christianity or of the Dalits had also been attempted.

An Assessment

Dalit Christian history has come a long way over the past half-century. What began as a mere subsection on the mass movements in mission and church histories has now become an important field of study in its own right, with a significant body of scholarly literature. Virtually all the regions with sizeable Dalit Christian populations have received at least some coverage, but Protestant Dalits have received far more attention than have Catholic Dalits. Perhaps, most important of all, in many of these histories, Dalit Christians were no longer viewed simply as the 'fruit' or beneficiaries of mission and church endeavours, but as subjects of their own histories with aims of their own, and the capacity to negotiate with those who were more powerful than they to realize those aims. In other words, the input–impact model of viewing Dalit Christian history had given way more and more to an interaction model, whether the 'others' were village landowners, missionaries or church leaders. In addition, Dalit Christian communities and Dalit Christian politics were being treated as worthy of study in their own right. In short, the earlier mission and church history approaches were being supplemented, although not yet replaced,

Encounter and Change in Western India; Camil Parkhe, *Dalit Christians: Right to Reservations* (Delhi: ISPCK, 2007).

by socio-cultural approaches in which new questions about the Dalit Christians themselves were being asked and new methods of answering them were being employed.

Conversion and conversion movements have constituted the main theme of Dalit Christian history so far. There is little difference of opinion among historians about the complex Dalit motives or reasons for conversion or about Christianity spreading among them along caste lines. Only a few historians have shed some light on the substance of the message which either (often Dalit) catechists and evangelists or Dalit inquirers and converts actually shared with fellow Dalits that persuaded many to convert, and even more not to. Also, the working hypothesis, drawn from the sociology of social movements, that conversion movements passed through several stages, with differing perceptions and motivations dominating each stage, has not been widely tested.

Closely related to conversion has been the key issue of the consequences of conversion, whether measured in terms of the converts' own aspirations for social emancipation and the more immediate gains to be made in that direction, or of the historians' chosen indicators for assessing psychological, social, cultural, economic or political change. Historians dealing with this subject have shown a sobering awareness of the powerful, change-resisting constraints which Dalits, whether converts or not, faced in village communities. Their selections of indicators of change have had much in common, but the questions which some, like Cederlof, have asked are more sharply focused than others. What becomes apparent from this survey is that change—occupational mobility, status enhancement, adopting some new and abandoning some old cultural practices, are the ones most frequently examined—takes time and may neither be visible in the first generation of converts nor remain permanent. I have noticed among Dalit Christians in the Punjab, considerable dynamism and much stagnation at the same time,[85] thus making generalizations about change of any sort extremely difficult.

A third major theme is Dalit Christian politics, broadly understood. As this survey has shown, Dalit Christians have engaged in

---

85 John C.B. Webster, *A Social History of Christianity*, p. 331.

power struggles of various kinds with local members of dominant castes, with missionaries and church leaders, with state and
federal governments, and with each other (as in caste rivalries).
These power struggles became increasingly pronounced in the
years following Independence, but can also be found, as Gladstone
and Oommen in particular have shown, earlier at the beginning of
the twentieth century. This theme is relatively underdeveloped in
comparison with the first two and deserves further attention.

All these three themes have been at the heart of much controversy over a long period of time, both within the churches and in
the public realm. Three other themes, which have been touched
upon in a few of the works mentioned here, have flown by largely
under the historians' radar. The most obvious of these is Dalit
Christian women's history. Another might best be labelled the
internal dynamics or functioning of Dalit Christian communities
and congregations. In both these cases, written source materials are
relatively rare, especially in the latter case, and often not directly
relevant to the questions historians would want to ask of them.
That is where anthropology can be of great help to the historian, as
Bayly, Mosse and Bauman have demonstrated. The other generally
neglected theme has been how best to integrate Dalit Christian history with the rest of the history of Christianity in India. Two recent
general histories treat it separately,[86] a practice—as this survey
has indicated—with a long history behind it. The other approach
adopted so far was viewing either caste or urban élite–rural poor
competition and conflict as a major motif running through all
aspects of the history of Christianity in India.[87] Since Dalits constitute a majority of the Christian population, historians might be
well advised to view Christian history in India through a Dalit lens.

How then did the field develop to this point? Certainly, the
conditions were propitious. Mission sources have been plentiful
and accessible. Public controversy over Dalit conversions and
Dalit Christian assertiveness in seeking recognition and justice

86 Leonard Fernando and G. Gispert-Sauch, *Christianity in India:
Two Thousand Years of Faith*; Robert Eric Frykenberg, *Christianity in
India: From Beginnings to the Present*.
87 John C. B. Webster, *A Social History of Christianity*.

from both the Church and the State has stimulated interest in their history and defined the issues to be researched. Dalit Christians have been trying to discover their roots and redefine their identities. One can discern the influence of the academy as well. Some key developments, not only in Indian historical studies generally—such as social history and Dalit history—but also in the allied disciplines of sociology, anthropology and theology (to say nothing of the influence of teachers upon their students), have helped to shape a focus upon Dalit Christians and the ways in which their history might best be studied. Seminars, conferences, and books have been organized around concerns and themes, and historians have been invited to contribute papers to them that forced them to look at this subject in new ways and ask fresh questions. All this has been part of the milieu, but in the last analysis it was individual historians who, for reasons of academic interest, social commitment, and/or personal relationships with Dalit Christians, have shaped this field of study and contributed to its growth. We need to study the historians too and not limit ourselves just to their publications.

Conclusion

Examining Basic Assumptions

The previous chapters have offered some overviews of the ways in which the history of Christianity in India as a field of study has developed over the past two hundred years, and a closer look at some of the key issues confronting historians who have been writing that history in more recent times. This chapter examines some of the changing, basic—generally unstated—assumptions which have provided intellectual foundations for that body of work over the years. There are at least four categories of assumptions which seem unavoidable and so bear further exploration in this concluding chapter.

The first set of assumptions concerns the purpose or value of studying the history of Christianity in India. This inquiry particularizes the more general question, 'Why study history?' by asking, 'What makes the history of Christianity in India important enough to warrant study and further research?' The second set of assumptions concerns the epistemological basis for such study and research. This addresses such questions as: 'How do we know that historical accounts of this particular past are reliable?' or 'What provides assurance that we can trust the accuracy of the information and insights which such histories present?' A third category consists of theoretical assumptions—especially concerning the nature and dynamics of Indian culture and society—which have provided the interpretative frameworks for such histories. Finally, since the history of Christianity is religious history, there are inevitable theological assumptions to be reckoned with. As indicated in Chapter 2, historians make theological choices in applying such labels as Christianity and Church to their subject matter, but those are only the most obvious of the theological assumptions that abound in historical writing on this subject. Each of these four categories of assumptions will be examined in turn.

ASSUMPTIONS ABOUT PURPOSE AND VALUE

The earliest histories of Christianity in India were written and published in the West to influence Western readers on what were Western issues. LaCroze's and Geddes's histories were polemical products of the religious controversies in a deeply divided European Christendom. Both seemed less interested in India's history of Christianity than in fighting the evils of Roman Catholicism at home; India simply provided them additional ammunition for that fight. Hough shared their views of Catholicism, but was more interested in defending and promoting the cause of Protestant missions in India, the efficacy of which had come under serious attack from Roman Catholic quarters. Kaye wrote his history to defend the British government's policy of religious neutrality against Evangelical criticisms in the post-1857 debates on the subject. Sherring and the authors of many denominational histories wrote theirs to garner support for their Protestant missions. Richter began shifting the emphasis away from the polemical and promotional to more 'scientific' comparisons of missionary policies and methods, and their consequences, in an early work in the emerging field of missiology.

Only at the beginning of the twentieth century were histories of Christianity in India published in India addressing, mostly intra-Christian, issues of concern to a readership in India. History was used to validate or justify ecclesiastical jurisdictions, lines of succession, and church or mission policies. Agur wrote a history so that fellow Christians might take greater pride in and responsibility for their churches. So, too, did Rajaiah Paul, but with an added nationalist emphasis upon the [Protestant] Church's Indian heroes and heritage.[1] Indian Church history textbooks sought to explain how the churches—which their readers would be serving—came to be as they were, while Baagø used history to press for what he considered to be a more culturally indigenous Christianity.

Thus, historians of Christianity in India have had a long history of being preoccupied with 'churchly'—or, more broadly, Christian—concerns with only a Christian readership in mind. This changed significantly when Christianity in India became a subject of academic history, both inside and outside Christian circles, starting in the 1970s. The 'New Perspective' of the Church History Association of India (CHAI), which had considerable influence within Christian circles in India, shifted attention away from the history of churches and missions towards the socio-cultural history of the Christian people so as to gain insight into their changing identity over the centuries. In university circles, the role of Christianity in the Bengal Renaissance and in the modernization of India generally, and also Christianity as a focal point for studying the East–West encounter became subjects of considerable interest. Dalit Christian history began to emerge at the same time in both church and university circles. Since then, historians of Christianity have addressed such 'hot button' issues as conversion, the 'Indianness' of converts, and the Scheduled Caste status of Dalit Christians, so as to challenge both scholarly and popular perceptions.

What this brief historical survey of intentions suggests is that histories of Christianity in India, like all other histories, have been written—whether to enlighten, to engage, or to motivate—for the sake of the present and the future. A good starting point for exploring reasons for studying the history of Christianity today is the aim which the CHAI editorial board had recommended back in 1974, namely, to gain insight into the changing identity of India's Christians down through the centuries, because this represented a

1 For Agur, see Supra pp. 40-1, 45-6. Paul believed that churches need heroes, saints and martyrs; the Indian Church should not forget hers but learn from their examples. *Chosen Vessels: Lives of Ten Indian Christian Pastors of the Eighteenth and Nineteenth Centuries* (Madras: Christian Literature Society, 1961), pp. vii-ix.

strategic shift towards gaining insight into historical identity more in relation to the rest of India than to the rest of Christianity, especially Western Christianity.

Is such insight important enough to anyone other than Indian Christians to warrant study and research? It seems not. Christians, as a rule, have been left out of histories of India. A few foreign missionaries such as William Carey, or the more generalized 'missionary threat', may be mentioned, but Indian Christians rarely appear in general histories. Certainly, as Chapter 1 illustrates, there is a long history of the writing of Christian history in India as something apart from Indian history as a whole, but, as Chapters 6 and 7 illustrate, for the past four decades, that has no longer been the case. India's Christians—like women, Dalits, and the tribal people (the very groups with whom Christian history in India has been most closely intertwined)—have been almost completely excluded from its history, not necessarily consciously and intentionally, but nonetheless excluded.[2] Apart from any enhanced self-understanding and perspective which may result from a deeper understanding of the Indian Christian 'others' in their midst, the larger issue of inclusive history is at stake. If historians aim at writing a history with which large diverse groups or categories of Indians can identify, in which they can locate their ancestors, and which they can claim as their own, then it is important to study the history of Indian Christians (like Indian women, Dalits, and tribal people) and include it in regional and national histories. Of course, underlying this question of inclusiveness in writing Indian history is the ideological debate—revealed in recent polemics about conversion—about whether India has been, and should continue to be,

---

2 There are several possible reasons for such neglect. Some historians rule Christians out as un-Indian. Others consider religious categories historically less important than categories of class or caste. In most parts of India, Christians have not constituted a large enough minority to be considered politically significant. Their history has been more closely related to histories of other neglected categories of Indians than to that of the 'history-makers' in the 'mainstream' and, so, it will probably not become 'important' until these other neglected histories also become 'mainstream' and 'important'.

a heterogeneous, pluralistic society, or a homogeneous society. To state this in another way, is India's apparent diversity real or imaginary? Is it India's glory or a blemish on it? The study of the history of Christianity, especially in its more recent academic forms, provides considerable insight into the changing nature of Indian society as a whole, as well as a more complex and comprehensive picture of it, as has been indicated in Chapter 6.

For Christians in India, gaining an insight into their changing identity over the centuries would probably be the first and primary reason for such study and research. The study of one's own history helps in gaining self-understanding and a heightened self-awareness; it may even assist in a liberating process of self-discovery and visioning for the future, at both the individual and the collective levels. As Chapter 3 indicates, Indian Christians have, in the past, faced a multiplicity of identity issues which, however, have not been the same for all Indian Christians. Social identity—unlike self-image or self-definition—is not simply a matter of one's own choosing; it is inherited and then constantly renegotiated through interaction with others in the same social environment where self-images and public images may clash with, complement, or reinforce one another. For example, as indicated in the section on 'Innovation, Encounter, and Change' of Chapter 6, by all accounts and in most parts of India, Christians, through their evangelistic and educational initiatives, played a very provocative role in challenging not just the religious but also the socio-cultural status quo, especially during the nineteenth century. This challenge did not go unanswered. Among the by-products of the ensuing controversies surrounding conversion—which continue in the present—Indian Christians have been stuck with public images ranging from scoundrels, to modern and progressive, to culturally and/or politically 'un-Indian', to pathetic seekers of 'loaves and fishes' from missionary hands. Dalit Christians, who comprise a majority of the Christian community, have also borne the stigma of untouchability, while tribal Christians—the second largest category of Christians—have had to live with the public image of being 'primitive'. Given those past images and social categorizations, the study of history holds out the possibility of helping Indian Christians to make better sense of their past and, from it, to gain some perspective on their present, as well as to get their inherited collective identity issues sorted out and, perhaps to some extent, resolved.

There are two specific things which history can do to create this possibility. One is to contribute to the discovery and public articulation of Indian Christian traditions. The first step in this direction was CHAI's strategic move to define Christian identity in relation to other Indian identities rather than to those of the Christian West. The present challenge is to find out and/or further articulate what the specifically Christian traditions within Indian frameworks have been, so that they might be strengthened, reformed, or abandoned for the sake of the present and future, theologically defined, well-being of India and of Christians in India. Given the debilitating Indian identities which most Christians have been assigned because of their social origins, there is much to be said for strengthening their sense of Christian identity through recoveries and reformulations of traditions that are not only Christian and Indian, but also expressed in words and symbols that are meaningful to Indian Christians today.[3]

The other step follows from the first. Social amnesia and/or distorted memories of key events in the Christian past can do serious damage to the body politic as a whole and to the Christian community in particular. India has already suffered considerably from communal readings of its past history. In recent years, India's self-image and international image have been hurt by the social strife and persecution of Christians fed by explanations of past Dalit and tribal conversions, which bear little resemblance to the conclusions arrived at by historians who have studied the origins and dynamics of those movements with some care. In short, poor quality history has played a role in fostering the social conflict in which Christians have been involved, primarily as victims.[4]

---

3 This seems to be the challenge which, for example, Dalit Christian theologians have been addressing. To date, they appear to have been more successful at the creative than at the traditioning aspect of the task. See John C.B. Webster, *The Dalit Christians: A History*, 3rd ed., pp. 248–315.

4 On the role of history in such conflicts, see the essays by K.N. Panikkar, Romila Thapar, and Sumit Sarkar in K.N. Panikkar (ed.), *The*

That is one side of the coin. The other is that the history of Christianity in India has considerable healing potential. As I wrote in the preface to my history of the Dalit Christians back in 1992,

> I discovered that Dalit Christians have come to believe things about their past which are not only either false or at best half-true, but are also very detrimental to their present well-being. Historical study under such circumstances becomes a form of group therapy, of casting out demons created by past controversy which still hold even educated Dalit Christians in their grip.[5]

More recently, in *Healing Wounded History*, Russ Parker described how group memories have been wounded by group conflicts. He saw reconciliation between wounders and wounded as a necessary step towards healing such memories. For reconciliation to occur, however, the stories of those wounding events had to be told publicly and in detail, with all their factual and emotional content, as well as with references to what those events did to those who were wounded by them and what it meant to them.[6] Even if the wounders have no interest in reconciliation or healing, those stories must still be told. Trauma therapists have pointed out that those who have suffered traumatic histories (for example, Christian and other Dalits who have suffered what one scholar has called

---

Concerned Indian's Guide to Communalism (New Delhi: Penguin Viking, 1999), pp. viii–33, 73–106.

5 John C.B. Webster, *The Dalit Christians: A History*, 1st ed. (1992), p. i.

6 Russ Parker, *Healing Wounded History: Reconciling People and Restoring Places* (Cleveland: The Pilgrim Press, 2001). Most of his illustrations come from England and Ireland. In 2009, *The American Historical Review* published five essays on 'Truth and Reconciliation in History', three of which were case studies of efforts by professional historians to promote reconciliation between religious and ethnic groups through reconciling histories which dealt with the issue of genocide. Their approach was to include historians representing all the groups involved, together with other specialists, to prepare single accounts of the alleged genocides. *The American Historical Review*, 114:4 (October 2009), pp. 899–977.

'institutionalized humiliation')[7] need to confront the horrors of the trauma-causing event(s) in their lives so that they can grieve over their losses, discover what still remains, and find the presence of restorative love in their lives. Without publicly telling this story, trauma survivors experience great difficulty in regaining control of their lives and reconnecting to ordinary life.[8]

However, in highlighting the therapeutic potential of historical study and research, I went on to point out that 'if history is to be therapeutic, it must bring us as close to the truth of past reality as possible, because that kind of truth has far greater capacity to heal and to empower for present and future action than does the ideological use of the past'.[9] Academic histories, which seek truth in accuracy, can serve as both resources and 'reality checks' in the retelling of wounded group histories and, thus, in the healing of those wounds. That assumes, of course, that historical study and research can, in fact, bring one close to the *truth* of past *reality*, an assumption which now needs further examination.

Epistemological Assumptions

The epistemological assumptions upon which historical writing on Christianity in India has been based have both changed and diversified over the past two centuries. The earliest historians treated their sources as authorities. They shared the outlook and the aims of the missionaries who provided their source materials and assumed that the information which those sources contained was accurate and reliable. From those sources, they selected the information which they felt shed the most light on their subject and then let it 'speak for itself'. Only the St. Thomas tradition provoked its historians to undertake major exercises in source criticism; that

7 Bhikhu Parekh, 'Logic of Humiliation', in Gopal Guru (ed.), *Humiliation: Claims and Context* (New Delhi: Oxford University Press, 2009), p. 31.

8 Judith Lewis Herman, *Trauma and Recovery* (New York: Basic Books, 1997), pp. 175–95.

9 John C.B. Webster, *The Dalit Christians: A History*, 1st ed. (1992), pp. i–ii.

tradition has been posing problems about the possibilities of historical knowledge ever since.

Fresh issues of epistemology arose in the years following Independence when academic historians began asking their own questions about the Christian past instead of simply following the narrative flow of 'mission work' built into their sources. To cite my own first major effort as an example, I posed these basic questions about converts to Christianity: Who were they? Why did they convert? What changes did they undergo as a result of conversion? To answer those questions, I had to decide what were the important indicators of identity (for example, religious background, caste, education, occupation); of motivation (by looking at the entire screening process through which inquirers had to pass prior to baptism); and of significant change (for example, in names, religious beliefs and practices, occupation, legal status, family and community relationships). Once I knew what I was looking for and, therefore, what constituted 'evidence', I went to my sources to see what I could find. I pieced together bits of information from here and there, but faced gaps in the evidence and found it problematic to generalize from small samples or illustrative examples.[10] While the determining and sharing of 'what really happened' remained the goal, I expressed varying degrees of confidence in the conclusions to which I had come.

This procedure followed E.H. Carr's definition of history as a 'continuous process of interaction between the historian and his facts, an unending dialogue between the present and the past'.[11] Carr was reacting against the positivism of the empirical 'commonsense' view of history and its claims of objectivity. This he considered to be based on a false separation not only of the inquiring subject from the object inquired into, but also of fact from interpretation. 'The historian', he pointed out, 'is necessarily selective', and the selection of facts to become historical facts is bound

10 John C.B. Webster, *The Christian Community and Change in Nineteenth Century North India*, pp. 46–92.

11 E.H. Carr, *What is History?* (Harmondsworth: Penguin Books, 1964), p. 30.

up with that historian's interpretation,[12] which is, in turn, bound up with the historian's present. There is, thus, an inevitable subjective element—the historian's personal subjectivity as well as that of the historian's historical and social environment—in all historical writing. Only the sources and the facts save historians from total subjectivity.[13]

In Carr's unending process of interaction and dialogue, the historian's questions are rooted in his/her own person and present. They may be provoked by the sources but they are addressed to the sources which may, in turn, indicate that there may be better or supplementary questions to be asked. (For example, I did not consider asking about the screening process through which baptismal candidates were put until I saw it described so frequently in my sources.) The answers which the sources offer up may have to be revised in the light of further questioning and further information. Through this interaction and dialogue, the historian arrives at an interpretation of the specific aspect of the past that is being focused upon.

The working assumptions of the historian described in Chapter 1, as well as most of the histories described in Chapters 6 and 7, were of this type. In the Preface or the Introduction, the author stated what the theme or the problem under investigation was, and explained why it was being researched with reference either to historical context, or to previous scholarship, or to both. Some posed the research questions which would guide their study and there was generally a reference to the sources consulted. The author's delimitation of the research topic under examination and choice of implicit or explicit questions to ask the sources constituted the present subjective standpoint from which the 'continuous process of interaction' and 'unending dialogue' would take place. While there might be some preliminary source criticism when describing

12 Ibid., pp. 12–13.

13 Carr distinguished between what he called 'basic facts'—the raw material common to all historians, and 'historical facts'—basic facts to which one or more historians attributed historical significance. Carr bypassed the epistemological status of the former and concentrated on the latter. Ibid., pp. 11, 120–3.

the materials from which evidence would be drawn,[14] there was no question about the capacity of the sources to yield 'basic facts' and 'historical facts'.

A sceptical post-modernism then posed a far more serious epistemological challenge to historians than Carr had, by calling into question the entire modern agenda, including the scientific approach to truth. For empirical inductive historians, this meant that not only were their interpretations of 'basic facts' considered a priori subjective and relative, but even their ability to get at the 'basic facts' was called into question. For many post-moderns, histories were basically fiction imposed upon alleged facts. Beverley Southgate has traced the origins of this development to three sources. Studies in the psychology of perception, he said, indicated that

What we see is determined not only by what is 'out there' in the external world, but also by the ways in which we personally respond to it; and that is dependent in turn upon what we are, what we have experienced and what we have come to expect. So that our own input is an indissoluble part of the total process of perception. . . . The main lesson of psychology for history is that any version of events, any explanation of what has happened, and perception of 'the past', is necessarily limited and contingent, and may therefore need to be revised.[15]

Thus, the subjectivity of the perceiver—both those who produced the historians' sources and of the historians who selected and used them—is unavoidable, and there is 'no privileged standpoint from which to assess the relative validity of [differing versions of the past], no way of achieving access to any past simply "as it was".'[16] Modern linguistic studies have reinforced this constructive (as opposed to objective) view of the historian's sources and task.

14 See, for example, Koji Kawashima, *Missionaries and a Hindu State: Travancore 1858–1936*, pp. 12–15.
15 Beverley Southgate, *History: What and Why? Ancient, Modern and Postmodern Perspectives*, 2nd ed. (London and New York: Routledge, 2001), pp. 71–2.
16 Ibid., p. 72.

Instead of simply describing an already existing situation, language itself serves to determine the construction of that situation: it outlines the parameters within which construction can take place, it places constraints on what at any time is considered possible, it bounds our very thoughts, perceptions, interpretations and experiences.[17]

Meanwhile, philosophers were examining how historians make 'truth claims', and the sceptics among them found no way out of this same bind of constructive subjectivity and relativism. History as hypothesis, construction, discourse, even as fiction, replaced history as objective, established knowledge in any sense of the term; a quest for historical truth was ruled out as impossible.

Chapter 5 contains a partial response to this challenge by providing an exercise in making the move to the external world from the internal world of the perceiver. 'Absolute truth', or total truth, has always been an impossible goal and few historians in recent times have made such claims for their accounts of the past. However, total subjectivity—including only subjective criteria for differentiating 'good' from 'bad' historical scholarship—is not the only alternative. Southgate pointed out the limitations of perception and language but not their possibilities. There are middle ways between empiricist and post-modernist history, in which perceptions and the language used to describe them do put the historian in touch with external realities, and the historian's task consists of far more than just deconstructing past narratives.[18] One middle way is what Appleby, Hunt and Jacob have called 'practical realism';[19] Rosenau characterized another one as 'affirmative post-

---

17 Ibid., p. 74.

18 '*Deconstruction* involves demystifying a text, tearing it apart to reveal its internal, arbitrary hierarchies and its presuppositions. It lays out the flaws and the latent metaphysical structures of a text. A deconstructive reading of a text seeks to discover its ambivalence, blindness, logocentricity.' Pauline Marie Rosenau, *Post-Modernism and the Social Sciences: Insights, Inroads, and Intrusions* (Princeton: Princeton University Press, 1992), p. 120.

19 'Knowing that there are objects out there turns scholars into practical realists. They can admit their cultural fixity, their partial grasp of truth, and still think that in trying to know the world, it's best not to divert the lens from the object—as the relativist suggests—but to leave it on and

modernism'.[20] In *Historical Theory*, Mary Fulbrook offered a third one which she called 'partial histories'.[21] All three take the post-modern challenge very seriously but do not surrender completely to it.

As the literature surveyed in the previous chapters indicates, the epistemology of post-modernism in its more sceptical forms has to date had little visible impact upon historical writing about Christianity in India. These historians have remained firmly grounded in the empiricist tradition but now follow a middle road between positivist objectivity and total scepticism and relativity. There has been some deconstruction of reigning metanarratives; some unwillingness to go beyond providing more than fragments or probes; and some reviewing of the sources from a sociology of knowledge perspective. However, the methods and the language used, indicate not only that the writers believe that aspects of the past external world can be described and explained with a considerable degree of accuracy, but also that their 'truth claims' are expected to

---

keep trying to clean it.' Joyce Appleby, Lynn Hunt and Margaret Jacob, *Telling the Truth about History* (New York: W.W. Norton, 1994), p. 268.

20 In her view, affirmative post-modernists are more optimistic than the sceptics and many consider 'certain value choices are superior to others'. With respect to epistemological foundations, they 'seek a philosophical and ontological intellectual practice that is nondogmatic, tentative, and nonideological'. Pauline Marie Rosenau, *Post-Modernism and the Social Sciences*, p. 16.

21 For Fulbrook, the fundamental issue was stated in the question, 'What are the implications of the fact that a multiplicity of interpretations (or stories) can be constructed out of the "same" past?' She then went on to say, 'We do not need to agree with the relativist and sceptical conclusions of postmodernists; nor do we need to accept simple empiricist assertions of faith. History is a far more complicated endeavour than either of these positions recognize. It seems to me that, on closer analysis, we can begin to distinguish grounds for accepting, rejecting, or amending different perspectives in more detail; and for determining whether in some areas at least a relatively broad scholarly community can collectively engage in closer approximations to adequacy in accounts of the past in the present, while certain issues will prove to be insurmountable stumbling blocks.' She then offered some guidelines, ground rules or commitments to follow. Mary Fulbrook, *Historical Theory* (London: Routledge, 2002), pp. 186–7.

meet with generally shared academic criteria used to distinguish good from bad historical scholarship. These criteria have changed over time, but today they would include diversity and comprehensiveness of the sources consulted; accuracy of information derived from them; quality of the questions posed; appropriateness of the warrants and qualifiers used for various kinds of generalizations and explanations; clarity and transparency in the use of concepts; and logic of argumentation—all of which are subject to international and multi-cultural peer criticism.[22] Thus, while qualities such as imagination, empathy, insight, and felicity of language, are important, faithful adherence to the fundamental disciplines of historical scholarship is the best guarantor available of the basic reliability and trustworthiness of the truth claims embedded in a historical account and, therefore, for fulfilling the aims of studying the history of Christianity in India as described earlier.[23]

THEORETICAL ASSUMPTIONS

With the post-modern challenge came an increasing awareness of how thoroughly theoretical assumptions have been embedded in even the most inductive empirical histories. Historians may eschew grand theory and metanarratives which offer explanations of the meaning, direction and dynamics of history as a whole, but then go on to use middle-range theories in framing their research

22 Fulbrook's study indicates that, while differences in the basic paradigms which determine the standpoints from which historians write often cannot be resolved by reference to facts or methodologies, the closer one gets to the more concrete and particular in historical research, the more likely the resolving of differences in that way becomes.

23 The three efforts at preparing 'reconciling histories' mentioned in footnote 5 did not result in perfect agreement, but in histories to which all those who were involved could sign on; it brought new (and often uncomfortable) facts to light; and it exploded many of the myths surrounding the events narrated. This was achieved by elevating professional academic standards above those of group interest and ideology. While appreciated by historians and other social scientists, these efforts were less well received by the politicians and the general public who had emotional stakes in the kind of conclusions arrived at.

questions, or even in the very technical work of selecting historical facts and relating them to one another so as to answer those
questions. This section cannot cover the full range of such theoretical assumptions, but will confine itself to those theories about
the nature and dynamics of Indian society which have been most
influential in shaping histories of Christianity in India.

Julius Richter's *A History of Missions in India* (1906, 1908)
exhibits two important theoretical assumptions informing nineteenth-century mission histories. One was that, while India was
diverse and complex, it was also basically unchanging. His introductory chapter on the land, people and religion of India, based on
the latest ethnographic data, categorized the people in static terms
of linguistic and physical affinities, and their religion in terms of
Hinduism, caste, and sects. In the narrative that followed, India
played a very passive, background role; the actors were Christian
missions and foreign governments until the end of the nineteenth
century. The other theoretical assumption was that the most
important thing about India was its religion. This assumption was
implicit in his narrative but quite explicit in his analyses of the
accomplishments and state of the missions at the time of writing.
This sharp focus on religion was probably a result of his view that
'The great problem of missionary work is: How can Christianity
overcome and supplant native forms of religion?'[24] Richter looked
only at religion (and caste) when assessing the forces at work in
assisting or inhibiting the progress of Christianity in India as well
as the leavening effect it was having there. In those chapters, he
treated religion as an independent variable, impacted only by other
forms of religion and, hence, an autonomous compartment of life
virtually divorced from politics, economics and social conflict.

These assumptions were largely abandoned when Christianity
became a subject of academic history in the 1960s and 1970s, and
the modernization of India became a major concern. As indicated in Chapter 6, a significant body of literature developed on
Christianity's role not only in those nineteenth- and twentieth-
century processes of structural and cultural change labelled (at
times, interchangeably) as modernization and Westernization, but

24 Julius Richter, *A History of Missions in India*, p. 241.

also in creating opportunities for individual and collective social mobility within those changing structures.[25] Moreover, while some of those historians used an input–impact model in describing the process of change, a larger number used an interaction model which had two distinct advantages over the former model. One was that it did not treat Indians as simply passive accepters, incorporators, or rejecters of missionary inputs, but saw change as a product of active interaction between Christians (whether missionaries or Indians) and members of other communities, defined by caste, class, and/or religion. The other advantage was that, whereas the former view tended to hide competition and conflict, the latter view highlighted them in their many forms: religious and cultural controversy; caste and class rivalry; and also, the clashing interests of women and men. This latter view, both in its research questions and in its findings, argued for a conflict model with multiple contradictions rather than for a more harmonious, organic view of Indian society.

With the post-modern turn came three important theoretical approaches to the study of Indian history that opened up new ways of studying the history of Christianity. All three were based on a conflict model of society; a sociology of knowledge approach to the past; an awareness that knowledge was an instrument of both domination and subversion; and liberative visions for the future. One was the Subaltern School which had its intellectual roots in Marxist historiography and began as a protest against the 'colonialist élitism and bourgeois-nationalist élitism' which had dominated historical writing on India. This school, therefore, decided to concentrate upon the subalterns and their politics. The subalterns were those groups or categories of people in Indian society—whether defined by occupation, caste, tribe, gender, or minority status— who were subordinate rather than dominant; unprivileged rather than privileged; marginalized rather than 'mainstream'; 'different'

25 In 1976, I made a deliberate attempt to correlate my findings in *The Christian Community and Change in Nineteenth Century North India* with the theoretical frameworks provided by Percival Spear, A.R. Desai, M.N. Srinivas, Bernard Cohn, and Yogendra Singh to arrive at my own conclusions. See pp. 263–71.

rather than 'one of us'. Their politics constituted 'an autonomous domain, for it neither originated from élite politics nor did its existence depend on the latter'.[26] The aim, therefore, was 'to understand the consciousness that informed and still informs political actions taken by the subaltern classes on their own, independently of any élite initiatives. It is only by giving this 'consciousness' a central place in historical analysis that we see the subaltern as the maker of the history he/she lives out'.[27]

This emphasis upon subaltern autonomy vis-à-vis the élite, upon subaltern agency, consciousness, and voice, had great potential for historical writing on Christianity in India because the vast majority of Christians was drawn from the 'subaltern classes'. However, this potential has been largely unrealized. As Chapter 7 indicates, Dalit Christian history got off to a somewhat earlier start than did the Subaltern School and developed independently of it. Like Subaltern School historiography, it emphasized Dalit autonomy vis-à-vis the missionaries (most notably in the Dalit mass conversion movements), as well as Dalit agency, consciousness and voice. Unlike the early Subalternists, it paid more attention to caste (jati); to caste hierarchy; to patron–client relationships between members of castes differently placed in that hierarchy; to individual and jati mobility; to inter-caste rivalries; and to the conflicting interests of Dalit and élite Christians, than to class analysis. As it matured, it became based increasingly on a conflict model of Indian society along, not Marxist but, Ambedkarite lines.

26 Ranajit Guha, 'On Some Aspects of the Historiography of Colonial India', in Ranajit Guha (ed.), *Subaltern Studies I: Writings on South Asian History and Society* (Delhi: Oxford University Press, 1982), pp. 1, 4. Gyanendra Pandey later noted that 'For a quarter of a century now, in this project of a new critical history that originated in India, the archetypal figure of the subaltern has been the revolutionary Third World peasant.' 'Introduction: the Subaltern as Subaltern Citizen' in Gyanendra Pandey (ed.), *Subaltern Citizens and their Histories: Investigations from India and the USA* (Oxford: Routledge, 2010), p. 2. Few Christians in India fit that archetype.

27 Dipesh Chakrabarty, 'Discussion: Invitation to a Dialogue', in Ranajit Guha (ed.), *Subaltern Studies IV: Writings on South Asian History and Society* (Delhi: Oxford University Press, 1985), p. 374.

It also drew more on specifically Dalit history than on subaltern history,[28] and some historians set their histories of Dalit Christians in the context less of Christian than of Dalit history—a significant theoretical choice.

Histories of tribal Christianity also preceded the Subaltern School and developed independently of it. They tended to be confined to either a single cluster of tribes (for example, Nagas, Mizos) or to all tribal people within a given region. They did not consider the tribal people to be subaltern groups within the Indian 'mainstream' but as having distinct societies of their own at its geographic margins. Their main focus was on Christianity's spread and influence upon the internal life, both of the converts and of the tribes to which they belonged. With one notable exception, which generated considerable controversy,[29] historians of Christianity treated these tribes as whole units, undifferentiated by social class or culture and, hence, free of internal class and/or cultural conflict.

Post-colonial theory has had more impact on histories of Christianity than has the Subaltern School. This approach has been characterized as 'a *process* of disengagement from the whole colonial syndrome'[30] and post-colonial studies as directing 'its critique against the cultural hegemony of European knowledges in an attempt to assert the epistemological value and agency of the non-European world'.[31] The special targets of post-colonial critique have been the images, stereotypes, representations, categories, theories, and underlying ideologies which colonial powers have used to define, classify, and 'understand' non-European peoples. Chapter 4 offers a description of the process by which the story of an Indian 'other' (Ditt) became totally swallowed up in Western mission theory and missionary hagiography, to be recovered and re-represented only recently. Other examples referred to in

28 On Dalit history, see Chapter 7, n35.

29 Vanlalchhuanawma depicted class and cultural conflict as combined in *Christianity and Subaltern Culture*.

30 Ania Loomba, *Colonialism/Postcolonialism* (London: Routledge, 1998), p. 19.

31 Leela Gandhi, *Postcolonial Theory: A Critical Introduction* (New York: Columbia University Press, 1998), p. 44.

Chapter 6 are found in the analyses of how the colonial legal system defined and classified Indian converts to Christianity, offered
by Gauri Viswanathan and Chandra Mallampalli, as well as (in
Chapter 7) my description of how similar colonial definitions and
classifications of Dalit Christians both misrepresented and trapped
them from 1919 until the present day.[32]

Post-colonial theory can also be applied to the churches in
India, for they, too (with the exception of the Syrian Orthodox
churches) were colonies complete with their own foreign rulers and Indian subjects—some collaborators, some dependents,
some rebels, some a combination of all three. Missionary rulers
not only shared much of the 'socio-cultural knowledge' of the
civil service but also had some more uniquely their own, rooted
in their Christian theologies, ethics, and missiologies. While these
have long since been deconstructed by Indian theologians, much
remains for the historian, including the myth of the 'masterful',
'guardian' missionary to whom all the virtues of the churches are
attributed and on whom all their faults are blamed. Post-colonial
theory also raises questions about whether, when the missionaries
left, the churches underwent regime changes or simply changes in
leadership personnel.

Like the Subaltern School, feminist theory is concerned with
agency, voice, and consciousness; like post colonial theory, it is
concerned with forms of knowledge and with the kinds of images,
stereotypes, representations, categories, inclusions, and exclusions
which they generate. While, for those theorists, the subaltern and
colonial experiences provide their respective starting points, for
feminists the starting point is women's experience, how it is constructed and with what consequences. The underlying premise is
that women's experience is not identical to, and therefore cannot be
subsumed under, men's experience. Because Indian women were
largely inaccessible to male mission personnel, Christian 'women's
work' developed as a separate, distinct, semi-autonomous (albeit

32 Gauri Viswanathan, *Outside the Fold*, pp. 75–117; Chandra
Mallampalli, *Christians and Public Life in Colonial South India, 1863–
1937*, pp. 19–84; John C.B. Webster, *The Dalit Christians: A History*, 3rd
ed., pp. 93–247.

subordinate) sphere of activity dominated by single women missionaries—a virtual guarantee that, at least among Christians, women's experience was seen as different from men's. Moreover, as Chapter 5 illustrates, there was a feminist component in the source materials which women produced, and evidence that, even in the nineteenth century, Christianity in India was being viewed through early feminist lenses.

In most of the histories surveyed in Chapters 6 and 7, women, when included, were treated separately, primarily as objects of evangelism, education, and/or social reform and uplift. Only a few histories were devoted exclusively to women and addressed such feminist issues as women's status, 'the social organization of gender', and constructions of 'Christian womanhood'.[33] In some more inclusive histories there are shorter treatments of dowry/ bride price, sex ratio, work in 'respectable' occupations outside the home, and leadership in the churches. However, a most basic feminist objective—that of making Indian Christian women visible, their voices heard, and their interests considered, whether in women's or more general histories of Christianity in India—is only just beginning to be realized, while studies of how Christian history in India has been gendered still lie almost entirely in the future.[34]

Although not a specific theoretical approach so much as a disciplinary focus in the study of society, cultural anthropology has also become an important interdisciplinary partner in studying Christianity in India. It examines particular communities, generally through participant observation, and then draws inferences about their culture by examining such things as myths, values, beliefs, symbols, as well as, 'honour, power, authority, exchange,

33 See the works by Eliza Kent, Frederick Downs, and Aphuno Chase Roy described in Chapter 6.

34 'Gender is a constitutive element of social relationships based on perceived differences between the sexes, and gender is a primary way of signifying relationships of power.' Joan W. Scott, 'Gender: A Useful Category of Historical Analysis', *The American Historical Review*, 91:5 (December 1986), p. 1056. See also, 'AHR Forum: Revisiting "Gender: A Useful Category of Historical Analysis",' ibid. 113:5 (December 2008), pp. 1344–429.

reciprocity, codes of conduct, systems of social classification, the construction of time and space, rituals',[35] not in isolation from, but in relationship to, structures and changes in other aspects of social life. Its theoretical frameworks in observing, questioning and inferring have changed over time and include those mentioned above.[36] This approach to studying the history of Christianity in India adopted by Susan Bayly, David Mosse, Rowena Robinson, Gunnel Cederlof, and Chad Bauman[37] has provided a necessary corrective to the overly social emphasis of historians following the socio-cultural 'New Perspective' advocated by CHAI. It has been especially useful in studying local Christian communities.[38]

This brief overview of some of the main theoretical orientations towards Indian society and culture which are evident in histories of Christianity leads to several conclusions. One is that these more recent theoretical approaches share a common concern to see and write history from the 'underside'. This is a healthy development for historians of Christianity because the vast majority of Christians in India are socially located on the 'underside', and these approaches have enhanced our understanding of them. Secondly, Christians should thus be compared with others similarly placed on the 'underside'—Christian Dalits with other Dalits; Christian tribal people with other tribal people; Christian women with other women; colonized Christians with other colonized Indians; Christian 'Indianness' with other local forms of it—in order to discover what is distinctive in the Christian experience. Thirdly, a conflict model of society is the one which best expresses not only the experience of society of those on its 'underside', but also

35 Bernard S. Cohn, *An Anthropologist among the Historians and Other Essays* (Delhi: Oxford University Press, 1987), p. 47.

36 See Fanella Cannel's Introduction to her edited volume, *The Anthropology of Christianity* (Durham, London: Duke University Press, 2006), pp. 1–50.

37 Supra, pp. 86–8, 161, 163–4, 165, 167–8, 177–8, 202, 204–5, 215–6.

38 Essential reading for anyone adopting this approach is Rowena Robinson's *Christians of India*, an anthropology of Christianity in India, which brings together the findings of other studies, and includes an historical dimension along with a focus on the present.

the aims of historical writing about them that are set forth in the first section of this chapter. Fourthly, while there is considerable compatibility and overlap among these newer theories, it is not possible to combine them consistently because of their differing starting points and priorities. Instead, one can use them in a more pragmatic fashion according to the dictates of the particular subject matter under investigation and the evidence in one's source materials. In the end, history is not a theory-building discipline, although it may rule out certain theories as either falsifying the evidence or being devoid of descriptive and explanatory power. For historians, theory serves to enhance understanding of people; it is not an end in itself. People take priority over abstractions.

THEOLOGICAL ASSUMPTIONS

Many of the early histories of Christianity in India were written within interpretative frameworks that were more theological than theoretical. For example, the purpose of God provided the framework for George Smith's historical overview, *The Conversion of India*. 'The one faith of Christ Jesus, the Son of Man, who said that He came to seek and to save the lost, prompting science, guiding colonisation, and using English speech, is working out the realisation of the unity of mankind by the very modern enterprise of Foreign Missions.'[39] Specifically, 'the historical and providential problem of missionary Christianity—the only true Christianity— . . . is to bring into the kingdom of Jesus Christ the elder branch of the great Indo-European family in India and Southern Asia'.[40] The Nestorians, the Roman Catholics, and the Dutch Protestants had failed to do this because of bad theology and/or bad methods, but English-speaking Evangelicals were succeeding within the context of religious liberty and equality set forth in the Queen's Proclamation of 1858. On the other hand, an unnamed Catholic priest did not set his history of the beginnings of Telugu Christianity in the Carnatic (1701–43) within a clear theological framework,

39 George Smith, *The Conversion of India: From Pantaenus to the Present Time, A.D. 193–1893* (London: J. Murray, 1893), p. 3.

40 Ibid., p. 6.

but he did include a number of lessons which that history had to teach concerning, for example, the distinctive Christian virtues; the work of Satan; God's grace and Christian fortitude in the face of persecution; and the lesser importance of the goods of this world as compared to those of the next.[41] In addition, both the author and the missionaries whose letters he quoted at great length made frequent references to divine interventions in the events about which they wrote.[42]

Such optimistic views of history could not last. In *Faith and History* (1949), Reinhold Niebuhr, the most influential American theologian of the twentieth century, faced with the devastation of World War II and the prospect of cold war nuclear annihilation, offered a theological critique not only of modern views of history but also of false absolutes in Christian interpretations of history, which might resonate well with later post-modernists.

> It is indeed one of the proofs of the ambiguity of man, as an observer of the historical process who transcends but is also involved in the process, that he cannot construct systems of meaning for the facts of history, whether of a particular story in it or of the story of mankind as a whole, without making the temporal locus of his observation into a falsely absolute vantage point, or without using a structure of meaning which seems to him to be absolutely valid but which is actually touched by historical relativism.[43]

Niebuhr did see provisional meanings and renewals, as well as judgements in history, the renewals being 'made possible by the very humility and love which is derived from an awareness of the limits of human virtue, wisdom and power',[44] but the end or culmination of history lay beyond and not within history itself. 'By the symbol of the Resurrection the Christian faith hopes for an eter-

41 A Father of the Mill Hill St. Joseph Society, *History of the Telugu Christians* (Trichinopoly, 1910), pp. iii, 77, 102, 139.

42 For example, ibid., pp. 20, 23, 24, 37, 83, 113.

43 Reinhold Niebuhr, *Faith and History: A Comparison of Christian and Modern Views of History* (New York: Charles Scribner's Sons, 1949), p. 112.

44 Ibid., p. 215.

nity which transfigures, but does not annul, the temporal process. The symbol of the Last Judgement, on the other hand, emphasizes the moral ambiguity of history to the end. . . . These eschatological symbols transcend the rational; but they do justice to the temporal and the eternal dimensions of man's historic existence.'[45]

Niebuhr's British contemporary, Herbert Butterfield, Professor of Modern History at the University of Cambridge, wrote extensively on Christianity and history as a Christian historian rather than as a theologian. While he saw divine providence (and not just mere chance) at work in history, especially when considering the unintended consequences óf human actions, he did not see the study of history as devoted to the larger theological/philosophical questions of God or of the meaning and purpose of life, but to the more mundane task of understanding the human past. Thus, 'the historian must play the game according to the rules. Within the scholarly realm that is here in question he is not allowed to bring God into the argument, or pretend to use him as a witness'.[46] However, the Christian can bring certain sensitivities to historical scholarship: intellectual humility; a sympathetic understanding of human personality, of historical forces and tendencies, as well as of their relationships with each other and with divine providence. Although he believed that history was undergirded by God's promise, Butterfield did not lay the same emphasis upon history moving towards a culmination point as did Niebuhr.

> If we want an analogy with history we must think of something like a Beethoven symphony—the point of it is not saved up until the end, the whole of it is not a mere preparation for a beauty that is only to be achieved at the last bar. And though in a sense the end may lie in the architecture of the whole, still in another sense each moment of it is its own self-justification, each note in its particular context as valuable as any other note, each stage of the development having its immediate significance, apart from the mere fact of any development that does

45 Ibid., p. 237.
46 Herbert Butterfield, 'Does Belief in Christianity Validly Affect the Historian?' in C.T. McIntire (ed.), *Herbert Butterfield: Writings on Christianity and History* (New York: Oxford University Press, 1979), p. 134.

take place....We envisage our history in the proper light, therefore, if we say that each generation—indeed each individual—exists for the glory of God; but one of the most dangerous things in life is to subordinate human personality to production, to the state, even to civilization itself, to anything but the glory of God.[47]

Niebuhr and Butterfield represent something of a watershed. Both saw Christianity as providing not only a theological anthropology and a view of history—which addressed the questions of overall meaning and purpose rather than offer an interpretative framework for specific past events and changes—but also a vantage point from which to critique and relativize all such frameworks, including those of a Smith or a Richter. Both viewed history as open-ended, morally ambiguous, full of mystery, and ever-present to an active God in ways that virtually require historians to follow 'the rules of the game' set by the academy in studying the human past in strictly human terms. Academic histories of Christianity in India, whether written by Christians or not, have followed those rules.

However, following the rules of academic history has not saved historians of Christianity from making a number of theological choices, even if those choices are not made for theological reasons. For example, in defining the parameters of one's inquiry, who is to be included and who excluded? The question, 'Who is a Christian?' has unavoidable theological dimensions. Within the churches, a baptized person is generally considered a Christian. But, does the historian include or exclude as Christians—and on what grounds—those who were baptized as babies but take no interest in Christianity as adults, or those Dalits who are full and faithful participants in the life of the churches but refuse to be baptized or placed on the church rolls lest they lose their Scheduled Caste benefits? There are Christians who use theological, spiritual or moral criteria to distinguish what they call 'real' or 'true' Christians from 'nominal Christians' or heretics. The historian cannot avoid using theological criteria while making these choices by simply including as Christians all those people who claim to be Christians, because

47 Herbert Butterfield, *Christianity and History* (London: Fontana Books, 1957) [originally published in 1949], p. 91.

that subordinates the criteria of the churches for membership to the historian's criteria.

The same problem of unavoidable theological assumptions arises when choosing to study the history of the Christian Church. Does the historian's view of 'the Church' include or exclude those Christian churches, fellowships, and *panths* of indigenous origin which are independent of and often 'unrecognized' by the older churches whose origins lie in the West? As an empirical reality, the Church is both multi-form and multi-dimensional, so, which form shapes the historian's approach to the subject and which dimensions does the historian treat as significant? All these choices may be made for pragmatic or even theoretical rather than theological reasons, but they favour some Christian theologies of the Church over others. Even the historian who seeks a neutral position on such theological issues by treating each church on its own terms has taken what amounts to a theological stand.

Moreover, the very subject matter of religious history begs the question of the presence of the divine and of mystery. How is the historian to treat that? For example, academic historians have generally treated religious conversion as a purely human transaction. They have analysed both individual conversions and large-scale conversion movements in terms of who the converts were, what their background circumstances were, what led them to convert, and what changed as a result. They have depicted conversion as a change of religious affiliation; an act of socio-cultural protest; an emancipatory act; a change in beliefs and relationships; a change in identity; a response to cultural conflict—all of which may well be true.[48] Nevertheless, is this not missing the point? By ignoring the specifically religious dimension of religious conversion, the historian reduces it to something else. That something else may be less mysterious, more manageable, and probably far better documented but, by ignoring the religious/theological dimension of conversion or ruling it out *a priori*, the historian has most probably failed to get to the heart of the matter.

The historian also faces unavoidable theological choices when making assessments of historical significance, especially

48 See Chapter 6.

in cases where social conflict and suffering are involved. At this point, historians confront profound mysteries that have held the attention of theologians and philosophers of all faiths and cultures for centuries. To say, for example, that Christianity in India has been aggressive, arrogant and exclusivist in its claims,[49] or that it has failed to win the quantity or quality (whatever that is) of the converts whom it sought to win,[50] or that it was one among several agents of India's modernization,[51] or that it was instrumental in raising the status of women, Dalits, and tribal people, as well as being a source of blessing to its adherents, might be warranted by the evidence selected. However, it would also be not only a partial judgement, reflective of the historian's own subjectivity but also one that is superficial, even one-dimensional, merely scratching the surface of events. Assessments of historical significance are based on preconceptions of what it means to be human; where this human enterprise we call history has been headed; and how it is going to get there—these remain mysteries which we glimpse only occasionally at best. Those preconceptions, glimpses, and their accompanying insights take us beyond the strictly empirical into the theological/philosophical dimensions of the human story, and have to be confronted at that level.[52]

The historian's own assumptions about diverse and changing Christian theological views on human nature and culture, on the nature of Christian ministry and mission, as well as on the status and relationships of the various world religions in the purposes of God, would also have a direct bearing upon any history of Christianity in India. Like theoretical assumptions, theological assumptions are to be found everywhere in dealing with this subject and there is no escaping them. Just as 'all historical writing is inevitably theoretical',[53] so all historical writing about Christianity

49 See pp. 4–5.

50 For example, Kanti Prasanna Sen Gupta, *The Christian Missionaries in Bengal, 1793–1833*, pp. 164–5, 193–4.

51 Supra, pp. 143–55.

52 For Fulbrook, these are the world views, paradigms, and philosophical anthropologies that historians bring to their work. Mary Fulbrook, *Historical Theory*, passim.

53 Ibid., p. 4.

is inevitably theological. Given this particular subject matter, even the historian who is an 'outsider' to Christianity is forced to make theological choices. While Butterfield was right in insisting that the historian's primary task is not to answer theological questions but to understand the human past, it is nevertheless inevitable that the historian of Christianity's theological choices will shape the understandings of that aspect of the human past she or he comes to.

As has been pointed out elsewhere, history has posed some very serious challenges to the work of Christian theology,[54] but the opposite is also true; theology poses some serious challenges to the work of writing history, and particularly the history of Christianity. How the historian chooses to deal with those challenges will depend in part on personal conviction and in part on the nature of the readership for which the history is being written. As far as theological assumptions are concerned, the 'rules of the game' are not quite the same in the churches as in the academic world. In writing for a Christian readership—whether academic or not—the historian can use an explicitly theological framework as well as a language which makes her or his theological assumptions concerning God, history, human nature, culture, Christian identity, the Church, quite explicit; the 'rules of the game' permit but do not require that. However, 'the rules of the game' are different when writing for the wider academic community and the general public. Therefore, the historian must, and in fact may much prefer to, use an interpretative framework and a language that make his or her theological assumptions and/or choices only implicit. Given the aims of studying and researching the history of Christianity in India which have been outlined in the opening section of this chapter, it would seem to be the wisest way to proceed.

LOOKING BACK AND AHEAD

The foregoing analysis of four clusters of assumptions upon which historical writing on Christianity in India has been based indicates that this field of study has not remained static, but has under-

---

54 See Euan Cameron, *Interpreting Christian History: The Challenge of the Churches' Past* (Oxford: Blackwell, 2005).

gone significant change, not just in the subjects being researched but in its core premises as well. Not only do historians today no longer live in the same intellectual world as their nineteenth-century predecessors, but both Christianity in India and India itself have changed in ways that those predecessors could not have anticipated. Hence, the reference points from which Christianity's Indian history could be written are now both very different from and more diverse than they were one or two hundred years ago. Furthermore, the history of Christianity in India has not been an autonomous, self-enclosed, field of study, impervious to outside influences. Instead, it has been shaped profoundly by developments in historical study generally, in the study of Indian history in particular, and, to a lesser degree, in the study of Christian history elsewhere, and also by such obvious events as India's Independence and the ecclesiastical autonomy of the churches in India.

This is as it should be. New historical situations beg new historical questions that may require fresh assumptions and new methods for answering them. At the same time, it is worth noting that, for example, CHAI's 'New Perspective' (now almost forty years old) has not yet exhausted its potential, especially when combined with the newer post-colonial or feminist theories, the disciplinary foci of the anthropologists, and/or the special concerns of Dalit and tribal history. The present historian of Christianity in India has plenty to work with and a solid base from which to move this field of study forward.

A final assumption on which this analysis has been based is that the historian is a public figure with a public responsibility that extends well beyond the academy. Historians are responsible first and foremost to the past and, in particular, to the people about whom they write their histories. Whatever the historian's personal likes and dislikes or agreements and disagreements may be, the dead deserve at least as much empathetic understanding and respect as the living, especially since they cannot answer back. This would include not just the Christians of the past but also their sympathizers and their critics. Historians who fail to be as true to past generations as they can be are also doing a disservice to the present generation for whom they write. Since, as was pointed out at the beginning of this chapter, the way in which the history of

Christianity in India is written helps to shape, reshape, and even heal the inherited identities of both Christians in India and India as a whole, their past must be presented as carefully as possible. The responsibility of the historian of Christianity to the present as custodian of collective memory, as critic of prevailing assumptions about the past, as reconciler and healer, can be further carried out by keeping both the Christian public and the general public in mind when writing. Identity issues are contested and sorted out far more in public arenas than in the academy. Bringing our histories into those public arenas where something of their fuller civic potential might be realized requires the use of clear, open-ended interpretative frameworks as well as jargon-free, non-technical language that the 'intelligent non-specialist' can understand and appreciate. In that way, the public will be both better informed and, at the same time, left free to decide what steps, if any, should be taken with the identity-shaping perspectives provided by the histories they read, without having those decisions imposed upon them by what particular historians consider to be the 'dictates' or 'lessons' of their past. This kind of history writing can be very liberating because it helps its readers realize that their future is shaped, at least in part, by their own decisions, however difficult they may be, rather than determined by a historical fate totally outside their control.

Glossary

bhakti	devotion to a personal God
bihishtin	female water carrier
biradari	caste brotherhood
cathanar	priest
Catechist	a person appointed to provide instruction in Christian teachings
Dalit	literally 'broken' or oppressed; a name which members of those castes considered untouchable have chosen to give themselves
dharma	sacred moral and religious duties prescribed for each caste
doolie	a seat surrounded by curtains carried on men's shoulders
Gaunkar	founder member of a village community
guru	religious teacher
hakim	practitioner of the classical system of Muslim medicine
Harijan	'child of God'; Gandhi's term for Dalits
Hindutva	literally 'Hinduness'
jati	caste group based on kinship and lineage; the jati-talaivan is the headman of a caste group in Tamil Nadu
*jhagrra*s	quarrels, disputes
Khristadharma	the Christian dharma

*kissa*s	stories
Lumbardar	village headman
missiology	the study of Christian mission and missions
muffassal	countryside
Munshi	clerk, teacher
Nain	female hairdresser
nautch	dance
panth	a group following a particular teacher or set of doctrines
pativrata	virtuous wife
pir	a Sufi religious guide
*puggerie*s	turbans
pundit	a Brahmin, learned person
Ryot	peasant cultivator
Sangh Pariwar	family of organizations promoting a Hindutva agenda for India
sati	a devoted widow who willingly burns herself on the funeral pyre of her husband
zamindar	landlord
zenana	female apartment or section of the house reserved for women

Bibliography

Abbott, Walter M. *The Documents of Vatican II*, New York: Guild Press, 1966.

Abraham, C.E. 'The Study of Church History in India', *The International Review of Missions*, vol. XXV, 1936, pp. 461–9.

Agur, C.M. *Church History of Travancore*, New Delhi: Asian Educational Services, 1990.

'AHR Forum: Revisiting "Gender: A Useful Category of Historical Analysis",' *The American Historical Review*, 113:5 (December 2008), pp. 1344–429.

Ali, Muhammad Mohar. *The Bengali Reaction to Christian Missionary Activities 1833–1857*, Chittagong: The Mehrub Publications, 1965.

Alter, James P. *In the Doab and Rohilkhand: North Indian Christianity 1815–1915*, revised and completed by John Alter; Delhi: ISPCK, 1986.

Anderson, Emma Dean, and Mary Jane Campbell, *In the Shadow of the Himalayas: A Historical Narrative of the Missions of the United Presbyterian Church of North America as Conducted in the Punjab, India 1855–1940*, Philadelphia: The United Presbyterian Board of Foreign Missions, 1942.

Annual Report of the Board of Foreign Missions of the United Presbyterian Church of North America 1906, 1911.

Appasamy, A.J. 'The Study of Church History in India', *National Christian Council Review*, LIII (March 1933), pp. 123–8 and (April 1933), pp. 185–93.

Appleby, Joyce, Lynn Hunt, and Margaret Jacob. *Telling the Truth about History*, New York: W.W. Norton, 1994.

Baagø, Kaj. *A History of the National Christian Council of India 1914-64*, Nagpur: National Christian Council, 1965.

Baagø, Kaj. *Pioneers of Indigenous Christianity*, Madras: Christian Literature Society, 1969.

――――. 'The Discovery of India's Past and Its Effect on the Christian Church in India', in John C.B. Webster (ed.), *History and Contemporary India*, Bombay: Asia Publishing House, 1971, pp. 26–45.

――――. 'The First Independence Movement Among Indian Christians', *Indian Church History Review*, I (June 1967), pp. 65–78.

Balasundaram, Franklyn J. *Dalits and Christian Mission in the Tamil Country: The Dalit Movement and Protestant Christians in the Tamil Speaking Districts of Madras Presidency 1919–1939 with Special Reference to London Missionary Society Area in Salem, Attur, Coimbatore and Erode*, Bangalore: Asia Trading Corp., 1997.

Ballhatchet, Kenneth. *Caste, Class and Catholicism in India 1789-1914*, Richmond: Curzon Press, 1998.

Barnes, Irene H. *Behind the Purdah: The Story of C.E.Z.M.S. Work in India*, London: Marshall Brothers, 1897.

Barraclough, Geoffrey. *Main Trends in History*, New York: Holmes and Meier, 1979.

Bauman, Chad M. *Christian Identity and Dalit Religion in Hindu India, 1868-1947*, Grand Rapids: Eerdmans, 2008.

Bayly, Susan. *Saints, Goddesses and Kings: Muslims and Christians in South Indian Society 1700–1900*, Cambridge: Cambridge University Press, 1989.

Brown, Judith M. and Robert Eric Frykenberg (eds.), *Christians, Cultural Interactions and India's Religious Traditions*, Grand Rapids: William B. Eerdmans, 2002.

Bugge, Henriette. *Mission and Tamil Society: Social and Religious Change in South India 1840–1900*, Richmond: Curzon Press, 1994.

Bulletin of the Church History Association of India, 1961–7.

Butterfield, H. *Christianity and History*, London: Fontana Books, 1957.

――――. 'Does Belief in Christianity Validly Affect the Historian?' in C.T. McIntire (ed.), *Herbert Butterfield: Writings on Christianity and History*, New York: Oxford University Press, 1979, pp. 133-50.

Cameron, Euan. *Interpreting Christian History: The Challenge of the Churches' Past*, Oxford: Blackwell, 2005.

Cannel, Fanella (ed.). *The Anthropology of Christianity*, Durham and London: Duke University Press, 2006.

Carr, E.H. *What is History?* Hammondsworth: Penguin Books, 1964.

Cederlof, Gunnel. *Bonds Lost: Subordination, Conflict and Mobilisation in Rural South India c. 1900–1970*, Delhi: Manohar, 1997.

Chakrabarty, Dipesh. 'Discussion: Invitation to a Dialogue', in Ranajit Guha (ed.), *Subaltern Studies IV: Writings on South Asian History and Society*, Delhi: Oxford University Press, 1985, pp. 364–76.

Chatterji, P.C. (ed.). *Self-Images, Identity and Nationality*, Shimla: Indian Institute of Advanced Study, 1989.

Chattopadhyaya, D.P. (ed.). *History of Science, Philosophy and Culture in Indian Civilization: Volume VII Part 6: Indian Christianity*, ed. A. V. Afonso, New Delhi: Centre for Studies in Civilizations, 2009.

Chaudhuri, Nurpur and Margaret Strobel. *Western Women and Imperialism: Complicity and Resistance*, Bloomington: Indiana University Press, 1992.

Cheriyan, P. *The Malabar Syrians and the Church Missionary Society, 1816–1840*, Kothayam: Church Missionary Society's Press & Book Depot, 1935.

Church of England Zenana Missionary Society, *Annual Reports*, 1880–1914.

Clark, Robert. *The Punjab and Sindh Missions of the Church Missionary Society Giving an Account of their Foundation and Progress for Thirty-Three Years, from 1852 to 1884*, London: Church Missionary Society, 1885, 2nd ed.

Cohn, Bernard S. *An Anthropologist among the Historians and Other Essays*, Delhi: Oxford University Press, 1987.

Copley, Antony. *Religions in Conflict: Ideology, Cultural Contact, and Conversion in Late Colonial India*, Delhi: Oxford University Press, 1997.

Coward, Howard (ed.). *Hindu–Christian Dialogue: Perspectives and Encounters*, Maryknoll: Orbis Books, 1989.

Cox, Jeffrey. *Imperial Fault Lines: Christianity and Colonial Power in India, 1818–1940*, Stanford: Stanford University Press, 2002.

Das, Sisir Kumar. *The Shadow of the Cross: Christianity and Hinduism in a Colonial Situation*, New Delhi: Munshiram Manoharlal, 1973.

David, Immanuel. *Reformed Church in America Missionaries in South India, 1839-1938: An Analytical Study*, Bangalore, 1986.

David, M.D. *Missions: Cross-Cultural Encounter and Change in Western India*, Delhi: ISPCK, 2001.

Dorairaj, J. *Springs of Hope: Dalit History*, Madurai: Tamilnadu Theological Seminary, 2009.

Downs, Frederick S. *Christianity in North East India: Historical Perspectives*, Delhi: ISPCK, 1983.

———. *Essays on Christianity in North-East India*, ed. Milton S. Sangma and David R. Syiemlieh, New Delhi: Indus Publishing Company, 1994.

Downs, Frederick S. *History of Christianity in India. Volume 5, Part 5: North East India in the Nineteenth and Twentieth Centuries*, Bangalore: Church History Association of India, 1992.

———. 'Identity: The Integrating Principle', *Bangalore Theological Forum*, vol. XXIV, March-June 1992, pp. 1–14.

———. *The Christian Impact on the Status of Women in North East India*, Shillong: North-Eastern Hill University Publications, 1996.

———. *The Mighty Works of God: A Brief History of the Council of Baptist Churches in North East India, The Mission Period 1836-1950*, Gauhati: Christian Literature Center, 1971.

D'Sa, M. *History of the Catholic Church in India. Volume I: 52–1652 A.D.*, Bombay 1910; *Volume II: 1652–1924 A.D.*, Bombay 1924.

Dube, Saurabh. 'Paternalism and Freedom: The Evangelical Encounter in Colonial Chattisgarh, Central India', *Modern Asian Studies*, 29:1, 1995, pp. 171–201.

———. *Untouchable Pasts: Religion, Identity, and Power among a Central Indian Community, 1780-1950*, Albany: State University of New York Press, 1998.

Dubois, J.A. *Letters on the State of Christianity in India*, London: Longman, Hurst, Orme, Brown, and Green, 1823.

Ebeling, Gerhard. *The Word of God And Tradition: Historical Studies Interpreting the Divisions of Christianity*, trans. S.M. Hooke; London: Collins, 1968.

Farias, Kranti K. *The Christian Impact in South Kanara*, Mumbai: Church History Association of India Western Branch, 1999.

Farquhar, J.N. *Modern Religious Movements in India*, New York: Macmillan, 1915.

A Father of the Mill Hill St. Joseph Society, *History of the Telugu Christians*, Trichinopoly, 1910.

Fernando, Leonard and G. Gispert-Sauch. *Christianity in India: Two Thousand Years of Faith*, New Delhi: Penguin Viking, 2004.

Firth, Cyril Bruce. *An Introduction to Indian Church History*, Madras: Christian Literature Society, 1961.

Fishman, Alvin Texas. *Culture Change and the Underprivileged: A Study of the Madigas in South India under Christian Guidance*, Madras: Christian Literature Society, 1941.

Forrester, Duncan B. *Caste and Christianity: Attitudes and Policies on Caste of Anglo-Saxon Protestant Missions in India*, London: Curzon Press, 1980.

———. 'Indian Christian Attitudes to Caste in the Twentieth Century', *Indian Church History Review*, vol. IX, June 1975, pp. 3–22.

Frykenberg, Robert Eric. *Christianity in India: From Beginnings to the Present*, Oxford: Oxford University Press, 2008.

—— (ed.), *Christians and Missionaries in India: Cross-Cultural Communication since 1500*, Grand Rapids: William B. Eerdmans, 2003.

Fulbrook, Mary. *Historical Theory*, London: Routledge, 2002.

Gandhi, Leela. *Postcolonial Theory: A Critical Introduction*, New York: Columbia University Press, 1998.

Geddes, Michael. *The History of the Church of Malabar*, London: Samuel Smith and Benjamin Walford, 1694.

Gladstone, J.W. '19th Century Mass Movement in Travancore—A Result of Social Liberation', *Indian Church History Review*, vol. X, June 1976, pp. 53–66.

—— *Protestant Christianity and People's Movements in Kerala 1850–1936*, Trivandrum: The Seminary Publications, 1984.

Goel, Sita Ram. *History of Hindu-Christian Encounters*, New Delhi: Voice of India, 1989.

Gopal, S. 'The Fear of History', *Seminar*, no. 221, January 1978, pp. 71–4.

Gordon, Andrew. *Our India Mission: A Thirty Year History of the India Mission of United Presbyterian Church of North America, Together with Personal Reminiscences*, Philadelphia: Andrew Gordon, 1886.

Grafe, Hugald. *History of Christianity in India: Volume 4, Part 2: Tamilnadu in the Nineteenth and Twentieth Centuries*, Bangalore: Church History Association of India, 1990.

Guha, Ranajit. 'On Some Aspects of the Historiography of Colonial India', in Ranajit Guha (ed.), *Subaltern Studies I: Writings on South Asian History and Society*, Delhi: Oxford University Press, 1982, pp. 1–8.

Hambye, E.R. *A Bibliography on Christianity in India*, Bangalore: Church History Association of India, 1974.

——. *History of Christianity in India. Volume 3: Eighteenth Century*, Bangalore: Church History Association of India, 1997.

Hansen, Bent Smid. *Dependency and Identity: Problems of Cultural Encounter as a Consequence of the Danish Mission in South India Between the Two World Wars*, Quebec: World Heritage Press, 1998.

Hardgrave, Jr, Robert L. *The Nadars of Tamilnad* (Berkeley and Los Angeles: University of California Press, 1969).

Hardiman, David. *Missionaries and Their Medicine: A Christian Modernity for Tribal India*, Manchester: Manchester University Press, 2008.

Harding, Christopher. *Religious Transformation in South Asia: The Meanings of Conversion in Colonial Punjab*, Oxford: Oxford University Press, 2008.

Harper, Susan Billington. *In the Shadow of the Mahatma: Bishop V.S. Azariah and the Travails of Christianity in British India*, Grand Rapids: Eerdmans, 2000.

———. 'The Politics of Conversion: The Azariah-Gandhi Controversy over Christian Mission to the Depressed Classes in the 1930s', *Indo-British Review*, XV:1, n.d., pp. 147–75.

Harvey, Van A. *The Historian and the Believer: The Morality of Historical Knowledge and Christian Belief*, Toronto: The Macmillan Company, 1966.

Hedlund, Roger E. (ed.), *Christianity is Indian: The Emergence of an Indigenous Community*, Delhi: ISPCK, 2000.

———. *Quest for Identity. India's Churches of Indigenous Origin: The 'Little Tradition' in Indian Christianity*, Delhi: ISPCK, 2000.

Herman, Judith Lewis. *Trauma and Recovery*, New York: Basic Books, 1997.

Hewlett, S.S. *Daughters of the King*, London: Church of England Zenana Missionary Society, 1886.

Hluna, John Vânlal. *Church and Political Upheaval in Mizoram: A Study of Impact of Christianity on the Political Development in Mizoram*, Aizawl: Mizo History Association, 1985.

Hough, James. *A Reply to the Letters of the Abbe Dubois, on the State of Christianity in India*, London: L.B. Seeley and Son, 1824.

———. *The History of Christianity in India from the Commencement of the Christian Era*, London: R.B. Seeley and W. Burnside, Vols. 1 & 2 1839, Vols. 3 & 4 1845, Vol. 5 1860.

Houpert, Joseph. *A South Indian Mission: The Madura Catholic Mission from 1535 to 1935*, Trichinopoly: St. Joseph's Industrial School Press, 1937, new ed.

———. *Church History of India and Ceylon* A.D. *52–1942*, Trichinopoly: The Catholic Truth Society of India, 1942, rev. ed.

Hrangkhuma, F. (ed.), *Christianity in India: Search for Liberation and Identity*, Delhi: ISPCK, 1998.

India's Women, 1881–1895.

India's Women and China's Daughters, 1896–1918.

Ingham, Kenneth. *Reformers in India 1793-1833: An Account of the Work of Christian Missionaries on Behalf of Social Reform*, Cambridge: Cambridge University Press, 1956.

Jackman, S.W. *Nicholas Cardinal Wiseman: A Victorian Prelate and His Writings*, Dublin: Five Lamps Press, 1977.

Jayakumar, D. Arthur. *Christians and the National Movement: The Memorandum of 1919 and the National Movement with Special*

Reference to Protestant Christians in Tamil Nadu 1919–1939, Calcutta: Punthic Pustak, 1999.

Jayakumar, Samuel. *Dalit Consciousness and Christian Conversion: Historical Resources for a Contemporary Debate*, Oxford: Regnum International and Delhi: ISPCK, 1999.

Jedin, Hubert. 'General Introduction to Church History', in Karl Baus (ed.), *Handbook of Church History. Vol. I: From Apostolic Community to Constantine*, Hubert Jedin and John Dolan (gen. eds.), New York: Herder & Herder, 1965, pp. 1–56.

Jones, Serene. *Feminist Theory and Christian Theology: Cartographies of Grace*, Minneapolis: Fortress Press, 2000.

Kammen, Michael (ed.) *The Past Before Us: Contemporary Historical Writing in the United States*, Ithaca: Cornell University Press, 1980.

Kananaikil, Jose. *Christians of Scheduled Caste Origin*, New Delhi: Indian Social Institute, 1983.

———. *Scheduled Castes in Search of Justice. Part I: Knocking at the Door of the Lok Sabha; Part II: The Verdict of the Supreme Court; Part III: Constitution (Scheduled Castes) Orders (Amendment) Bill, 1990*; New Delhi: Indian Social Institute, 1986, 1986, 1993.

Kawashima, Koji. *Missionaries and a Hindu State: Travancore 1858–1936*, Delhi: Oxford University Press, 1998.

Kaye, John William. *Christianity in India: An Historical Narrative*, London: Smith, Elder and Co., 1859.

Keay, F.E. *A History of the Syrian Church in India*, Madras: SPCK in India, 1938.

Kent, Eliza F. *Converting Women: Gender and Protestant Christianity in Colonial South India*, New York: Oxford University Press, 2004.

Kim, Sebastian C.H. *In Search of Identity: Debates on Religious Conversion in India*, New Delhi: Oxford University Press, 2003.

Kipgen, Mangkhosat *Christianity and Mizo Culture: The Encounter Between Christianity and Zo Culture in Mizoram*, Aizawl: Mizo Theological Conference, 1997.

Kooiman, Dick. *Conversion and Social Equality in India: The London Missionary Society in South Travancore in the 19th Century*, Delhi: Manohar, 1989.

Kuriakose, M.K. *History of Christianity in India: Source Materials*, Madras: The Christian Literature Society, 1982.

Kopf, David. *British Orientalism and Indian Renaissance: The Dynamics of Indian Modernization 1773-1835*, Berkeley: University of California Press, 1969.

La Croze, M.V. *Histoire du Christianisme des Indes*, La Haye, 1724.

Laird, M.A. *Missionaries and Education in Bengal 1793-1837*, Oxford: Clarendon Press, 1972.

Lalsawma. *Revivals the Mizo Way: Forty Years of Revival Movements in Mizoram*, Aizawl: The Author, 1994.

Latourette, Kenneth Scott. *A History of the Expansion of Christianity, Vol. VI: The Great Century A.D. 1800-A.D. 1914 in Northern Africa and Asia*, New York: Harper & Row, 1944.

Lobo, Lancy. 'Conversion, Emigration and Social Mobility of an Ex-Scheduled Caste from Central Gujarat', *Social Action*, vol. 39, October-December 1989, pp. 423–37.

Loomba, Ania. *Colonialism/Postcolonialism*, London: Routledge, 1998.

Majumdar, R.C. 'Nationalist Historians', in C.H. Philips (ed.), *Historians of India, Pakistan and Ceylon*, London: Oxford University Press, 1961, pp. 416–28.

Malhotra, Anshu. *Gender, Caste, and Religious Identities: Restructuring Class in Colonial Punjab*, New Delhi: Oxford University Press, 2002.

Mallampalli, Chandra. *Christians and Public Life in Colonial South India, 1863–1937: Contending with Marginality*, London: Routledge Curzon, 2004.

Manickam, Sundararaj. *The Social Setting of Christian Conversion in South India: The Impact of the Wesleyan Methodist Missionaries on the Trichy-Tanjore Diocese with Special Reference to the Harijan Communities of the Mass Movement Area 1820–1947*, Wiesbaden: Franz Steiner Verlag, 1977.

Martin, E. Josephine. *A Father to the Poor*, Descendants of Dr & Mrs Samuel Martin, n.n. (1956?).

Massey, James. *Religion as a Source of Bondage or Liberation, with Special Reference to Christians*, Delhi: Manohar, 1995.

———. *Towards Dalit Hermeneutics: Rereading the Text, the History and the Literature*, Delhi: ISPCK, 1994.

Mathew, A. *Christian Missions, Education and Nationalism: From Dominance to Compromise 1870-1930*, Delhi: Anamika Prakashan, 1988.

McIntire, C.T., ed. *God, History and Historians*, New York: Oxford University Press, 1977.

Menachery, George (ed.) *The St. Thomas Christian Encyclopedia of India. Volume 1: Indian Christianity by Chronological, Denominational, Geographical and Ecclesiastical Divisions*, Trichur: The St. Thomas Christian Encyclopedia of India, 1982.

Menachery, George (ed.) *The St. Thomas Christian Encyclopedia of India. Volume 2: St. Thomas, Kerala, Malabar Christianity*, Trichur: The St. Thomas Christian Encyclopedia of India, 1973.

Metcalf, Thomas R. *The Aftermath of Revolt: India 1857-1870*, Princeton: Princeton University Press, 1964.

Mingana, H. *The Early Spread of Christianity in India*, Manchester: The University Press, 1926.

Moraes, George Mark. *A History of Christianity in India. From Early Times to St. Francis Xavier: A.D. 52–1542*, Bombay: Manaktalas, 1964.

Mosse, David. 'Idioms of Subordination and Styles of Protest among Christian and Hindu Harijan Castes in Tamil Nadu', *Contributions to Indian Sociology*, 28:1 (ns), 1994, pp. 67–106.

———. 'The Catholic Church and Dalit Christian Activism in Contemporary Tamil Nadu', in Rowena Robinson and Joseph Marianus Kujur (eds.), *Margins of Faith: Dalit and Tribal Christianity in India*, New Delhi: Sage Publications, 2010, pp. 235–62.

Mundadan, A. Mathias. *History of Christianity in India. Volume I: From the Beginning up to the Middle of the Sixteenth Century*, Bangalore: Theological Publications in India, 1984.

———. *Indian Christians Search for Identity and Struggle for Autonomy*, Bangalore: Dharmaram Publications, 1984.

———. *Sixteenth Century Traditions of St. Thomas Christians*, Bangalore: Dharmaram College, 1970.

———. 'The Changing Task of Christian History: A View at the Outset of the Third Millenium', in W.R. Shenk (ed.), *Enlarging the Story: Perspectives on Writing World Christian History*, Maryknoll: Orbis Books, 2002, pp. 22–53.

Natarajan, Nalini. *The Missionary among the Khasis*, New Delhi: Sterling Publishers, 1977.

Neill, Stephen. *A History of Christianity in India: The Beginnings to AD 1707*, Cambridge: Cambridge University Press, 1984.

———. *A History of Christianity in India 1707-1858*, Cambridge: Cambridge University Press, 1985

———. *The Story of the Christian Church in India and Pakistan*, Madras and Delhi: CLS-ISPCK, 1972.

Neog, Maheshwar (ed.), *The Resusitation of the Assamese Language by the American Baptist Missionaries*, New Delhi: Omsons Publications, 2008.

Niebuhr, Reinhold. *Faith and History: A Comparison of Christian and Modern Views of History*, New York: Charles Scribner's Sons, 1949.

O'Connor, Daniel. *Gospel, Raj and Swaraj: The Missionary Years of C. F. Andrews 1904-14*, Frankfurt: Verlag Peter Lang, 1990.

Oddie, Geoffrey A. 'Christian Conversions in the Telugu Country 1860-1900: A Case Study of One Protestant Indian Movement in the Godavery-Krishna Delta', *Indian Economic and Social History Review*, vol. XII, January-March 1975, pp. 61–79.

Oddie, Geoffrey A. 'Christianity and Social Mobility in South India 1840-1920: A Continuing Debate', *South Asia*, vol. XIX, Special Issue 1996, pp. 143–59.

————. 'Christianity in the Hindu Crucible: Continuity and Change in the Kaveri Delta, 1850-1900', *Indian Church History Review*, vol. XV (June 1981), pp. 48–72.

————. *Hindu and Christian in South-East India*, London: Curzon Press, 1991.

————. 'Protestant Missions, Caste and Social Change in India', *Indian Economic and Social History Review*, vol. VI, September 1969, pp. 259–91.

————. *Social Protest in India: British Protestant Missionaries and Social Reform 1850–1900*, New Delhi: Manohar, 1979.

———— ed., *Religion in South Asia: Religious Conversion and Revival Movements in South Asia in Medieval and Modern Times*, Delhi: Manohar, 1977.

———— ed., *Religious Conversion Movements in South Asia: Continuities and Change 1800–1900*, Richmond: Curzon Press, 1997.

Oommen, George. 'Communist Influence on Dalit Christians—The Kerala Experience', *Bangalore Theological Forum*, XXVI: 3&4 (September & December 1994), pp. 43–62; reprinted in Kanichikattil Francis (ed.), *Church in Context: Essays in Honour of Mathias Mundadan CMI*, Bangalore: Dharamaram Publications, 1996, pp. 31–55.

————. 'Dalit Conversion and Social Protest in Travancore 1854–1890', *Bangalore Theological Forum*, vol. XXVIII, September-December 1996, pp. 69-84.

————. 'Christianization or Dalitization: The Twentieth Century Experience of Dalit Christians in Kerala', *Indian Church History Review*, XXXVII:1, June 2003, pp. 1–22.

————. 'The Struggle of Anglican Pulaya Christians for Social Improvement in Travancore, 1854–1966', Unpublished PhD Dissertation, University of Sydney, 1993.

Oommen, George and John C.B. Webster (eds.), *Local Dalit Christian History*, Delhi: ISPCK, 2002.

Pachuau, Lalsangkima. *Ethnic Identity and Christianity: A Socio-Historical and Missiological Study of Christianity in Northeast India with Special Reference to Mizoram*, Frankfurt: Verlag Peter Lang, 2002.

Pandey, Gyanendra. 'Introduction: the Subaltern as Subaltern Citizen' in Gyanendra Pandey (ed.), *Subaltern Citizens and their Histories: Investigations from India and the USA*, Oxford: Routledge, 2010, pp. 1–12.

Panikkar, K.M. *Asia and Western Dominance*, New York: Collins Books, 1969.

Panikkar, K.N. *The Concerned Indian's Guide to Communalism*, New Delhi: Viking, 1999.

Parekh, Bhikhu. 'Logic of Humiliation', in Gopal Guru (ed.), *Humiliation: Claims and Context*, New Delhi: Oxford University Press, 2009, pp. 23-40.

Parker, Russ. *Healing Wounded History: Reconciling People and Restoring Places*, Cleveland: The Pilgrim Press, 2001.

Paul, Rajaiah D. *The Cross Over India*, London: S.C.M. Press Ltd., 1952.

Perumalil, H.C. and E.R. Hambye (eds.). *Christianity in India: A History in Ecumenical Perspective*, Alleppey: Prakasam Publications, 1972.

Philip, E.M. *The Indian Church of St. Thomas*, Nagercoil: London Missionary Sovciety Press, 1950.

Philipos, Edivalikel. *The Syrian Christians of Malabar Otherwise Called The Christians of S. Thomas*, edited by G.B. Howard, Oxford and London: James Parker & Co., 1869.

Pickett, J. Waskom. *Christian Mass Movements in India: A Study with Recommendations*, New York: The Abingdon Press, 1933.

Placid, Rev. Fr. *The Syrian Church of Malabar*, edited by K.E. Job, Changanacherry: St. Joseph's Orpjhanage Press, 1938.

Potts, E. Daniel. *British Baptist Missionaries in India 1793–1837: The History of Serampore and its Missions*, Cambridge: Cambridge University Press, 1967.

Powell, Avril Ann. *Muslims and Missionaries in Pre-Mutiny India*, Richmond: Curzon Press, 1993.

Prabhakar, M.E. 'In Search of Roots—Dalit Aspirations and the Christian Dalit Question: Perceptions of the Telugu Poet Laureate, Joshua', *Religion and Society*, XLI:1, March 1994, pp. 2–20.

——. 'The Dalit Poetry of Poet-Laureate, Joshua', in Joseph Patmury (ed.), *Doing Theology with the Poetic Traditions of India: Focus on Dalit and Tribal Poems*, Bangalore: PTCA/SATHRI, 1996, pp. 3–20.

——. (ed.), *Towards a Dalit Theology*, Delhi: ISPCK, 1988.

Rae, George Milne. *The Syrian Church in India*, Edinburgh & London: William Blackwood and Sons, 1892.

Ranson, C.W. *The Christian Minister in India, His Vocation and Training*, London: United Society for Christian Literature, 1946.

Report by the Committee for the Propagation of the Gospel in Foreign Parts Especially in India to the General Assembly of the Church of Scotland, May 1875.

Report of the Seminar on Postgraduate Research and Teaching in History, New Delhi: University Grants Commission, 1964.

'Report: The Church History Association of India (A History of the Association from 1935 to 1960)', *The Indian Journal of Theology*, vol. IX, 1960, pp. 166-68.

'Reports: Church History Association of India, Burma and Ceylon Report for the Year 1935', *National Christian Council Review*, vol. LVI, March 1936, pp. 160–6.

Richter, Julius. *A History of Missions in India*, trans. by Sydney H. Moore, Edinburgh and London: Oliphant, Anderson and Ferrier, 1908.

Robinson, Rowena. *Christians of India*, New Delhi: Sage Publications, 2003.

———. *Conversion, Continuity and Change: Lived Christianity in Southern Goa*, New Delhi: Sage Publications, 1998,

Robinson, Rowena and Sathianathan Clarke (eds.). *Religious Conversion in India: Modes, Motivations and Meanings*, New Delhi: Oxford University Press, 2003.

Rosenau, P.M. *Post-Modernism and the Social Sciences: Insights, Inroads and Intrusions*, Princeton: Princeton University Press, 1992.

Roy, Aphuno Chase. *Women in Transition: Angami Naga Women from 1878 to the Present*, Kohima: The Author, 2004.

Sarkar, Sumit. *Beyond Nationalist Frames: Relocating Postmodernism, Hindutva, History*, Delhi: Permanent Black, 2002.

'A Scheme for a Comprehensive History of Christianity in India' (mimeographed); also *Indian Church History Review*, VII (December 1974), pp. 89-90.

Scott, Joan W. 'Gender: A Useful Category of Historical Analysis', *The American Historical Review*, 91:5, December 1986, pp. 1053–75.

Sen Gupta, Kanti Prasanna. *The Christian Missionaries in Bengal 1793-1833*, Calcutta: Firma K.L. Mukhopadhyay, 1971.

Sharma, Raj Bahadur. *Christian Missions in North India 1813-1913: A Case Study of Meerut Division and Dehra Dun District*, Delhi: Mittal Publications, 1988.

Sherring, M.A. *A History of Protestant Missions in India from their Commencement in 1706 to 1871*, London: Trubner and Co., 1875.

Shourie, Arun. *Missionaries in India: Continuities, Changes, Dilemmas*, New Delhi: ASA, 1994.

Shyamlal. *Tribals and Christian Missionaries*, Delhi: Manak Publications, 1994.

Singh, Maina Chawla. *Gender, Religion and "Heathen Lands": American Missionary Women in South Asia (1860s–1940s)*, New York: Garland Publishing, 2000.

Smith, George. *The Conversion of India from Pantaonus to the Present Time A.D. 191–1893*, London: John Murray, 1893

Snaitang, O.L. *Christianity and Social Change in Northeast India: A Study of the Role of Christianity in Social Change Among the Khasi-Jaintia Hill Tribes of Meghalaya*, Calcutta: Firma K.L. Mukhopadhyay Private Ltd., 1993.

Snaitang, O.L. (ed.). *Churches of Indigenous Origin in Northeast India*, Delhi: ISPCK, 2000.

Soares, Aloysius. *The Catholic Church in India: A Historical Sketch*, Nagpur, 1964.

Southgate, Beverley. *History: What and Why? Ancient, Modern and Postmodern Perspectives*, London and New York: Routledge, 2001, 2nd ed.

Spear, T.G.P. 'British Historical Writing in the Era of the Nationalist Movement', in C.H., Philips (ed.), *Historians of India, Pakistan and Ceylon*, London: Oxford University Press, 1961, pp. 404–15.

Stewart, Robert. *Life and Work in India: An Account of the Life, Work, Conditions, Methods, Difficulties, Results, Future Prospects and Reflex Influence of Missionary Labor in India Especially in the Punjab Mission of the United Presbyterian Church of North America*, Philadelphia: Pearl Publishing Co., 1899, new edn.

Stock, Eugene. *The History of the Church Missionary Society: Its Environment, Its Men and Its Work*, London: Church Missionary Society, 1899.

Stock, Frederick and Margaret Stock. *People Movements in the Punjab, with Special Reference to the United Presbyterian Church*, Pasadena: William Carey Library, 1975.

Sundarsingh, J.G. Jacob. 'The "Outcastes" and the Lutheran Church in Tamil Nadu: Towards an Alternative Historiography', *Sathri Journal*, 2:1, May 2008, pp. 90–136.

Swaro, Dasartathi. *The Christian Missionaries in Orissa: Their Impact on Nineteenth Century Society*, Calcutta: Punthi Pustyak, 1990.

Tanneti, James Elisha, 'Madiga Christians and the Subversive Gospel', in C.I. David Joy, ed., *Transforming Praxis: God, Community, and Church (Essays in Honour of Dr. I. John Mohan Razu)*, Bangalore: United Theological College, 2008, pp. 133–44.

Thaliath, Jonas. *The Synod of Diamper*, Rome: Institutum Orientalium Studiorum, 1958.

The Church of England Zenana Missionary Society Jubilee Souvenir 1880–1930.

The Constitution of the Church of South India, Madras, 1972.

The United Presbyterian, 1858–86, 1906–9.

Thekkedath, Joseph. *History of Christianity in India. Volume 2: From the Middle of the Sixteenth to the End of the Seventeenth Century (1542–1700)*, Bangalore: Theological Publications in India, 1982.

Thomas, George. *Christian Indians and Indian Nationalism 1885-1950: An Interpretation in Historical and Theological Perspectives*, Frankfurt: Verlag Peter Lang, 1979.

Thomas, M.M. *Some Theological Dialogues*, Madras: C.L.S., 1977.

——. *The Christian Response to the Asian Revolution*, Lucknow: Lucknow Publishing House, 1967.

Thomas, P. *Christians and Christianity in India and Pakistan: A General Survey of the Progress of Christianity in India from Apostolic Times to the Present Day*, London: George Allen and Unwin, 1954.

Thomas, V. V. *Dalit Pentecostalism: Spirituality of the Empowered Poor*, Bangalore: Asian Trading Corporation, 2008.

Tisserant, Eugene. *Eastern Christianity in India*, adapted from the French by E.R. Hambye, Bombay: Orient Longman, 1957.

'Truth and Reconciliation in History', *The American Historical Review*, 114:4, October 2009, pp. 899–977.

United Theological College, Bangalore, *Yearbook July 1940, Year Book July 1941, Year Book 1969–70*.

Vander Werff, Lyle L. *Christian Mission to Muslims: The Record. Anglican and Reformed Approaches in India and the Near East, 1800–1938*, Pasadena: William Carey Library, 1977.

Vanlalchhuanawma. *Christianity and Subaltern Culture: Revival Movement as a Cultural Response to Westernization in Mizoram*, Delhi: ISPCK, 2006.

Visvanathan, Susan. *The Christians of Kerala: History, Belief and Ritual among the Yakoba*, Madras: Oxford University Press, 1993.

Viswanathan, Gauri. *Outside the Fold: Conversion, Modernity and Belief*, Princeton: Princeton University Press, 1998.

Webster, John C.B. *A Social History of Christianity: North-West India since 1800*, New Delhi: Oxford University Press, 2007.

———. 'Christians and the Depressed Classes in the 1930s', in D.N. Panigrahi (ed.), *Economy, Society and Politics in Modern India*, New Delhi: Vikas, 1985, pp. 313–44.

Webster, John C.B. *History for College Students*, Chandigarh: Panjab University, 1966.

———. 'Leadership in a Rural Dalit Conversioin Movement', in Joseph T. O'Connell (ed.), *Organizational and Institutional Aspects of Indian Religious Movements*, Delhi: Manohar, 1999, pp. 96–112.

———. 'Missionary Strategy and the Development of the Christian Community: Delhi, 1859-1884', in Selva J. Raj and Corinne C. Dempsey (eds.), *Popular Christianity in India: Riting Between the Lines*, Albany: State University of New York Press, 2002, pp. 211–32.

———. *The Christian Community and Change in Nineteenth Century North India*, New Delhi: Macmillan, 1976.

———. *The Dalit Christians: A History*, Delhi: ISPCK, 1992 (2nd ed. 1994, 3rd ed. 2009).

———. *The Study of History and College History Teaching*, Patiala: Punjabi University, 1965.

———, 'Understanding the Modern Dalit Movement', *Sociological Bulletin*, vol. 45, September 1996, pp. 189–204.

———. 'Towards Understanding the Modern Dalit Movement', *The Fourth World*, vol. 7, April 1998, pp. 13–36.

Wilson, H.S. 'Involvement of the Wesleyan Kanarese Mission in the Mysore Territory in the Nineteenth Century', *Indian Church History Review*, vol. XX, June 1986, pp. 54–73.

Wiseman, Nicholas. *Lectures on the Principal Doctrines and Practices of the Catholic Church*, London: Joseph Booker, 1836.

With the King's Heralds: A Short Report of the Work of the C.E.Z.M.S. for the Year 1909.

Young, Richard Fox. *Resistant Hinduism: Sanskrit Sources on Anti-Christian Apologetics in Early Nineteenth-Century India*, Vienna: De Nobili Research Library, 1981.

Index

Wauton, E. 126, 130–1, 133
Webster, John C.B. 88–92, 148–9,
    160, 173, 196–7, 199–200,
    212–3, 214
Westernization 148, 233
Wiseman, Nicholas 16
Wolf, H.H. 75–6
women 8–9, 30, 79, 81–2, 94,
    115–24, 126–32, 134–40, 144,
    149, 159, 168–9, 180, 222, 237;

of Amritsar 8, 116, 120–40;
in churches of North-east
168; and conversion 38, 159;
Muslim 122, 130, 134; status of
94, 144, 168–9, 245; work of 30,
198, 237

Xavier, Francis 12, 153

Yakoba Christians. *See* Jacobites
Young, Richard Fox 150